The Chenango Kid

THE CHENANGO KID

A Memoir of the Fifties

Roger K. Miller

authorHOUSE

AuthorHouse™
1663 Liberty Drive
Bloomington, IN 47403
www.authorhouse.com
Phone: 1-800-839-8640

© 2012 by Roger K. Miller. All rights reserved.

No part of this book may be reproduced, stored in a retrieval system, or transmitted by any means without the written permission of the author.

The author's rights are fully asserted. The right of Roger K. Miller to be identified as the author of this work has been asserted by him in accordance with the Copyright, Designs and Patents Act 1988.

First published by AuthorHouse   2012

ISBN: 978-1-4685-5330-7 (sc)
ISBN: 978-1-4685-5329-1 (hc)

Library of Congress Control Number: 2012902994

Printed in the United States of America

Any people depicted in stock imagery provided by Thinkstock are models, and such images are being used for illustrative purposes only.
Certain stock imagery © Thinkstock.

Because of the dynamic nature of the Internet, any web addresses or links contained in this book may have changed since publication and may no longer be valid. The views expressed in this work are solely those of the author and do not necessarily reflect the views of the publisher, and the publisher hereby disclaims any responsibility for them.

Also by Roger K. Miller

Invisible Hero
Dragon in Amber

For "the kids"
Krista, Jennifer, Ian

"After being Turned Down by numerous Publishers, he had decided to write for Posterity."

—*George Ade*

CONTENTS

Foreword xiii

Prelude xv

Chapter 1   The Moon Block Fire 1

Chapter 2   The Five-Finger Discount 10

Chapter 3   North of the Viaduct 22

Chapter 4   Christopher Columbus and Thomas Edison 30

Chapter 5   Anyone Lived in a Pretty How Town 46

Chapter 6   Raggedy Man 65

Chapter 7   East Junior 80

Chapter 8   Uncle Russell's Reckless Romance 96

Chapter 9   The Prevalence of Linoleum 104

Chapter 10   Another Damn'd, Thick, Square Book 118

Chapter 11   The Silver Screen 133

Chapter 12   The Little Screen 144

Chapter 13   Portrait of the Would-Be Artist as a Boy 167

Chapter 14   Lopez 176

Chapter 15   North High 193

People and Places Appearing in the Book 215

Acknowledgments 217

FOREWORD

Speak, Memory
—Title of memoir by Vladimir Nabokov

No Book Without a Foreword, Erich Kästner said in his memoir of his childhood in Dresden, Germany, and anything Erich Kästner suggests should be good enough for any writer. So, forward . . . .

When his publisher suggested to Don Marquis, the great newspaper columnist and humorist, creator of Archy and Mehitabel, that he write his autobiography, Marquis replied, "I'm entitled to a better subject."

Well said, and true of any writer. I would only alter it or add to it in my instance to say, "*Readers* are entitled to a better subject." When you are old, people do not want to hear your stories. They grow wary when it sounds as if you are about to tell them something interminable about when you were a kid. Their eyes flick rapidly left and right as they mentally calculate how much of their life this tale is going to use up. Or possibly they are looking around for the nearest exit. This attitude is understandable. After all, your life probably has been as boring as theirs, and they would rather be bored by their own.

Me too. I set these thoughts down as a way of talking to myself. My life, though ordinary and conventional, has not been dull. This does not mean there weren't spells when I could have screamed with boredom—U.S. Army basic training and Infantry Officer Candidate School, for all their frantic and violent activity, were particularly long stretches—but on the whole I have been granted an un-dull existence. Despite its ordinariness and conventionality, its beginnings were, in my estimation, peculiar. I have been talking to myself for decades in an attempt to make sense of the peculiarity and to understand how it made the adult me. This talking

Roger K. Miller

to myself has always been sporadic and unsystematic. *The Chenango Kid* attempts to bring some order to it.

I don't know how it was for Kästner; it is hard for me to believe that people would not want to listen to his stories, but maybe so. Certainly, however, when he wrote them down in *Als ich ein kleiner Junge war* (When I Was a Young Boy), readers paid attention. Maybe the same kind fate will befall *The Chenango Kid*.

For those who might read this and wonder how anyone can write about the 1950s without discussing certain high-profile topics, such as McCarthyism or *West Side Story*, I can only say that my rule in writing was to bring up only those things that I remember touching my life then. While I wanted this book to be not just a memoir in the "and then I did this" genre, but an appreciation of the cultural life of the decade that made me, I also did not want to stretch it into a history of that decade; there are enough already. McCarthyism and *West Side Story* and hundreds of other phenomena I did not become aware of until later.

And now, with a brief nod of acknowledgment to cowboy actor Charles Starrett, whose nickname, the "Durango Kid," gave me, through the similarity in sound and syllables, the title for this book, I say, as Kästner said at the end of his foreword, No Foreword Without a Book . . . .

PRELUDE

This is how it was in those winter days in Upstate New York in the late 1950s that few of us can now recall. This is how it was for a silly adolescent male in that decade that anguished over a new species of beings called teenagers.

The boy sat in the warm classroom, feeling calm, at peace with the world. A heavy, somnolent atmosphere, not uncomfortable, exuded an air of laziness that increased his sense of privacy in the midst of twenty-some other human beings. The room, while drowsily and unwillingly ahum with the business of a high school English class, seemed nevertheless still and undisturbed. The teacher talked, feet scuffled, whispers rustled, sighs soughed every few minutes or so, but all these sounds added to rather than detracted from the floating stillness of the hour.

Rattling his ancient, initial-carved desk in the back of the room, he pulled himself out of the diagonal position—feet straight out front, shoulders propped against the back of the chair—and drew his legs and feet far back under the seat and hunched himself over the arm of the desk, resting on his elbows. He looked out the windows on the other side of the room. It was snowing, snowing hard, an Upstate small-city snowfall that would gladden the heart of any Christmas card manufacturer.

It was becoming a storm of heroic proportions, a storm to make wolves howl and bury their noses deep into their tails and whimper with delight. It was a whirling thickness of snow with big soft flakes that obscured the trees only a few dozen feet from the side of the building. It heightened the colors inside: the brindled, scarred desks, the chemical mahogany of the cupboards and bookcases, the begrimed reds and greens of the book covers. The boy could tell from the look of the snow that it would continue falling for hours and he was glad of it, for it added to the pervading sense of warmth and privacy. He thought ahead to the dismissal of school later in the afternoon when the

Roger K. Miller

school buses would be lined up their yellow row, engines idling and windows steaming. Waiting for others but not for him; he lived in town and would walk home.

The radiator hissed and water dribbled from its regulating valve. He pushed himself further over the arm of the desk and brought his attention back to the classroom. Miss Heffron was expounding again. That meant she worked while the kids sat in quasi-respectful silence. He heard her mention something about Pegasus. "Wing-ed Pegasus," she said, making two syllables. Good old scholarly Genevieve Heffron.

The boy understood. This was his world, his province. There were brighter and more intellectual students, and there were many more who were less intelligent than he. There were students who were far more popular. But none felt so at ease in the classroom, none moved so effortlessly and contentedly through the school routine as he did. The school and its environs and activities—the basketball and football games that he went to (though he cared for neither sport), the school plays that he attended (but that others more self-confident than he performed in), the dances that he did not go to but wished he could if he were not so shy, the Wigwam luncheonette on the corner of East Frederick and Moeller streets—formed the focal point toward which the others brought their lives each day, while he carried his province with him outward into the rest of his life.

He was liked and moderately well-known throughout the school though for no particular reason or accomplishment. He had an equally undistinguished group of friends, all liked and generally well-known in much the same way. He was appreciated for a quick wit, even by those outside that band with whom he roamed the halls during the lunch hour—there being, in those less parlous, more secure days, nothing intimidating or even unusual about students walking the halls of their own school. Being shy, he had no girlfriend. He never had the courage to press an advance on any girl, always being discouraged by the fear of ridicule from his peers or a sense of inadequacy that he felt the girl could easily detect. A male born too soon, into the since-discarded genteel tradition of romance in which the male is, however uncertainly, the pursuer.

The heat had increased and was growing dry in the room. It and the approaching end of the day were making the class restless. Miss Heffron, aware of the imminent clatter of the bell, was beginning to wind up the period in that stuttering, unsure way she sometimes had.

A fortuitous bit of scheduling: a double study hall at the end of a Friday. While others might doze, or read a magazine, or toss wads of paper at each other, the boy normally would have used this golden stretch of time to clean up his homework for the weekend. But today was his day and he could not work. He was locked snugly and securely into his world by the snow, the gentle, buffering routine of the schoolday, and by the structure of relationships, student and teacher, that kept him where he was, a contented member of a closed and provincial society.

But most of all, today, the snow. When he walked through the wooden, swinging double doors into the large third-floor cafeteria where the study hall was held, he was struck by the long rectangular expanse of eye-dazzling white on one side of the building. It was the snow outside the row of windows: whirling, buffeting, climbing upon and doubling within itself. From his distance the blasting, whirlpooling thickness blocked out sight of any outside objects. He could imagine that the snow blew not only around and over the school, but underneath, too, as if the school were suspended there with him and all his friends, teachers, enemies. Then, standing close to the windows, the heat from the radiators on the lower half of the wall warming his knees and crotch and the radiating cold from the window panes cooling his nose and face, he looked down upon the snow-covered pavement immediately below and the athletic field across from it. The open wooden bleachers had piled up ascending thick slices of snow. Frequent strong gusts of wind created a sea storm, almost, with the wind whipping off long thin trails of dusty snow from the drifts like spray from the tops of waves. Only a few people could be seen. A barely discernible man reeled across the field with a seaman's gait, a lone mariner rolling with the tempestuous sea. A few people struggled up the streets, their steps creating wakes of snow on the unshoveled sidewalks. An occasional car chugged and lurched like a tugboat through the unplowed streets. Over it all hung the only ominous element—a washed-out, benday sky.

He sat down, took up Call of the Wild, stretched out over the table with his head supported in his hands, and began to read. Steam rose from the stainless steel and glass fixtures and cauldrons of the kitchen, presided over by harried women in grease-spotted white who now and then gave their pots and pans an irritated rattle and bang to show that they, and not just the students and teachers, were members of this privileged society. One of them went up and down the rows of tables, washing them off with a rag reeking of ammonia that she slapped around negligently and joylessly. Someone strode through the doors and down the cafeteria, clattering his heels, to and through the doors at the other end. Somewhere far to the north wolves stirred, snapped at one another, and dozed on.

CHAPTER 1

The Moon Block Fire

"Mule train, h'yah, h'yah.
"Mule train, clippetty-clopping over hill and plain."
  —*Mule Train,* No. 1 song in December 1949, sung by Frankie Laine

I cannot remember much of my existence before the age of eight-and-a-half; that is, before the huge fire that destroyed the Moon Block apartment building on the corner of Chenango and Lewis streets in Binghamton, New York, on December 6, 1949. My mother and I and my half-sister Louise, and sometimes my mother's brother, Russell Sheridan, lived there at the time. I remember scattered details of that conflagration and a lot of my boyhood from then on, but not much before, other than snatches of scenes, widely separated in time, that are wispy and sepia-colored in my memory.

My father did not live with us then. I do not know when he moved out. He and my mother were not legally separated yet; that came in 1951. Divorce was not as common as it has become; I have read that in the mid-2000s married adults divorced four times as often as they did fifty years earlier. Technically, it was not a divorce, which at the time in New York could be granted only on limited grounds, including adultery, and apparently that was not the marital problem. Officially it was called a legal separation. My memory does contain scenes of his living with us, nothing extensive, only of his lying on a bed in a narrow bedroom in the front of our apartment, newspapers and magazines strewn all around him, which would be a typical position for him for the rest of his life. For years—decades—afterward I never thought of the situation as unusual, that he slept there and my mother elsewhere. Or presumably she did, because, again, I cannot summon up where it is she did sleep in that shotgun-style apartment. Only in hindsight do I put two and two together and assume that I must have been in the middle of an ongoing estrangement.

I was born July 9, 1941, in what was then called City Hospital in Binghamton to Keith Geist Miller and Mae Elna Sheridan. They were not then married; that came later, in September, and I have always been partial to Edmund's line in *King Lear*, "Now, gods, stand up for bastards!" Illegitimate birth then was even rarer than divorce. In 1950, nine years after I was born, fewer than four births in one hundred were to unmarried women; fifty years after that the rate had risen to almost one-third. My mother's given name may have been reversed, Elna Mae. Her gravestone in the cemetery in Clifford, Pennsylvania, reads Elna M. Miller. Most of her life I knew her as and heard her called Mae, except by her eight siblings, who usually called her Elna, or sometimes Hattie. I do not know where the nickname came from. I once heard it said it came from the Cole Porter musical *Panama Hattie*, but knowledge of a Cole Porter musical sounds too sophisticated for my family. My father was born August 19, 1904, outside of Wyalusing, Pennsylvania, my mother May 5, 1912, in Clifford.

The dime-store psychology that we all like to practice, even after Freud has been discredited, tells me I have suppressed much that happened before the fire because what I saw or experienced was emotionally or psychologically disturbing. I may not be far off the mark. Louise used to tell me that the reason for their separation was that my mother deceived my father as to her—Louise's—identity, and once he learned the truth of that, he decided to put an end to the marriage that had come about primarily, I'm sure, not because of mutual love but because my mother was pregnant with me. But then, Louise may not be the best authority on this, for she had her own issues with our mother.

The Moon Block fire, though, that was a big deal. The Moon Block was a big old four-story gray stone structure dating from 1880 or earlier. There must have been more than three dozen apartments in the place. Newspaper reports say the fire displaced thirty-two families and more than sixty residents. We lived on the second floor. It was called the Moon Block because it had been owned by the family or firm of George Q.

Moon, who used to run a feed or grain company, but it had been bought a few years before by Charles and Victor Rosen. The neighborhood wasn't upscale, but neither was it rundown, because across Chenango Street from the Moon Block sat the city's premier hotel, the Arlington, handy to the railroad station, which was across Lewis Street from the hotel. Rail was an important mode of travel. Neither was Chenango a bad street. Running roughly north and south and paralleling the Chenango River for much of its length, it was—and is—one of the city's two main thoroughfares, the other being the east-west Court Street/Main Street, into which Chenango runs. There were many thriving stores and other commercial establishments along it, as there were in most cities in those antediluvian times before the malling of America. Some were housed in the ground floor of the Moon Block. I recall Jimmy Lake's grocery/delicatessen on Chenango Street, where we did most of our shopping, and the Douglass & Bradley dry cleaners where my mother worked part-time. And the Johnston drugstore with its corner entrance where you had to walk up three stone steps to enter. Around the corner on Lewis Street was an old-fashioned barber shop where you could see them singeing men's back hairs. I don't know why they did that and I never wanted to get my hair cut there. No, it wasn't a bad street at all.

The Moon Block, though, was a queer place, in a way. It was a kind of anti-*You Can't Take It With You* world peopled by eccentrics. Or maybe a parallel eccentric world, where the eccentrics were sour and mean and shady and intermittently happy, rather than delightful and funny and eternally happy. The former are more often characteristic of the poor than the latter, and no wonder, because being poor is neither delightful nor funny. Funny and delightful, however, play better on Broadway. I had a friend around my age—not a real close friend, but a friend—who fell from the fourth-floor back porch of the apartment building onto the roof of a peddler's van below and apparently suffered nothing that required more a few stitches in his forehead. I heard adults say the boy had been pretending he was Superman and took a header off the back porch with a crimson cotton bath towel safety-pinned around his neck. True or not, it fits the place.

Anyway, the Big Fire. Louise and I discovered it. It's true. You could look it up in the defunct *Binghamton Sun*, the rabidly Republican rag in town. Our role is not mentioned in the *Binghamton Press* (for which, twenty-one years later, I would go to work as a copy editor when it was known as the *Evening Press*). Over the decades I have thought about that fire hundreds of times and tried to reconstruct the sequence of events, but nothing comes to me beyond a few short scenes of Louise and I and a friend walking home along Chenango Street and entering the apartment house and discovering smoke. From those scenes and from the newspaper account I have imagined the following. The dialogue is made up, though it is close to the sort of things we did say to each other in the way we would have said it. The physical background is quite real.

The apartment house was quite a warren. Ma and Louise and I—and occasionally Uncle Russell—lived in an apartment over Jimmy Lake's store. The block was so big it had several entrances, both front and back. When I have read German novels, such as Hans Fallada's *Wolf unter Wölfen*, that feature the huge *Mietskaserne* that housed the poor of Berlin I always mentally place the novels in a sort of Germanized Moon Block. In the back was the courtyard/wasteland of cinders, a makeshift playground, loomed over by a four-story-high framework of back porches covered in scabrous green paint and dotted with signs for the iceman—25 pounds, 50, 75, and 100. The icemen lugged the big blocks of ice on their backs. I'll bet they loved the people on the fourth floor. But to get to our place from the front, you entered through a doorway next to Jimmy's and climbed a flight of stairs lit by a dim bulb as old as Edison and covered with linoleum from Harding's administration. Our door was at the top of the stairs. Ma's wringer washing machine sat just to the right of it. Everybody in all the apartments kept stuff in the halls and on the landings, things that weren't easily stolen.

The door opened into the kitchen. The apartment was a variant on the shotgun or railroad flat, most of the rooms lined up one behind the other and the only windows were in the front and back. A short hall that ran alongside the middle rooms—Ma's bedroom (I think) and the bathroom with its pull-chain toilet that released a Niagara of water from a cistern high up on the wall when the chain was pulled. In the front of the apartment, facing onto Chenango, were a living room and a small bedroom, the one my father used to sleep in. I suppose Louise slept there, or maybe Russell, when he was with us. In the back, facing the porch and the cinder courtyard—the one into which my friend had pitched—was a small dining room that may also have served as my bedroom for it wasn't used as a dining room; we had no dining room furniture. I can't remember where I slept. Sometimes I slept with my mother, later in childhood than could have been healthy for me. Make of that what you will; I certainly have, my entire life. The only other exterior door was also in the kitchen; it opened onto the back porch.

So there we were on that cold gray December afternoon, walking home north on Chenango from Christopher Columbus School, me, Louise, and Louise's friend Francine. I don't know if that really was the girl's name, but Louise had a good friend and Francine sounds like the name she might have had. Big, soft, slowly drifting flakes fell onto Louise's and Francine's headscarves as they walked along, heads bent toward each other, arms cradling textbooks and notebooks—not that either was what you might call a scholar—and talking animatedly. I trudged alongside them, puffy in my thick winter coat and with the earflaps on my cap dangling loose around my ears, truculent at being ignored and letting out an occasional "*Wee*-zee!" for attention.

"*What?*" Louise finally snapped, turning abruptly to face me on the snow-covered sidewalk. "Will you for God's sake stop dinging me?"

"Dinging me." She got that from our mother, who was always saying that.

"You weren't listening to me. I asked if you'd take me to see Abbott and Costello. The new one with that Frankenstein guy."

"No, you little pest," Louise said, walking again. "They're stupid. Besides, you're old enough to go by yourself. Go with your snot-nosed little friends."

It's true. I could have gone by myself. Kids regularly went to "the show," alone or in groups, without adult supervision in those days. Beforehand we stopped in at the Karamel Korn (it may or may not have been spelled that way) shop on the corner of Henry and Chenango to load up on cheap kiddie komestibles to take into the theater, which did not ban "outside" food as theaters try to do today

"I don't have any money."

"So how am I supposed to get you in, for crying out loud? On my looks? Ask Ma for some money. Turn in some milk bottles for the deposits."

"I already did. There's none left. I can't find any more."

"That's tough titty, then. Maybe Santa will bring you a movie ticket." Despite her sarcasm and belligerence, Louise was protective of me. The year before, in a fury, she broke the nose of an older boy who had pushed me down and rubbed my face in the snow. It cost Ma almost one hundred dollars in medical reimbursement to the boy's angry parents. The parents would have sued for other damages, too, but they knew a bloodless turnip when they saw one.

"Here we are," Louise said. We had reached Francine's entrance to the Moon Block.

"You want to come up for a while?" Francine asked. "You can see our Christmas tree. We just put it up last night. It's pretty nice. My Dad's not home yet. I think my Mom's over to my grandma's."

"Sure. Might's well. I can't stay long, though. Ma wants me to feed the ball-and-chain here." She nodded her head in my direction. I scrunched up my face at her.

"God," Francine said as they turned toward the door, "I hope we don't run into that creep Lonny." Lonny was in the eighth grade with Louise and Francine. He also lived on the second floor, though in an apartment on another side of the building. Francine's family lived in an apartment on the third floor on the same side.

"He's always creeping around," Francine continued. They started up the stairs. "I hate to go past his door. I think he watches for you. He's always trying to sneak a peek up my skirt whenever I go up or down the stairs, pretending he just happened to be there by accident. He's a disgusting little pervert."

"Louise," I said, trailing behind as they reached the landing, "what's a pervert?"

"Never mind. You'll find out soon enough." Francine, leading the way, looked back at Louise and the two girls broke into snorts of laughter.

"What's so funny?" I asked. Once the three of us were walking along the banks of the Chenango River and I darted away to pick up what I thought was a deflated white balloon lying in the grass. "Don't touch that!" Louise shouted at me. "That's what men put on their willies!" I'm sure I must have asked why men did that, because they gave out a loud, conspiratorial burst of laughter, just like today's.

We started up the next flight of stairs to Francine's apartment on the third floor, where my friend Johnny also lived. I cocked my head and sniffed. "Hey, I smell something."

Halted, with her hand on the banister, Francine said, "You know what? The little twerp's right." We ran up the remaining steps to the next landing. Francine sniffed and looked around. "I think it's coming from Johnny's place." She looked at the door. "I think it's smoke."

"Jesus!" Louise yelped. She ran to the door, lowered her head close to it, and sniffed, placing the flat of her right hand on the door for support. "You're right, it's smoke. Jesus!" She pulled her hand away and looked at it, and then at Francine. "The door's warm."

"Ohmigod!" Francine screamed. "It's a fire! Ohmigod! What if they're in there?" She twisted the doorknob, then tugged on it. "Johnny!" The girls pounded on the door while continuing to yell.

"Jesus, where *is* everybody?" Louise whined. She looked up into the murky recesses of the stairwell and shouted, "Fire!" And again, "Fire!" She looked at Francine, who had given up on the door and was shifting agitatedly from one foot to the other in a frenzy of indecision. For an insane moment it looked to me as if she had to go to the bathroom. I was whimpering. Tiny curls of smoke were coming out from under the door. We could hear crackling inside the apartment. "Isn't anybody home?"

"Oh God," Francine said, "our apartment, our stuff."

Louise quickly took hold of her arm and stopped her from heading toward her apartment. "No," she said. Her breath came hard and fast. "We need to call. You don't have a phone. We need to tell somebody." Keeping hold of Francine with her left hand and grabbing hold of me with her right, she began pulling and pushing us down the stairs.

"Downstairs! Downstairs! Down to Jimmy's!" We clattered, half-tumbling, down one flight of stairs, then the other. "Jimmy's got a phone. He'll know what to do."

We slammed flat-footed onto the white tiles of the ground-floor entrance-way. In doing so Louise's scarf, flying loose behind her, snagged onto one of the metal mailboxes on the wall. She tugged on it furiously and ripped it loose. Louise pushing me, I tore open the door and, turning left, raced to the store, followed by the girls, all of us skittering on the snowy sidewalk. Through the plate glass window, in which hung a small, sputtering neon PeeWee soft drink sign, surrounded by small, hand-written cardboard signs advertising various specials, I could see Jimmy, a short man with thinning hair in his mid-thirties, standing behind the worn wooden counter. A soiled white apron covered his slight paunch, and he was resting his right arm on the big roll of brown wrapping paper and talking to Mrs. Simmons, who lived with her railroader husband in an apartment on the second floor on the Lewis Street side.

I tore open this door, too, Louise hot on my heels.

"Jimmy!" Louise shouted. Jimmy and Mrs. Simmons turned to look at the disturbance, she irritated, he startled. "Call the fire department, Jimmy. Call quick. There's a fire in Johnny's place upstairs!"

§

It was no use. Looked at now, we must have been pretty quick-witted kids, but by early that night the Moon Block lay in smoking ruins. Every fireman and every piece of fire equipment from every station in Binghamton eventually responded to the three-alarm fire. Units came from nearby Johnson City and other places, but it was no use. The first engine was there within minutes, but by that time the fire, still showing only small wisps of smoke to the outside, was roaring up to the third and fourth floors inside and moving to other parts of the block. Residents were streaming out or, like Ma and Francine's mother and father, coming home to calamity from work or other places. By 4:15 that afternoon, an hour after we smelled the smoke from Johnny's apartment, flames were shooting out of third- and fourth-story windows. Thousands of people gathered on the streets and on the Viaduct, the bridge over the railroad tracks to the North Side of town, to watch the show, the most dramatic part of which was over by 5:30 when the firefighters got the inferno under control.

Miraculously, as the newspapers say, no resident was seriously injured, though several firefighters were. The newspaper says my Uncle Russell carried an elderly woman out to safety, and if the newspaper says it, it must be true, but I cannot think where he might have been at the time. Probably in our apartment—chances are better there than at work, where he rarely was. But everything was gone—Jimmy's store, Douglass & Bradley, Elgin's rug store, Johnston's drugstore, the barber shop, every precious piece of cheap furniture in every apartment.

There we sat, the sixty-some residents of the Moon Block, or most of us, in the lobby of the Carlton Hotel, across Chenango Street from the Moon Block—on the same side as the Arlington, though further south. People fleeing the fire or coming home from work or school to encounter it initially had flocked to the Arlington directly across the street as a place to gather, but the Arlington wouldn't let us stay there. We had to go to the Carlton. Why the Carlton let us congregate and the Arlington did not I never knew. Both hotels are now gone. But I always felt gratitude to the place, picked up from my mother, who forever after expressed her surprise and thankfulness at the hotel's generosity. At that moment she was sitting on one of the huge leather sofas in its lobby, amid all the noise and confusion of the milling homeless and the prowling newspaper reporters, weeping softly over the loss of all her worldly goods, completely uninsured, a situation shared by nearly all the Moon Block residents. Former residents.

CHAPTER 2

The Five-Finger Discount

"O tempora, o mores."
—Cicero

Now that I think of it, it is not accurate to say I cannot remember much of my existence before the Moon Block fire. Of my pre-fire existence, bits and pieces are lodged in my brain that now and then come to the fore. They are foggy and make only partial sense. You might say I was forged in fire, for after the fire I have a sense of a continuing existence with its own story in which all the bits and pieces fit together. Before that I do not; the bits and pieces are just bits and pieces, scenes.

For instance, I have a distinct memory of a very embarrassing incident when I was five or six years old walking by myself down a street, perhaps Fayette, near Christopher Columbus School and crying floods of tears. I won't describe it further except that if, say, a twenty-five-year-old man had done it, crying or not, he would have been arrested on the spot. The tears are so thick and vivid that sparkles of sunlight flash through them even now. As I walk I am conscious that this is wrong. Did it really happen? If so, why? To get attention for some slight? To protest in some way conditions that I found unbearable and wanted others to know about but didn't know how else to draw attention to? It couldn't have been an accident, could it? Not even a five- or six-year-old makes that mistake. Did somebody see me and stop me? Did they then report me someplace—to the school, maybe?—where the incident was put on my permanent record? Would I not have been examined by some professional as to my mental and emotional state, even in the 1940s? Or have I suppressed that, too? Where do they keep your permanent record? If I went to the Binghamton School District would I find a record of that? Would they show it to me, or would they insist it cannot be revealed to the public, even to the member of the public whose record it is, out of the natural conservatism of bureaucrats, who would keep everything under wraps if they could? If it cannot be revealed to anyone ever, what is the point of keeping it? So that future bureaucrats can read it? Is some New York state bureaucrat heading to the files to look me up even as he or she reads this? It is remotely possible that this is a "borrowed" memory, something that I read or heard elsewhere and incorporated into my own past. What makes me think that this is not the case is the clear reality of those sparkling, jewel-like tears.

§

I date things by where I was in school at the time. This is a roughly reliable calendar of my past. I started kindergarten at Columbus School in 1946 and can remember little before the fourth grade, aside from the tyranny of handwriting exercises in second grade—the teacher got angry at my complete inability to make perfect ovals—and being lifted up off the floor by the neck by an Italian immigrant kid in the third grade, nearly choking in the process. I dreaded being weighed and measured (information that went on report cards) in the third grade because I could not tie my shoes that late in life and would have to suffer the humiliation of that becoming known when it came to putting my shoes back on after getting off the scales.

I had a secret "girlfriend" around this time, the first in a long line of girls who did not know they were my girlfriends. I know her name but will not mention it, except to say it was the same as that of a famous Italian city, for if she is still alive she might not welcome being outed as the object of second- or third-grade lust. She was Italian, as were many residents of that area of town, and walked with a slight limp, the result, perhaps, of a childhood bout of polio. Years later—1956, to be exact—when I entered North High School I was startled to see her again, for, given where we went to elementary school she should have gone on to Central High, not North. Her family must have moved in the meantime. Not surprisingly, she did not recognize me, and, equally unsurprisingly, I did nothing to rekindle a romance that had never caught fire. By that time I had gone through more than a few other love interests who never had an inkling that that is what they were, so I was quite inured to unrequited love. She became part of the glamorous clique of the high school—cheerleader, and all that—and I went on to pal around with a group of lovable if undistinguished schlubs.

My mother told me that I had a "little friend" who died of leukemia and we went to the viewing for his funeral. Not the least remarkable thing about this, if it is correct, is that the boy was black and that his name was also Roger—Roger Harris, if I remember right. That is what sticks in my head, the name Roger, for I considered it, now as then, a fairly uncommon name, even a "rich kid's" name like Reginald or Rollo. It wasn't a "real boy's" name like John, Bob, Tom, or Bill. My mother's story may be true, for Columbus School was close to a "black area" of Binghamton—Susquehanna Street—and I had more than a few black classmates. Indeed, all through Binghamton public schools—Columbus, Thomas Edison Elementary, East Junior High, and North High—I probably had more black schoolmates than is the case six decades later in these more enlightened and integrated and suburbanized days.

§

Louise was what in those days was called "wild." What was considered "wildness" in the late 1940s and what would be labeled wildness in our own more vicious times . . . well, it is no comparison at all. Louise must have been on the leading edge of what became one of the scourges of the 1950s—juvenile delinquency. I guess our mother could not control her, or maybe, given their mutual history, she did not try. Capturing this situation in detail is difficult, because a sense of our living together—our mother, Louise, and I—is another blank or at least opaque space in my past. At any rate, she hung out with the "wrong crowd," and Francine, or whatever her real name was, was not a good influence. They shoplifted together. At one time they tried to involve me. They stole something and tried to get me to return it to the store, the F.W. Woolworth's on Court Street, and ask for the "return" of the purchase price. What, were they *nuts*? A seven- or eight-year-old returning a "purchase" without a receipt? But then, to be a fourteen- or fifteen-year-old girl in any time period is its own form of nuttiness, exacerbated when given almost no moral or domestic guidance. I don't think I did what they asked; I can still sense the fear I had of what they wanted me to do. Or the fear may have come from having done it and gotten caught, a sort of way-under-age accomplice to petty theft.

My life has always been wrapped up with the movies, and I think of Louise and me and shoplifting every time I see a certain scene in *The Best Years of Our Lives* in which Dana Andrews, the returned aviator hero working as a postwar store clerk, is dressed down by his boss, patently a wartime draft shirker, who sits in a chair sniffing an inhaler. When I see that mustachioed little ferret face sticking the inhaler up one nostril while compressing the other with the index finger of his other hand, I think of the manager at Woolworth's in Binghamton grilling Louise and Francine. Art validates life.

At some point they were caught. And, on a different occasion, so was I. In his first, magnificent novel, *Appointment in Samarra*, John O'Hara tells how his main character, Julian English, as a boy got involved with his small gang of friends—all, like him, sons of the town's more affluent citizens—in a "game" of dare they called Five-Finger Grab. It was nothing more than shoplifting at either Kresge's or Woolworth's. They did it not to obtain items they particularly wanted, but just to see if they could get away with it. And they did. By a tactic of wandering through the store and distracting clerks and assistant managers, they grabbed what they could at the opportune moment and left. Julian came to like it and became good at it—until one day the manager put the arm on him and he was caught. But with the aid of a swift kick to the manager's shin by one of his fellow thieves, Julian wrested free and both of them ran out of the store. If Julian faced any long-term consequences, O'Hara does not reveal them.

In the game of what we kids all called, with a slight variation on O'Hara, the Five-Finger Discount, I and a friend, Dickie, were not so fortunate in playing it at the Western Auto store, which was at the other end of Court Street from Woolworth's. We may have been doing it like O'Hara's Gibbsville boys, purely for the dare, or we may have been doing it to obtain stuff we really wanted. I suspect the former, for I realized that if I brought home items that I could not account for buying, Ma would be suspicious. Some of it I stuffed feverishly into what I now want to see as a large pipe or some other kind of opening on the grounds of the First Presbyterian Church on Chenango Street. Did I put it there for safekeeping until, having thought up some reason to give Ma for possessing it, I could take it home? It may be there still, whatever it was, sixty years later, moldering and rusting and deteriorating in some obscure little ground-level cavern near a north wall of First Presbyterian.

If so, it is not the merchandise on this occasion, because before Dickie and I could sidle oh-so innocently and casually out the front door, I found my way blocked by a pair of gray-cloth-covered legs.

"Got you this time, you little shit!"

I looked up into a livid, ugly face contorted by an angry smirk. My heart pounded. Out of the corner of my eye I was conscious of Dickie being detained by a woman clerk.

"We've had our eye on you," the livid, ugly, smirking face said. "We seen you two in here before, stealing. Now we've got you. What've you got in your pocket?"

"I haven't done anything wrong," was all I could think to say. I was trembling, tears were forming.

"Don't give me that, ya snot-nosed brat." He was right; snot was beginning to bubble out of my nose. While keeping a painfully tight hold on my left bicep, he shot his left hand down to my right-hand pants pocket and pulled out its illicit contents, a black, circular, wind-up carpenter's ruler of the kind that you don't see much anymore.

"A carpenter's ruler? What the hell does a kid want with a carpenter's ruler?" He bent over slightly, looking at me fiercely and accusingly with red-rimmed eyes astride an oddly bent and shiny nose. The thrill of the catch was in his demeanor; this must have been a big moment in a dreary managerial existence.

He straightened up again. "I know. You thought you could sell it. That it?"

"I don't know how that got there," I said, shifting my glance to the scuffed toes of my shoes, my voice quavering. Then, weakly: "I was gonna pay for it."

"Sure you were. And I'm gonna win the Irish Sweepstakes." I can hear the delight in his voice at throwing a scare into a little kid. "We'll see what your mother and father have to say about this. And the cops."

"My father doesn't live with us." What ever possessed me to offer this needless bit of information?

"Really? Why am I not surprised? The way society's going, I don't know, kids running wild on the streets."

I'll bet he was a wife- and child-beater himself. Major authority on raising children.

"So c'mon," he said, putting a hand on one of my shoulders and turning me toward the back of the store. "We'll call your mother, see what she thinks about having a thief for a son. She home now? You on the phone?" Before I could answer that we didn't have a phone and she wasn't at home but at work, he pushed me roughly forward. "I just hope for your sake they don't put your skinny ass in jail."

They didn't put my skinny ass or any other part of me in jail. My mother, who must have thought she had another delinquent offspring developing, had to go down to the store with me, but beyond that the consequences of my larceny seem to have been nil. Except for probably being on my permanent record somewhere.

§

That Western Auto incident, when I was seven or eight years old, was not the end of my life of crime. Jumping ahead a couple of years, I got caught trying to steal comic books from Williams' cigar store. This establishment, which I patronized frequently until I was unmasked as a thief, was near the corner of Chenango and Eldredge streets; the Skat bar and grill was smack on the corner, and just north of it was a barber shop, and then Williams'. I don't know that Williams' specialized in cigars; the name may have been a holdover from an earlier era in The Cigar City, one of the civic nicknames by which Binghamton once recognized itself (The Parlor City, The Valley of Opportunity were others). There were many such stores like that in those days, small Mom and Pop places that sold a wide range of small items—candy, smoking materials, toiletries, "notions." And comic books. Williams' was kind of a kids' hangout. Across from the counter was a wide, wide rack of comic books and we kids always knew when the new ones were due to come out. Comic books were a staple of kids' life and were available in a glorious variety of subject matter and genres: Cowboys (Roy Rogers, Dale Evans, Trigger—yes, Trigger had his own comic book), war (Sergeant Rock), horror (*Tales of the Crypt*), superheroes (Batman, Superman, Captain Marvel, Plastic Man—I really liked Plastic Man and his sidekick, Woozy Winks), children's fantasy (Mary Jane and Sniffles), humor (Little Lulu, Archie), romance, crime, comic books from comic strips (Joe Palooka), comic books of celebrities (Dean Martin and Jerry Lewis, Bob Hope), comic books from animated characters (Mickey Mouse, Donald Duck, Baby Huey). And, starting in 1952, that most inventive of all comics, *Mad* ("Humor in a Jugular Vein"). That is not even the beginning of a beginning of a listing of the garish-hued, pulp-paper delights, and I read them all except romance. And all for only ten cents each.

Trouble was, there weren't enough dimes to satisfy my habit. New issues of most of them came out every month. I roamed stores up and down Chenango searching for interesting or odd specimens—3-D comics, for example—that might not have made it to Williams' eclectic inventory. I know that two or three times I had tried a little dodge—slipping one comic inside another—to make my money go further at other stores and gotten away with it, but one evening at Williams' I was caught red-handed.

It may have been because I got greedy and tried to slip *two* other comics inside a third. Pretty bulky, that. Innocent as an angel I walked up to the fogged-glass case that served as a counter and put my purchase and a dime on the little rubber circle of tiny rubber spikes. The guy behind the counter looked at me silently and knowingly for no more than three seconds and then pulled one comic, then the other, from their defective protective covering, splaying them out across the glass accusingly. I see him now; he was the one generally behind the counter. Maybe he was the owner, maybe he was Williams himself, if there still was such a person. He seemed even to my precocious understanding to be the eternal clerk, living when he was not working in a dim and dusty cheap one- or-two-room apartment with the bath down the hall. He always wore an out-of-fashion double-breasted gray suit with pointy lapels and a tie—why?—and had slicked-back hair above a pinched, narrow, weasely face and a moustache that could have been the underfed understudy for film actor William Powell's. His eyes had a constant suspicious look, given them, perhaps, by the lid of the left that was always at half-staff. Or perhaps it was the result of constantly having to keep a lookout for sneaky kids and other larcenous customers. It was disconcerting, those one-and-a-half eyes boring into me with unspoken question.

"Oh gosh," I said, "I must've, I don't know, I was looking at so many comics and I couldn't decide. I must have got mixed up, looking at them all. I don't know . . . ."

"Which comic did ya want, kid? Ya got three here and ten cents."

"Oh, yeah, I . . . ." I felt sweat breaking out and was conscious of the two old duffers sitting on a ledge of the plate-glass window. I could sense they were smiling, enjoying the unexpected show that was the reward for sitting on their ass for hours, chewing the fat with Weasel-Face. They probably had to move to this perch when the barber shop closed, ending that day's entertainment there. "The Scrooge McDuck," I said, choosing the one that had been the "wrapper."

Weasel-Face took the dime and picked up the two other comics and placed them somewhere behind the counter.

I took the Scrooge McDuck and was about to say something as I prepared to skulk out of the store.

"Get out of here, kid, and don't let me see you in here again. I see you in here again, I *will* call the cops on you." For a weasel, he sounded convincingly menacing.

With that, and to the sound of the duffers' snorting laughter, I beat my retreat, effectively ending my criminal career. A couple of years later, when my literary tastes had risen somewhat, I contemplated not paying for a copy of Hans Hellmut Kirst's *The Revolt of Gunner Asch* that the Studio Book Shop on Court Street had let me take with only partial payment and the promise to pay the rest later, because they could see I desired it so much but didn't have sufficient funds. But an improved sense of honesty, or more likely the knowledge that stiffing the store would cut me off from a—to me—increasingly important resource in a one-bookstore town, impelled me to go back with the balance. As for Williams', I didn't stop going there entirely; it had too expansive a stock of comics. I simply waited for the times that Weasel-Face wasn't around. And I paid for each and every comic.

My loss of interest in comic books roughly coincided with a sudden decline in the industry, brought about by widespread, not to say hysterical, fears that comic books were rotting the minds and morals of American youth. There were protests and comic-book-burnings around the country. There was even a burning in Binghamton, in 1948, the culmination of a protest that began at St. Patrick's Academy on Oak Street. But the greater moralistic crusade came in the early 1950s. Its self-appointed national leader was psychiatrist Fredric Wertham, who spread his misinformation in an anti-comics tome, *Seduction of the Innocent*. David Hajdu has effectively discredited Wertham's work in his *The Ten-Cent Plague: The Great Comic-Book Scare and How It Changed America*, but that came decades after the damage was done and the comics industry was forced to emasculate itself through a "comics code." I have always maintained that my lifelong love of, even obsession with, reading began with comic books—and the Freddy the Pig novels of Walter R. Brooks.

§

Louise hung out with a guy named Earl on Prospect Avenue, not far from the back entrance of the Greyhound bus station. Sometimes she took me along when she went to see him. His house and most of the houses around there were crappy—unpainted, uncared-for, bleak. When I see certain Dorothea Lange photos they make me think of those houses. Her subject matter and time frame were different, but the "look" is the same as in her photographs—shabby, scabrous, listing, most of all *poor*. I can scarcely think of the houses there and those we lived in later on the North Side in anything but black-and-white.

Was Louise, at the age of fourteen or fifteen, having sex with Earl? I doubt it. Louise was daring, but she wasn't stupid. Daring and foolish: Once she burned Earl's name into the skin of her forearm. There may have been some short, nutty, teenage-girl fad of burning names or mottos into your skin. Francine and another of her girlfriends did it, too, there in our kitchen, somehow using a pin and the flame from the ancient gas range. The other girl may have been the daughter of the owner of a small jewelry store. How did that come about, that the daughter of a jeweler and a girl from the Moon Block were pals? But they were.

At some point Louise was "sent away" because of her shoplifting and, probably, other undesirable habits. For which I do not and never have blamed her; she received even less guidance and support than I did from those who were supposed to support and guide us. She was placed in a reform school of some sort run by Roman Catholic nuns in Albany. We visited her once, traveling there in the lime-green Henry J car (a kind of early American answer to the Volkswagen) owned by Ma's sister Jean and her longtime boyfriend and later husband, Alex Duby. I was both awed by and drawn to the friendly, black-clad nuns. Louise must have gone away shortly after the Moon Block fire, because she did not live with Ma and me for the next couple of years. I figure she must have been gone from about 1950 to 1952. If the episode is fuzzy, it is in part because it was little talked about. Louise was not ashamed of it—she used to say it was lucky it happened to her because it turned her around—but neither did she broadcast the information. Louise always gave me the impression that she did not talk about it with her three children.

§

What was Ma doing at this time? Was she already into the pattern that she followed for the next several years, going to bars and drinking with men? If so, I was not aware of it as I was later. Even now I have no sense of her having been an active part of my life, involved in it. She was *there*, in a much closer sense than my father, and she provided for me and took care of me and presumably even loved me—though my whole life long I cannot recall one instance of her saying so or indicating it physically, as with a hug. She did not hug nor did she encourage hugs—until her grandchildren came along. Them she hugged, I am happy to say. If she did not hug or show love, it probably is because she herself had not been hugged or shown much love. Odd families, both Ma's and Pa's, but in different ways.

One of my earliest sustained memories is of being baby-sat during the day by a woman named Mrs. Hinckley. I would have said Ma "hired" her to watch me, except she could not have afforded much in the way of child care with her paltry wages from working at the Endicott-Johnson shoe factory. What probably happened was that Ma paid her a nominal amount to come from her apartment to ours to listen to her string of soap operas—about three dozen were broadcast each day from studios in New York City at the time—and incidentally keep an eye on me, for that is what she did. She was enormously fat and sat in a chair in the kitchen where the radio was and listened the mid-day through to *The Romance of Helen Trent* and *When a Girl Marries* and the like, while I sat there and played quietly, for she forbade me to make any noise while the sacrosanct programs were on the air.

But with the Moon Block fire she was gone and so was everything else, an entire existence. Pre-fire was old, post-fire would be new, symbolized for me by the icebox and the refrigerator. In the Moon Block we had an icebox and ice haulers to fill it. In the new existence we would have a bright new white Norge refrigerator with a clock on the front of the door.

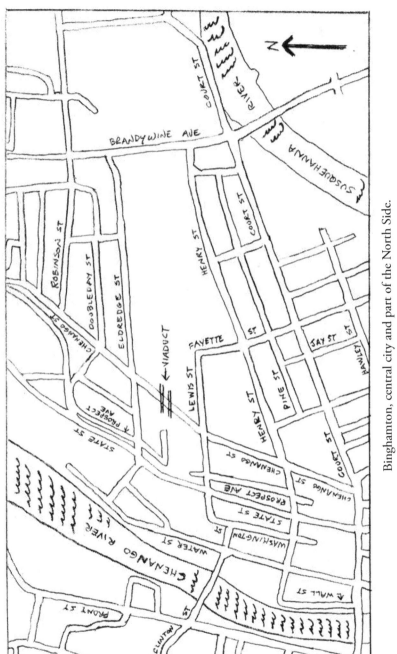

Binghamton, central city and part of the North Side.

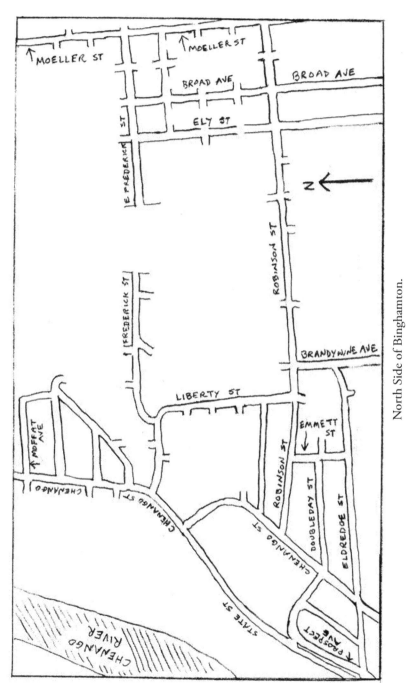

North Side of Binghamton.

CHAPTER 3

North of the Viaduct

"Put another nickel in
"In the nickelodeon."
    —*Music! Music! Music!*, No. 1 song of 1950, sung by
    Teresa Brewer

For fifteen of my first seventeen years, from 1943 to 1958, I lived on Chenango Street, with a yearlong interregnum on Eldredge, the first street that crosses Chenango north of the Viaduct. The Viaduct now is just a plain old concrete bridge arching over a shrunken railroad yard, looking out upon the stadium of the Binghamton Mets baseball team. Then the Viaduct carried Chenango Street across a steel tangle of railroad tracks of the Erie Railroad and the Delaware & Hudson and the Delaware, Lackawanna, and Western (the DL&W, a nice combination of sounds, Dee Ell and Double-Ya) and was a massive, forbidding structure of thick, black iron plates bound together with rows and rows of big rivets whose fat, rounded tops looked like strips of licorice button candy on black paper. These big flat black iron sections, or walls, separated the sidewalk from the roadway. On either end the sections were low, knee-high, and we kids liked to try walking them—not an easy or safe task because of the buttons. Some even climbed the higher sections, toward the middle of the bridge, where they could look down on the traffic whizzing by as they wobbled along across the buttons. In the very middle of the bridge the wall on either side of the street ended abruptly and there was an open space of thirty or forty feet before the wall resumed and continued to the other end. Thus to walk the high sections of the wall was extra perilous because of the difficulty of getting down from a height of maybe eight feet.

From the middle of the Viaduct, on one side of the street, we could see a tall, bright-red-brick structure shooting upon from the railroad station below it, a kind of minaret of the rails. It probably was used to view and control rail traffic, but I thought of it as a castle tower (never mind that there was no castle). In the middle of the Viaduct on the other side of the street, wide, heavy black iron stairs led down to the rail platforms and the Railway Express Agency office. Everything was heavy, iron, and black. When I was *very* young and steam still propelled locomotives I liked to pretend that I was emerging like a genie from the white steam or smoke that billowed up to the roadway and sidewalk from an engine as it passed underneath. On the west side of the north end of the Viaduct roadway were buildings housing businesses, apartments, and a tavern (the Iroquois bar & grill, which may also have been known as Lynch's).

The east side was open to the rail yards, but directly underneath the road was a concrete wall with an iron door. We thought it was where bums and winos hid out and slept. The big kids told us it was where you could take girls to do whatever it was you did with girls. If so, the bums and winos and big kids and girls must have had keys, because the door always was locked.

When the circus came to town it was by rail, and from these railroad yards the animals were led north up Chenango Street to Stow Flats where circuses and carnivals were held. Ma took me to a couple of carnivals. She liked to play the game where you tossed coins into saucers, trying to get a prize. I avoided looking at the "carnies," the carnival workers, when we walked past the booths and attractions. If I made eye contact they looked scary to me, like they knew something extremely vile and wouldn't hesitate to introduce me to it if they got the chance. Smiling menaces. Tent religious revivals were also occasionally held there. Stow Flats was named for the founder of Stow Manufacturing, a maker of flexible shafting, which sounds like what I got when the military draft came calling. Later it became the city dump before being developed into the Binghamton Plaza shopping center.

It is not unusual for a person to spend his or her entire childhood on the same street, but it most often is in the same house. Ma and I, however, were constantly on the move. I can count eight physical places of residence from birth until graduation from high school. Six of those apartments were on Chenango Street and three were in the same building. People ask me why we moved so often. I don't know; it's one of the many questions I should have asked my mother. I assume it must have been because she found a monthly rent that was a few bucks cheaper. Whatever it was, it must have been transmitted in the blood, for in my lifetime I have moved household—bag, baggage, and human beings—twenty-six times since being burned out of the Moon Block in 1949; eighteen of those moves were since Nancy and I have been married.

Immediately, the night of the fire, we—Ma, Louise, and I—spent at the home of my cousins Ken and Ruth Smith on Lawton Avenue on the West Side, the children of my father's sister Mima and her husband Walter, a worker at the Link flight simulator company (one of the first workers, in fact, for Ed Link, founder of the company). Ken, who is three months younger than I, says he can still see us there that night; he was wide-eyed at our bedraggled appearance and the strong smell of smoke. Ken says my father was there, also. Why he was there I do not know, since he did not live with us. Presumably it was the sense of protectiveness he felt for me.

We cannot have remained there long. For one thing, they had little room in their turn-of-the-century two-story house that was home to the four Smiths and an old lady boarder and, I think, my Aunt Frances Miller, youngest sister of Mima and Keith. For another, the differing lifestyles of my devoutly churchgoing evangelical Aunt Mima and that of my easygoing, decidedly unchurched mother were hardly simpatico, though Mima would not have let that get in the way of her Christian duty. (The depth of Ma's religious sensibilities went no further than the comment I heard her make several times, "If you go to church you have more luck," but she never made any effort to improve her luck that way.) What Walter might have felt about it I cannot imagine. What the mostly silent Walter Smith thought about anything at any time was hard for anyone to imagine.

Thus, after the fire and the move north of the Viaduct we lived on the proverbial "other side of the tracks." Funny thing, I cannot remember any of the actual, physical moves. Who moved us and how and when is lost in the mists of time. Probably it was one or both of Ma's frequently drunken younger brothers, Russell and Walter Sheridan, though both were usually without personal vehicular transport about as often as they were drunk. In any case the first move, after the brief stay at the Smiths', would not have been difficult since everything we owned had burned to a crisp. It was, in fact, into the apartment rented by Walter Sheridan and his first wife, Lena.

Lena all but disappeared from view at some point in the 1950s; she and Walter got divorced. She was a thin, intense, dark-haired woman who seemed to me too refined, relatively speaking, to be associated in any way with Walter Sheridan, though admittedly she did share his liking for liquor. If Walter moved us, it was in Lena's car; perhaps it was for her car he married her. They had a small second-floor apartment at 289 Chenango north of the Viaduct (and thus north of the late Moon Block) in one of the three or four wooden buildings, firetraps all, that stood approximately across from St. Paul's Roman Catholic Church. Mercifully, all of the buildings were torn down decades ago. The apartment consisted of a living room facing the street, a room behind that which served as a bedroom when the Murphy bed was folded down. Off of that room was a kitchenette and off of the kitchenette an even smaller bathroom. I remember it well because Ma and I moved into it ourselves within about a year after Walter and Lena moved out.

Before that, however, we moved a couple of cross streets down from that apartment, to a second-floor apartment on Eldredge. I don't know how it is now, but then once you crossed the Viaduct you were definitely on the North Side. I grew to be perversely proud of being a North Sider, as it was, besides being a poor side of town, also the "tough" side—though "tough" to the same degree that Louise was "wild," comparing both concepts with standards today.

But where *was* Louise? Surely she cannot have gone off to that "reform school" *immediately* after the fire. Yet she was not with Ma and me when we moved in with Walter and Lena nor when we moved from there to Eldredge Street. Ma was chary of talking about Louise's situation, and I, sensitive to matters that were sensitive (as well as being self-absorbed), did not bring it up. For decades afterward Louise and I mostly avoided the subject, too. It could be that, given our lack of adequate living accommodations, Louise *had* been hustled off prematurely to the reform school she probably had already been assigned to. Or it could be she had been "farmed out" with relatives once again. This, then, is the point at which to try to explain Ma, me, and my sisters.

§

Earlier I wrote that Louise had told me that my parents broke up because Ma had deceived Pa as to Louise's identity. Actually, to her identity *and* to that of my other half-sister (and Louise's half-sister), whose name I do not give here because all her life she seemed embarrassed by the situation and I will not embarrass her in death. She died in 2009 in Pennsylvania, a fact I learned only by googling her name, which indicates the degree of our disconnection. I had seen her only once since the late 1950s and that was at the gravesite of our mother's funeral in 1994. Early on I was conscious that she felt uncomfortable with my presence; later, contemplating her reaction, I assumed that I reminded her of something she preferred to forget.

Here are the sordid facts: Each of us had different fathers. Mine was the only man our mother married. The two girls, Louise said, were "farmed out" to live with Ma's brother Ralph and his family in Pennsylvania when Ma came to Binghamton to work. Indeed, for most of my life I thought the other sister was my cousin, one of Ralph's children. As an adult I began to suspect the truth, but it was not confirmed until I was about fifty years old when Louise said to me, "You know, she's your sister, your half-sister." That is how delicately all of us danced around the outer rim of the matter, never even looking at the core. Ma never acknowledged to me that she was my half-sister. I doubt that she ever referred to her as my "cousin"; I probably was allowed to assume it from her living with Ralph's family. No one in the family ever spoke openly about it, not even Ralph's family when I visited them occasionally during a couple of summers in the early 1950s. Why did Ralph even put up with what must have been a burden? Did Ma pay him to "keep" Louise and our sister? Were my summer visits a prelude or trial run for also being farmed out? (My father thought so and would not countenance it.)

One thing is for sure, the farming out was a source of lifelong anger for Louise, fierce anger at our mother and jealous anger at me for having had a better deal than she (about which she rarely lost an opportunity to remind me). "You stole my childhood!" she blazed at Ma, and with some justice. She lived in near-poverty with Ralph's family, she told me, and never had a doll until my father bought her one. If she exaggerated, it could not have been by much. Ralph was not exactly rolling in dough, even when I knew him, and he would have been unlikely to lavish any of it on his sister's bastards. Life must have been stark for the two girls. Indeed, as a girl she was told rather brutally by Ralph who her father was when he took her into a tavern with him one day. "See that man sitting over there on the bar stool?" he said to her. "That's your father."

Louise never forgot that and told it more than once. (Louise said she never knew the identity of our sister's father; perhaps our sister never did, either.) By contrast, all her life she also never forgot that Pa bought her that first doll. This is where the marriage-ending deceit that Louise spoke of enters the picture. According to Louise, Ma told Pa that her daughters were her younger sisters. They would have had to be *much* younger, as Ma was then in her early thirties and the girls no older than twelve and ten, perhaps even younger. Apparently Pa bought it, for at some point both girls came to live with us in the Moon Block. I do not recall my younger sister being there—nor do I remember Louise until the later 1940s—but Louise was insistent in praising Pa's kindness to them.

Until the truth came out. When it did, my father must have exploded in outraged anger, the girls were shipped back to Pennsylvania, and he moved into that narrow front bedroom until he could move out of the Moon Block. The marriage, which I imagine never was within hailing distance of perfect, was over. Once he moved out, Louise, but not my other sister, came back to live with us. This is where my remembered life with Louise begins; she and Pa (not to mention my other sister) are never in my mental Moon Block together, however much they may have been in reality.

Louise was a quite pretty young woman; she inherited many of our mother's features, more than I did. When I look at photos of her I feel an ineffable sadness that is more than remembrance of bittersweet things past. It pierces my heart that she had to endure the girlhood that she did and, more, that she could not overcome the bitterness about it. On the one hand, the adversity of that girlhood contributed to making her the ambitious, hardworking woman she became; on the other hand, the bitterness warped her enjoyment of the life she made for herself and her family.

So little is known; so much more could be known if only questions had been asked—but I never asked because it was a subject whose outlines were cloudy and that I sensed was to be avoided. No one ever volunteered information, not my mother's family nor my father's. In the latter case it was a not-nice subject and why bring up not-nice things? You might have to explain them. Even decades later when everybody was grown up and most of the principals were dead, when I deliberately referred to my unconventional upbringing, members of my father's family quickly hurried past it to nicer things. In my mother's family, it was just another shabby circumstance not much different from other shabby circumstances, so what's the big deal? And I lost contact with that side early on.

§

A little bit about Mae Miller, then. As a young woman she was quite good-looking, about five feet four inches tall, with a good figure and reddish hair that I inherited but lost to mouse brown after my second year, but that I passed on to my older daughter, Krista, who kept it. All her life she was a demon for work. Thirty-three years she worked in the Endicott-Johnson shoe factory in Johnson City, the last years in what they called the rubber mill. She professed to like it, and I believe she did. She liked the camaraderie, the joking back and forth with her fellow workers, male and female. The Triple Cities Traction bus she caught from Chenango Street got her into Johnson City early enough to stop in the Dipsy Doodle restaurant for coffee with friends. I visited her at the rubber mill once or twice, and she was proud to show me off. When she retired in 1974 at age 62—later she regretted retiring so soon—she received an EJ pension of ninety-six dollars a month, and when she died twenty years later it was still ninety-six dollars a month. Ma also worked frequently on weekends cleaning other people's houses. Usually they ended up being her friends.

Ma smoked and drank. It just occurs to me: What effect did that have on her unborn children? If it had any effect, I and my sisters had plenty of company, because pregnant women were not cautioned then the way they are now about not smoking and drinking. At about age fifty her drinking (and tavern-going) dropped off precipitously and she drank only the occasional beer, but she smoked cigarettes up until her late seventies, when the need to use an oxygen tank for breathing put a stop to it. That's what she died of, really, smoking-induced emphysema.

What her life was like in Pennsylvania I do not know—again, those unasked questions. Her father was Frank Sheridan and her mother Jenny Race. My Grandfather Sheridan I barely remember; he died around 1950. My Grandmother Sheridan died before I could know her. Ma had eight siblings, four brothers and four sisters. Not necessarily in order of birth, they were: Roscoe, Ralph, Walter, Russell, Anna, Jean, Viola, and Romayne.

Ma was not a great intellect, far from it, but she was an extremely nice person. It would seem her niceness extended to easy virtue, for Louise was born when Ma was twenty-one and our sister two years later. Louise once said, "Who knows if she didn't have other bastards that we don't know about?" But I think that was just bitterness talking. Nevertheless, easy virtue was a trait that she had not entirely shed when I lived with her.

At some point in the 1930s she found her way, like so many unemployed northeastern Pennsylvanians looking for work, to Binghamton. There (or somewhere) in the winter of 1940 she gave her by now easy virtue to Keith G. Miller, and nine months later, give or take a month or two, I was the unintended result.

CHAPTER 4

Christopher Columbus and Thomas Edison

"The past is a foreign country: they do things differently there."
—L.P. Hartley, *The Go-Between*

I went to school with boys with green teeth. I have the photo of my sixth-grade graduating class in front of me as I type and, though the black-and-white photo is not big enough to reveal it despite their smiles, I can still identify two boys who did not practice good—or any—dental hygiene. Not that my own teeth were all that dazzling. Few people in that area at that time had money to spend on what were considered frills like dental care. The assumption was that your teeth went bad early, and as a grown-up you had them pulled as soon as you could and got dentures (a fate that fortunately I avoided). Teeth aside, all twenty-one of us in that photo tried to make a neat, uniform appearance (as we were instructed to do by our teacher). Nearly all the boys (in the back rows) have on a suit or sport jacket and tie, and the girls wear frilly white or light-colored dresses. In the front row their eleven-and-twelve-year-old legs are demurely crossed at the ankles. One of them is another of my serial, unwitting girlfriends.

This was Thomas Edison Elementary School, a two- or three-story brick pile that sat almost on the corner of Robinson and Chenango streets. It fell to the wrecker's ball decades ago. I should have entered Edison in January 1950, right after the fire, as we now lived in a different part of town, or at least by September 1950, the start of the new school year.

The Binghamton school district was strict about that, I believe; you were required to attend the school for the area in which you lived. But for some reason I continued to attend Christopher Columbus through all of fourth grade—that is, until June 1951. My memory has erased essential parts of a year and a half of school—the long walk down Eldredge Street, over the Viaduct, onto Lewis Street, then Fayette, and ultimately to Columbus School. I must have walked it two hundred times each way.

I am certain I am not mistaken. For one thing, Ma saved my early report cards and a few school assignments that show I was at Columbus through fourth grade. For another, I can clearly see myself sitting in Mrs. Brown's fourth-grade classroom in Columbus. High on the wall, above the blackboard and running around the room, were black cards with white writing, showing examples of proper Zaner Bloser penmanship. I can see her getting up to answer the buzzer for the intercom system mounted near the door. It was of one of those old black metal dinguses, with the mouthpiece on the wall portion and the earpiece suspended from a hook. From her I learned about Egypt, which I had thought was pronounced Egg-pit, and about how Chinese women bound their feet so that they would not grow and thus stay dainty (I think our textbook may have been a few decades old). Once I made a pest of myself by showing off my "David Harding, Counterspy" badge that I had gotten by responding to a mail offer made on the radio espionage drama, *Counterspy*. It was gold-covered and had a drawing in the center of David Harding, the series hero, that glowed in the dark. Mrs. Brown finally made me give it to her and I never got it back.

On Valentine's Day a large cardboard box covered in white paper and decorated with red, stretchy crepe paper sat on a table near Mrs. Brown's desk in the left front corner of the room. Into it I dropped the cards I had bought at Wilber's, a small department store on Chenango. The cards came in books or folders made of several pages of stiff paper, from which you cut or punched them out on perforations. I agonized over which one to give to my current unwitting girlfriend; it should indicate romantic interest far beyond what was contained in the cards I gave to others—though how would she know that?—but not strongly enough to be accused of it should my classmates see it. It was a futile effort, for fine discrimination of that degree was not to be found outside a tool-and-die-maker's shop. In Mrs. Brown's class I first learned to read properly, sparking the joy that has remained with me all my life.

Our common reader was not the ubiquitous Dick and Jane series, but a rival pair called Alice and Jerry and their dog Jip. I was fascinated by, but did not read, a book on a classroom shelf, *Little Brother*. I have searched for it since, but cannot be sure what it was that I gazed upon day after day. Perhaps it was William J. Long's *A Little Brother to the Bear*. And it was in fourth grade that I discovered the Freddy the Pig books by Walter R. Brooks.

There was a prescribed format for writing our schoolwork. On a sheet of loose-leaf paper we had to place the school number and the grade and semester on the top line at the left, our names on the right. The subject went on the second line at the left, on the right the date. Thus:

5-4A	**Roger Miller**
Arithmetic	**June 4, 1951**

This must have been a school-district-wide practice for some time, for I have examples of it from my two elementary schools from third grade through six. We wrote with and only with—no outside pens allowed—steel-nibbed pens that we dipped into the small round inkpots sunk into the upper right corner of our desks.

Yet most other school-related memories of that part of my childhood have retreated to an unreachable region of my brain. I know that I walked for lunch each day to my Aunt Florence's apartment on Court Street, near the old Walking Shoe store whose neon sign depicting a series of moving footsteps dazzled me. But I do not know what I did with, how I played with, Columbus School friends I had, boys with last names of Montone and Torto, and others. I may not have done much playing with them, as they lived in one area and I in another. There is a scene, late afternoon or early evening, in which I am nearly weeping as they are standing around me next to a scraggly, balding front-yard hedge, probably on Fayette Street. Presumably this is when I took leave of them, having been told that I was to be cruelly dispatched to the Siberia of Thomas Edison School. I never saw any of them again, except for a skinny, curly-headed Italian kid named Anthony, a particularly close friend who lived on Carroll Street with what I considered to be aged immigrant parents. Him I discovered by accident as we both were about to graduate from Harpur College (the forerunner of today's Binghamton University) a decade and a half later. I did not know he was also attending Harpur. I did not introduce myself.

The Chenango Kid

Ma and I lived on Eldredge Street no more than a year and a half. We had a small, low-ceilinged, second-story apartment in the back of a house approximately halfway between Chenango and Emmett streets. The entrance was by way of an outside set of wooden stairs, which led to the hallway of the apartment, on one side of which was the kitchen and bathroom, on the other a living room and bedroom. I slept on a rollaway bed in Ma's bedroom. For the first time we had a telephone. The number was 2-7557. Later, when the city got phone exchanges, it became RAymond 2-7557. Having telephone service was by no means universal six-plus decades ago; the question asked was not, "What's your phone number?," but, "Are you on the phone?" So look at us, on our way into the middle-class on Ma's EJ pay of thirty-some dollars a week. We had that snazzy new Norge refrigerator in the kitchen and a "living room set" consisting of a green couch and a gray chair of cheap, rough, synthetic fabric patterned with scratchy swirls. Setting off this modern décor was a pair of ebony, turbaned heads disguised as table lamps. All purchased, on the installment plan no doubt, at Olum's furniture store on Main Street in Johnson City. It never occurred to me to wonder how we now could afford to have a refrigerator and a phone when we couldn't before, or where the new furniture came from to replace that destroyed in the fire. Kids just live. Only when I did a bit of newspaper research on the fire decades later did the question and answer come to me at the same time: The Red Cross, the newspaper said, tried to get donated clothing for the fire victims and cash contributions to help them purchase furnishings.

This could have been when I first tried writing a book, a Freddy the Pig adventure or a not very cleverly disguised imitation thereof. I wrote it on lined, loose-leaf-notebook paper. However much I wrote—it could not have been much—I was mostly concerned about getting the front matter correct: copyright, dedication, list of previous books (I fretted about having none), the ISBN or whatever the number was called then. I asked my Uncle Will about this—he had been to college and read a lot—but he gave me a dismissive answer.

I was alone a fair amount of time, including in the evening. Ma was out on the town—i.e., the bars on Chenango. She couldn't do it too often, because she had to get up for work early in the morning and she was conscientious about that, but when opportunity offered, such as on weekends or holidays. I fretted over being alone. Sometimes if the fret level got too high I would call around to the bars, asking if Mae Miller was there. In the background when the bartender answered I could hear loud talk and laughter and juke-box music and the clink of glasses. The bartender did not have to holler out "Mae Miller here?" because everyone knew Mae Miller so if she was not there he said so and if she was it was simply "Mae? Phone," and then I heard the soft thud of the receiver being put down. After a few moments she would answer and I would ask when she was coming home and she would say, "I don't know, Roger. Soon. Don't ding me." There it was again, that word, "ding."

I did not go into the bars much and when I did I did not like it. They were not the trendy sports bars where today's middlebrow suburbanites go to swap exaggerations about their children's achievements nor the quiet, dimly lit Third Avenue caverns that John McNulty wrote about affectionately in *The New Yorker* where lonely men sat brooding over their unhappiness. They were grungy working-class watering holes where working-class people went to get drunk and have a noisy good time. I did not and do not get that idea of a good time nor the ambience, to use a word the patrons never would, in which it was pursued, one that was a mixture of pungent odors—spilled beer, sweat, cigarette smoke, stale perfume, greasy food being fried to a fare-thee-well—and raucous sounds. I *should* have liked it because when I did enter one invariably I was treated like The Little Prince by maundering inebriates who meant well in saying things like, "So this is the hope of the future, eh, Mae?" and buying me soft drinks or giving me coins, scooped up from the beer rings on the bar, to play the shuffleboard. Russell tended bar at a couple of the places. Once I made him a sign to replace an older one, curling and browning and fly-specked, taped against the mirror behind the bar: "I May Be Under the Alcofluence of Incohol, but I Am Not as Drunk as Some Thinkle Peep I Am." Ho ho; my dislike of the barfly culture notwithstanding, that was wit to me. I embellished it with a picture of a man, his eyes the X's of a traditional cartoon drunk, holding a martini glass from which rose the traditional cartoon bubbles indicating an intoxicating drink.

So, alone, I read comic books. I was heavily into Walt Disney product at this time (which was when I got nabbed by the beady-eyed little worm in Williams' cigar store), Donald Duck and his nephews Huey, Dewey, and Louie; Scrooge McDuck. The piles of money in Scrooge's vault grabbed and held my attention; I studied the way the coins were drawn and the way the effect of immense wealth was created. I listened to the Lone Ranger on radio: "Return with us now to those thrilling days of yesteryear!"

Eldredge Street, neat and bland, is a relative nullity when I weigh it against it all our dwelling places. Yet it sticks in my head and will come back sometimes when I am reading a novel, and my imagination will site that novel there, I suppose because of an association triggered by mention of time or a name or emotion. The people who walked in and out of Edward Newhouse's *The Temptation of Roger Heriott*, for instance, walked in and out of the Eldredge Street apartment where once another Roger dwelt.

§

Muted, vaguely upsetting noises were coming from the dark in the next room, the one with the Murphy bed. A scuffling of feet, the rustling of cloth, hoarse and excited whisperings. "Unh, unh," someone said repeatedly and sporadically, and someone else, or maybe the same person, made suppressed moaning sounds. I sort of knew what was going on and I sort of didn't, and I didn't want to know more.

A girl, about fifteen years old, had come out of the room and sat down near me, looking concerned. Her name was Lorena and she was babysitting me while Ma was out. She was the daughter of a friend of Ma's named Leona, who possibly was with Ma at that moment in the North Side Tavern or Dud & Tom's or the Wales Hotel. Lorena was supposed to be babysitting by herself, but her older sister Lorna, sixteen or seventeen, had come along and brought with her a male friend, both of whom were in the darkened other room. Lorena looked back at the room, listened to the muffled sounds, and then at me, sitting by the window.

"You OK, kid?" she asked.

I nodded, saying nothing and not looking at her. The sounds came faster.

"It's just Lorna and her boyfriend. You know. She thinks they might get married, but I think she's crazy if she thinks that."

Did she expect me to understand that? Did she expect me to take that as a rationalization for something I didn't even understand? I pretended not to heed what was going on by listening intently to and watching the rush of traffic on Chenango Street below. It was a soft summer night and a warm wind blew Ma's lace-like curtains into the room and across my face. They were noisily in one room; I remained resolutely as far away as I could in the other. What did I know? I was ten years old.

Roger K. Miller

§

That occurred when we lived in the "Walter and Lena" second-floor apartment at 289 Chenango that I described earlier, in a building just about across from where Robinson Street runs into Chenango, diagonally opposite the A&P market on the corner. I think of it as the "green building," though it may actually have been gray, if its shabbiness had any identifiable color at all. I specify the second floor, because later we lived in two other apartments—directly across the hall from each other—on the first floor of that same three-story building. It was dusty and gritty and peeling, and a set of wide wooden steps led up to the first floor, for there were basement or semi-basement apartments underneath. We lived there two years, all the while I attended fifth and sixth grades at Thomas Edison Elementary. Thus my mother must have moved us in the summer, after I completed fourth grade at Columbus. Now that I think of it, all of our moves must have been in summer, for I can associate each apartment with a specific grade or grades in school. In the summers I usually was not at home but at my grandparents' in Lopez.

Into this apartment we brought our first television. It is where I put together one of the early examples of the new hobby, plastic models, specifically a red Model T Ford. I had to apply heat to the end of the axles to hold the wheels on. It is where I read an astonishing number and variety of comic books, from *Little Lulu* (I liked to read the "Dear Diary" feature in the center pages) to *Tales of the Crypt*, the latter of which scared me silly with its gore-dripping skulls yet drew me back again and again. And where, kneeling in front of the couch on the linoleumed living-room floor, I drew detailed pictures of the interiors of big, fancy yachts and houseboats, daydreaming that if I sent the drawings to the patent office—whatever that was—they were required to build the boat and give it to me, its creator. It would be cool to live on it, I thought. I never got a boat; perhaps I sent my drawings to the wrong office. This was where another boy, living in an apartment on the same floor, brought his drums to play because his parents, having insensibly bought them for him, would sensibly not let him play them in their apartment. He was older and an oaf and was able to bully me into letting him in, until Ma came home one day while he was still there and put an end to that. I know his last name still; I won't mention it here, but it was the name of a country.

It was also where—I still smile to think about it—a salesman tried to sell me a British luxury automobile. I had requested a catalog or brochure through the mail, having seen an advertisement somewhere that listed an address. I don't believe it was for Rolls-Royce, but something a peg or two down-market from that, possibly Wolseley. The brochure arrived, a surprisingly expensive-looking publication, a fitting vehicle for promoting gorgeous vehicles. Again and again I leafed through its thick, creamy pages, marveling at what some faraway people could afford to drive.

And then one evening came a knock on our door. It was a man seeking a Mister Roger Miller who had expressed interest in his motorcars. Ma and I were floored. The man must have seen his error right away, but even then I thought he should have seen it even earlier. Could he not have twigged that someone living behind a scabrous door on the second-floor of a dingy, smelly apartment building was unlikely to be in the market for an automobile that was accustomed to being parked in a multi-stall garage or on great circular gravel driveways in front of stately homes and not on the street with Chevys and Fords and DeSotos from the 1930s and '40s? For that matter, could he not have twigged still earlier, when he first hit our dusty, gritty neighborhood of depressing apartment buildings and woeful little single-family houses? Maybe he thought an eccentric rich guy lived here. The more I think about it, I wonder, was there *anyone anywhere* in Binghamton who could afford such a vehicle, and, if they could, would be likely to buy it instead of a Cadillac? From how far away did the poor guy have to travel to scout out a possible sale to Roger Miller? Surely there was no Wolseley dealer in the environs of Binghamton.

§

When I think of that building now, it is usually of warm weather: Residents sit on the sagging, splintery, footstep-worn steps in shirtsleeves or undershirts, smoking and talking with each other or with passersby. In that aspect it has some appeal, in that people engaged with their surroundings and with each other. Sometimes, admittedly, they engaged to the point of fisticuffs. Cars with windows rolled down whiz by other cars parked at the curb, honking at the traffic or at friends seen on the sidewalk. Kids play, nothing special or organized, just jumping, shouting, laughing. There is little or no breeze. The buzzing sound of cicadas fills the air.

§

None of the public schools I attended have survived as they then were. Two are gone completely: Thomas Edison Elementary and East Junior High. North High is now East Middle School; Christopher Columbus is for some sort of special education. I hold a special affection for Thomas Edison as it is the place that, in my head, I locate all stories I read of pre-adolescent schooling, such as Walter Van Tilburg Clark's wonderful *The City of Trembling Leaves*. It does not matter that sparsely treed Chenango Street in the 1950s was a far cry from aspen-shaded Reno, Nevada, in the 1920s, Edison is the place in my mind that Clark's Tim Hazard and all his friends attend school. The interior and exterior have to be mentally adjusted to accommodate differences between my and the author's realities, but everyone fits.

The school year was divided into A and B semesters, B starting in September and A in January. The pedagogical rationale must have been that if you flunked you had to repeat only the semester, not the entire year. I had two teachers in fifth grade, first, in the B semester, a nice, gray-haired lady in her fifties (or so I guess; at the age of ten, who knows?) named Mrs. Casey. We read *Dr. Doolittle*. It was, I am sure, an early if not indeed the original edition that contained derogatory terms for and depictions of blacks and other ethnic groups. If so, it didn't seem to bother us; we just liked the animals and the idea of talking to them. Though there were black children in my fourth- and sixth-grade classes, there may not have been any in Mrs. Casey's fifth grade. For her I wrote a story, "The Magic Flute," that she praised extravagantly.

The second semester, Grade 5A, was led by a different sort of teacher altogether. Tall, and bronzed from the Arizona or New Mexican sun, she floated up and down between the rows of desks in the classroom as if every moving part in her was fitted with well-oiled ball bearings, clanking turquoise-encrusted silver bracelets on both arms, smelling of God's heavenly scent, and smiling the inviting smile of a dark-haired Doris Day. Her name was Miss Barbara Schilling and she was a breath of fresh Western air in the middle of a slushy Upstate New York winter, and all of us boys, and probably the girls, too, were instantly in love with her. She seemed to know that and think it sweet. To receive her touch—teachers could touch students then—was better than getting an A on a spelling test. The only thing about her that I did not like was that she made us diagram sentences. I didn't like, and in fact was incapable of, diagramming sentences for *any* teacher. And the only time this Southwestern angel expressed disapproval of me was when, during warm weather toward the end of the school year, she caught me throwing paper airplanes out the window. Actually, she didn't catch me, but the janitor, who brought the incriminating evidence up to her. I had been stupid enough to make my airplanes out of schoolwork that bore my name. I wasn't angry at her for being disappointed in me, but at the janitor for ratting me out for such a puny infraction. What? A few lousy pieces of paper on his precious schoolyard?

A schoolyard that, as at Christopher Columbus, was of the finest asphalt, surrounded by a ten-foot high chain-link fence. Not a blade of grass. At recess during warm weather we sometimes played dodgeball and Red Rover, Red Rover (I dare you to come over). For a brief spell we boys played something called "Yankees and Confederates," a game that consisted chiefly in yelling and charging at each other and taking prisoners. Some of us even had cheap little Civil War-style forage caps with either a Union or Confederate flag on the tops. Where did they come from? Some movie promotion?

On June 24, 1952, I appeared in a radio production of WNBF's children's series, "The Story Road." We did "Lenka's Little House" by Fan Kissen from the book *The Straw Ox and Other Tales*. I played the Father. Other players were: Lenka, Lillian Gleason; Dorla, Sharon Kolanda; Stepmother, Gretta Reynolds; Old Man, Gerald Walker; Narrator, Linda Lynn. It was directed by our captivating fifth-grade teacher, Miss Barbara Schilling.

With that we took our leave of our pedagogical darling and, after the intervening summer vacation (in my case spent with my grandparents in Lopez), moved on to Mrs. Tice's sixth grade.

§

A school nurse came every so often and checked us for head lice, flicking through our hair with what looked like knitting needles for "nits," as we called them. How marvelously socially responsible we were then as a society. Each year we even received a brief physical exam, boys and girls, by a doctor, free of charge, because a decent society wanted to make sure its children were basically healthy and to head off at the schoolyard pass any potential outbreaks of disease. Today I suppose the neo-cons and libertarians and Hayek disciples and distributists—whatever the hell *they* are—would say we have no business using other people's money to palpate the bodies of public schoolchildren for their (and our) own good. I would have agreed with them then, for I dreaded the exams. A couple of weeks ahead of time you were sent a slip to let you know the date and hour of your appointment down in the nurse's office, and I fretted about it until the time of the exam. Usually they had to take my blood pressure two or three times to get a true reading, once my nervousness had abated.

(Years later, in 1960, when I worked as a teller at First-City National Bank I saw how this same "white-coat hypertension" kept a fellow worker out of the draft. He had been called up to Syracuse for a Selective Service physical multiple times, but he always failed it due to "high blood pressure" caused by nervousness in the presence of medicos. They even kept him overnight in the hope of getting him to relax. Why they thought that staying overnight in a cheap hotel in Syracuse would relax anyone I do not know. Of course, he may really have had high blood pressure, but the doctors seemed to recognize what it was and he always claimed that in normal circumstances his blood pressure was normal. Years after that, when I was called for my own Selective Service physical, I thought of that fellow—his name was Kenny—with disgruntled envy.)

We also had music, conducted by a teacher who traveled from school to school. She was a jolly lady of some proportions and once or twice a week she came to Edison and held sing-a-longs in the school auditorium. She played the piano, we sang. Songs that remain in my head six decades later, such as:

> *Oh lovely meadows green and fair*
> *High the grass is growing*
> *High the grass is grow-oh-ing*
> *Oh lovely meadows green and fair*
> *High the grass is growing everywhere.*
>
> *Mountains of melting snow*
> *Circling around they go*
> *Circling around they go*
> *Calling to me, HEY!*

And:

> *Oh for the days of the Kerry dancing*
> *Oh for the sound of the piper's tune . . .*

Her name was Margaret Connolly and she decorated her signature with little musical symbols ♫ ♪.

We had drills, fire drills in which we scurried outdoors, shivering in the winter months, and what must have been air raid or nuclear drills. I say "must have been," for they were not the "duck-and-cover" kind that are mocked today, though we had been shown the animated film of that title featuring Bert the Turtle put out by the Civil Defense Administration. Our exercises were equally hopeless as possible life-savers. We trooped down the stairs to the basement and stood with our noses against the wall. What was that all about? It could not have been a fire drill, for we would not have been directed to remain in the building in a fire. So I assume it was a drill in the event of some other sort of disaster.

Those were the days when radios had a little triangle-within-a-circle symbol at 640 and 1240 on the AM dial. (For that matter, those were the days when the AM dial was practically the *only* dial.) The symbols, established as part of CONELRAD, the emergency broadcasting system, were for easy identification of the stations that we were to tune to in the event of a civil defense emergency. I wondered why those two stations. Did that mean all the others could go on broadcasting their regular programs while the bombs fell on our heads? (No; it had to do with an intricate system of confusing enemy aircraft that might be navigating by radio direction finding.)

No one on the North Side could afford to build a bomb shelter. Not many people anywhere could; by the turn of the 1960s little more than 1,500 had been built in the country. But they were much in the news, how to build the best one and the pros and cons of doing so. If you built one and there was a nuclear attack, wouldn't your shelter-less neighbors kill you to get at it? And even if they didn't, after the attack was over how could you survive in the desolation and the atmosphere of heavy radiation fallout? The only person I have known to possess a bomb shelter was the note teller at the bank where I worked after high school; he was said to be building one. He was a nervous, fussy fellow and the object of amused derision behind his back.

Roger K. Miller

§

Florence King, the wittily acerbic writer and commentator, has rightfully praised the self-abnegating contributions of old maids and other spinsters to American life and history. For a long time they formed the essential cadre of our national teacher corps; typically they were required to resign their teaching positions upon marrying. Who knows how many of them spurned marriage in order to hang on to an assured income rather than tie themselves to the dubious fortunes of a possible future town drunk? Even as late as the 1950s, when I was in high school, about half of the women faculty was unmarried (which we could tell because they were designated either Miss or Mrs.; this was decades before Ms). They usually weren't gentle in the manner of making their contributions ("Sit up straight!"; "Stop whining!"), but that was the point: We needed to sit up straight and stop whining. We need it even more now.

Mrs. Sarah Ann Tice was obviously not a spinster. How old she was I do not know, but she wasn't young—at least in her late fifties. Somehow she, like some of her sisters (such as Mrs. Casey and Mrs. Brown), managed both marriage and avoiding the requirement to give up her job to be supported, so the theory went, by her husband. I probably should not make too much of this, for there were younger women teachers who were unmarried and remained unmarried, probably—again—on the understandable notion that being yoked to a man for life was not necessarily the best offer going.

Nevertheless, I place Mrs. Tice in Florence King's admirable-spinster category because of her vintage and her effectiveness. She probably was a good teacher and she wasn't very nice. That is, we kids thought she wasn't nice, and kids' complaints are not always of the self-pleading variety. A friend reminds me of the time she rapped a classmate's hand pretty smartly with a ruler. The next day the boy's mother came to the classroom and laid into Mrs. Tice with her tongue. Still, if she did her job in an arbitrary manner, who among us does not? She chastised me for making a drawing, either of an American Indian or a medieval battle scene, in which all the arrows flew through the air in neat formations; she contended with some justification that they should be random, haphazard. She also did not like my drawing of a car with a band of headlights all across its grill. Ridiculous, she said; car headlights were set atop, or into, the front of each fender and had been since the dawn of time.

She was of that era of teachers—today's teachers likely would contend it is not over yet—who tried to augment an anemic paycheck with outside income. She sold *Compton's Pictured Encyclopedia* and somehow cajoled Ma into buying a set, presumably for their educational value and on the installment plan, just a few dollars each week or month out of Ma's puny paycheck. I read the section on animation and Walt Disney over and over and over, each time hoping that it would reveal the secret of how one became a cartoonist or animator. Beyond that, the encyclopedia actually turned out to be useful. My seventh-grade English teacher at East Junior, Mr. Bernstein, once showed up at our door, trying to sell us a stove/range, but did not succeed.

For some reason we got stuck—which is the way we kids saw it—with Mrs. Tice for a whole year. We were supposed to move on to Mr. Church in 6A. It was highly unusual in the early 1950s to have a male teacher in elementary grades, but we did not get to experience it.

Our principal was, of course, male. Female principals were as rare as male elementary teachers. I don't retain a good impression of ours, Mr. Munson. I'm sure he must have been decent enough fellow, but my only run-ins with him were not pleasant. He verbally took a strip off my hide when I had to report to him over that petty paper-airplane incident. I was a school-crossing guard—indeed, at one time the captain of the guards, with a shiny silver-and-blue badge to stick on my white canvas, Sam Browne-style belt—and he withered me with his contempt for my self-pity when I complained that no one would obey me. You can't *make* people obey you, he said, drawing I suppose on recent military experience, but show them by your bearing and actions that they need to.

A bit more serious was the time I and another boy stood in front of his desk, heads bowed miserably downward, as he yelled at us while angrily waving in our faces a limp little eight-page booklet that he had just taken from us. It was one of those wretchedly drawn, wretchedly printed bits of pornography that sometimes popped up in schoolyards from God knows where. I think we called them "Toby books," but I have since learned that the more common term is "Tijuana bibles." Like the one, titled "Dick Tracy's Dick," that was causing Mr. Munson to nearly leap over his desk at us, they were filthy parodies that took popular comic strip figures, such as Archie and Betty and Veronica, and put them in eye-popping sexual situations—Archie screwing Betty and Veronica, Dagwood screwing women at work while the milkman took care of Blondie at home, that sort of thing (which, as ten- or eleven-year-olds I am sure we barely understood). If there were any consequences of our vice I have managed to suppress them. I am quite sure we did not get the booklet back. Maybe Mr. Munson kept it?

Speaking of eye-popping situations, a girl classmate once saw a female faculty member and a male family member, both married but not to each other, kissing in the teachers' lounge. They saw that she saw, and ever afterward they were *very* sweet to her.

§

I must have had an iron sense of responsibility and self-discipline to do what I was expected to do and not get into trouble. I got myself off to school each morning, from as early as the fourth grade on. Ma was out the door by 6:00 a.m. to catch the bus to work. She woke me up just before leaving, I dressed myself, made breakfast (milk and cereal), and was out the door in plenty of time to leg it to school. I was very conscientious in that regard. Also, I was a scaredy-cat. I was too scared to do anything wrong. Those two characteristics, conscientiousness and fear, probably kept me from going off the rails in an unstructured and at times unhinged upbringing.

One morning in fifth grade Mrs. Casey pulled me aside in a kind manner and asked me what was wrong, as she saw that I had been crying. She thought it was because I did not have the money for some school project or other. I may or may not have told her that the real reason was that it had suddenly come over me at breakfast that morning that my mother had to go to work every day at EJ and the realization made me feel bad. I cannot explain why I happened to break out of my normal state of self-absorption to be concerned for a moment about my truly hard-working mother. Or was it not that, but a perverse form of selfishness that I—*I*—had to live in circumstances with a poor mother and with the little that being poor could bring? Poor little me, in other words. I don't think so. I did not like friends to see where I lived, because I was ashamed, but I never was uncomfortable living there. I was pretty happy.

§

The Chenango Kid

While I was finishing up sixth grade Louise came home from her "reform school" to live with us. The apartment was too small for us, so, with Louise's added income once she started working, we moved to a much bigger apartment in a building two doors down at 285 Chenango, and I moved on to East Junior High School.

CHAPTER 5

Anyone Lived in a Pretty How Town

> *Where Did You Go? Out. What Did You Do? Nothing.*
> —Title of book about childhood by Robert Paul Smith, 1957

A fine but gritty, golden dust overlays the American 1950s, when the country had a population slightly above 150 million. Not a dust of nostalgia, but of a sense that for all the irregularities of any individual childhood, and the shortcomings of American society as a whole, it was a good time to be alive and we were moving, or lurching, in the right direction.

Binghamton's population, at 85,000, was almost twice what it is today. In the vaguest and most imaginative of senses Chenango Street resembled Edward Hopper's 1930 painting *Early Sunday Morning*. If you squinted just right as you looked at the buildings, and if you were in a melancholic mood, and if the sunlight fell upon the sidewalk at just the right time of day at the right time of the year and with the right slant—if all of those factors were in play at the same time, Chenango Street on the North Side in the 1950s might slightly resemble *Early Sunday Morning*. For a minute or two.

Terence Davies' short film *Of Time and the City* is an elegiac, wistful remembrance of, and lament for the loss of, his native Liverpool. The early images in that film, the black-and-whites of grubby streets and forlorn housing of the late 1940s and the 1950s (which had been built decades earlier), call up for me similar feelings about Chenango Street and the North Side of Binghamton. They are called up, as Proust said, through the "involuntary memory" that drives our remembrances of things past. Accident and serendipity, not conscious memory, are the agents of personal history.

Of course, there is the occasional madeleine that jogs the "involuntary memory." For me it is often television. Something on television—a reference to or the rerun of an old program—will drive me to a remembrance of some similar thing past. We got our first television in 1951 or '52, a seventeen-inch Majestic table model but with a detachable bottom with which you could make it look like a fancier floor model if you wanted. I can see the deliveryman lumbering it into our second-floor apartment at 289 Chenango. God knows what a dent it made in Ma's paycheck to buy it. It lasted a long time, until the mid-1960s, when Ma got a color set. She gave the old one to Louise, where it ran in their basement as a secondary set for several years more.

§

I cut my left wrist badly while playing on Chenango Street. "Cut" is too plain a word. "Ripped" is what I did, ripped it on a chain-link fence as I ran, shouting happily, with other kids, chasing them or they me. I must have been eleven, twelve years old, something like that. I was running through a yard—hard to believe that there were yards, but there were a few, scraggy and mangy and spotted with dog shit, occasionally interspersed between the ramshackle apartment houses—and as I went out through the open gate of the fence, I grabbed one of the gate's metal posts to steady myself as I swung through. But in the act of swinging, or rather whipping, myself around the post and out onto the sidewalk, my wrist caught on the gate latch. Immediate pain, and blood everywhere! I fell to the ground screaming, and instantly kids were all around me, looking as scared as I did as I saw my life's blood pumping out of the raw, pulpy gash.

Someone must have run to tell my mother. Why was she even home? It must have been either a weekend or late in the afternoon of a weekday and she was already home from work. No one called an ambulance because ambulances usually weren't called then for anything less severe than a car crash. Once an epileptic kid named Julius fell suddenly to the ground and lay there on the asphalt-patched sidewalk quivering in a seizure—or fit, as we said. No one knew what to do. We just stared at him as he stared glassily at the sky. Finally some grown-ups came and took charge, and in that instance an ambulance did come. Who paid for it is anyone's guess, because the point is ambulances cost money, and no one on Chenango Street had money for ambulances, certainly not Mae Miller. Which is why she and I ended up in a Yellow Cab taxi, heading for Dr. Mossew's office on Henry Street, with me holding my still badly bleeding, bandaged left wrist in my right hand and bawling, "Am I going to die, Ma?" I have always leaned toward the dramatic, especially in anything involving me.

Dr. Mossew. He was "our" doctor. More than that, he was an EJ doctor. Endicott-Johnson employees didn't have much, but they and their families did have medical care as long as they went to a doctor who agreed to accept EJ patients. Medical insurance was even rarer then than it is becoming now, so we were lucky in that regard. I remember Dr. Mossew sewing up the wound and bandaging it. Even more I remember having to go back to have the stitches taken out once it had healed. I went by myself. I had to wait a long time in the office for my turn. It was a dim, depressing place as I sat on the hard cushion of a straight-back chair, but doctor's offices then were generally pretty severe, without the bright, open waiting areas they have now adopted. Doctors usually were sole proprietors, not part of a multiple-physician office controlled by Medimess Corp. in Mussel Shoals, Alabama. The stitches came out neatly, leaving a jagged and, for a time, rosy scar. "Jagged" makes me think suturing was not one of Dr. Mossew's strengths. The scar is still faintly visible. For a time when I was younger and it was more visible I used to think that anyone noticing it might wonder whether I had tried to commit suicide. I wondered that when I filled out one of the many forms that the Army made you fill out before they consented to draft you. It asked about any visible scars, but possible indicators of a possible suicide attempt apparently were not enough to keep a warm body out of the Army at the height of the Vietnam War. I don't think anyone looked at those forms, anyway, unless you said you were a communist. Why didn't I think of that? A communist, scarred or not, made the authorities hyperventilate.

§

But that's what kids did then, played outside. Nancy and I are amazed at how few children we see playing when in fine weather we take walks around our or other suburban neighborhoods. They even have snazzily equipped playgrounds that they don't play in. We played in the streets or in cinder- or asphalt-covered lots. The voice of the child was heard in the land, along with the voice of the adult from a second-floor window telling him to shut up. It was always *him*; I can't remember playing with girls.

We led play lives more like what Robert Paul Smith, the title of whose 1957 book is cited at the beginning of this chapter, was used to than what he complains of. He opens by saying, "The thing is, I don't understand what kids do with themselves anymore." He contrasts the overscheduled, oversupervised lives of children in 1950s suburbs with the freedom of his own boyhood. (It has only gotten worse in the past half-century, Mr. Smith.)

The flight from the cities to the suburbs was in full swing; by the midpoint of the decade 4,000 families were making the flight each day. But things were different for those of us who remained on the concrete sidewalks of the North Side. What did we play? Nothing organized, like Little League baseball. I was not and never have been terribly sports-oriented, so I may have been unaware, but I doubt that such organized sport filtered down to the unchic recesses of the North Side. We played stickball, dodgeball, marbles, yes, but more often made-up games on the order of hide-and-seek, cops-and-robbers, cowboys and Indians. Mumblety-peg? Not so much; maybe if we had known what it was.

Occasionally on Saturday I played at my cousin Ken's house on Lawton Avenue on the city's West Side, close to the Johnson City line. I would call up and ask, "Aunt Mima, can I come over and play with Ken?" and she would always say yes. I took the city bus, No. 27 Leroy Street, I believe it was. I knew exactly where to get off the bus, Schubert Street at West End Avenue. Once, though, I became engrossed in reading a book, and upon looking up suddenly I didn't recognize my surroundings. I panicked. Had I missed my stop? Or had I not reached it? Panicking further at the prospect of having to ride the bus forever, I convinced myself that the stop coming up looked like mine. I got off, but it was the wrong place. I wandered up and down streets, close to the tears that actually did flow when I finally knocked on a door and asked the woman who answered if she knew where I was. She did, and where I was supposed to go when I explained it to her. My father was so angry at my inattention-caused misadventure when he learned of it that he made me ride the route with him to make sure I learned it and forbade me to read then or whenever I rode the bus in the future. I'm certain I did not comply. Reading had become too important to me.

Playing at Ken's was great fun. The Smiths owned their own small Victorian-style house in an area that, while not upscale, was more residential than the North Side. Ken and Ruth had several of the low-tech games of the time: Cootie, Mr. Potato Head, pickup sticks, jacks. He had his own band of friends he let me join. The Smiths had a TV set fairly early; Ken and I liked to watch ventriloquist Paul Winchell with his dummies Jerry Mahoney and Knucklehead Smiff. We listened to *Space Patrol* with its adventures of Commander Corey and Cadet Happy on the radio; I don't believe that the TV version was yet available. Ralston Purina, the sponsor of *Space Patrol*, ran a contest to name the planet on which dwelt the bad guy of the series. The company built a large mock-up of Commander Corey's rocket ship and toured the country with it to promote the contest (and its products). The prize to the winner was to be the thirty-foot mock-up itself, and while I desired it madly, I worried about where I would put it since I lived in an apartment not much bigger than it (and that slept far fewer than its eight). My worries were for naught, for I did not win, though I still think my entry, "Telestroid," suggesting "far-off planet," was a pretty imaginative concoction for an eleven- or twelve-year-old.

When we were a bit older Ken and I walked to the new-car show held each fall at the West End Armory. The annual model-year changeover was a more exciting event then than it is now. Each new year's models then usually looked noticeably different from the year before—and from the models of other brands—than is the case now. Dealerships often soaped their windows or covered them with newspapers, the purpose being as much to boost that excitement as to prevent early peeks at the new models. A Ford designer, George Walker, said, "We design a car to make a man unhappy with his 1957 Ford 'long about the end of 1958." Ken and I had a great time tramping about the huge hall, grabbing whatever shiny brochures we could and surely making life difficult for the men trying to sell cars.

Aunt Mima was always kind to me as she was to everyone and everything, but she worried about the state of my soul. A few times she managed to get me to attend church with Ken and the rest of her family at the First Church of the Nazarene on Main Street, just up the street from

The Chenango Kid

the Crest Theater (formerly the Suburban), but it never took, though I don't think I disliked the experience (until later in life). Once she asked me if I attended church. This was unlike her, as she surely knew I did not and she never treated anyone meanly; apparently she was attempting to get me to expose the barrenness of my soul, an exercise that she probably thought could only be good for me. But rather than disappoint her, and in an absurd attempt to keep a good impression in her eyes, I lied to her and said, Yes, at North Presbyterian. Oh, she responded, interested: And what is the pastor's name? Well, I hadn't expect her to carry it that far, but I quickly made up the name Rev. Delanoy, or some such. She let it go at that, having learned what she already knew. Another seriously uncomfortable religious moment in her presence was when I happened to be there when her minister, Rev. Fallon, visited. The three of us had to kneel down at a living room chair or couch and pray. Hell, I didn't know how to pray and I certainly did not want to. It's embarrassing.

§

Besides outside, another thing kids don't play anymore is with yo-yos. Every year in yo-yo season every other boy had a yo-yo spinning on a string from his middle finger. Was it in the spring, or was it autumn? Spring, I believe, when the yo-yo experts spread across the land. I think they were Filipinos, who apparently had an inborn gift for yo-yoing, dispatched by the yo-yo manufacturers. Suddenly, one day, a short, black-haired, whip-thin young Filipino would appear, leaning against a storefront or housefront, working his magic with a yo-yo—"walking the dog," "around the world," making it "sleep"—before our wondering eyes. Just as suddenly we all had to have one and just as magically they appeared in the stores. Duncan yo-yos were the brand to have, especially the more expensive models with "diamonds" (bits of glass or possibly plastic) embedded in each side. You wanted to get the rims nicely roughed up—they were made of wood—showing that you knew how to walk the dog.

§

A couple of summers I stayed for a week or two at Ma's brother Ralph's place in Pennsylvania. I liked that because it was fun playing with my cousin Johnny, who was my age within a couple of months, and his older brother Aubrey. The first place they had that I went to was a rented house at Gunn Hill near Lenoxville in Susquehanna County. The kindest thing I can say is that a watercolorist on the lookout for stark rural simplicity would have stopped and put up his easel immediately upon seeing this rundown, unpainted, barely-two-story clapboard house with sagging roof and front porch to match. In shambolic ambience it was hardly different from our apartments in Binghamton, except that the toilet facilities were outside and the water came from a springhouse by means of a handheld bucket. But what did that matter to a kid? Besides, in plumbingless, unfurnaced rusticity it was not far different from my Miller grandparents' house in Lopez.

I can't call up much of what we did. We "played cars" with plastic and rubber cars and trucks in the dirt underneath a tree just off the front porch. We ate mustard-and-sugar sandwiches. We went exploring in the nearby fields and woods. We pretended to drive—*vroom, vroom*, push the gear-shift lever—the clapped-out 1934 Chevy sedan with glassless windows that sat on tireless wheels in the tall grass of a field not far from the house. Whatever we did was occasionally so noisy that it irritated our grandfather, Frank Sheridan, who lived with Ralph and his wife, my Aunt Audrey. He would come out of his bedroom off the living room and shout about the kids making such a goddamned racket. Once our behavior must have been so raucous that, tottery as he was, he chased us out of the house and into the yard, shaking his fist angrily in the air and swearing. We ran from him, laughing, and climbed up on the springhouse roof. There we were, dancing about on the roof and taunting, "Ya, ya, can't catch me." Grandpa died not long after that, and when the undertaker came to the house he ran over the dog. Not deliberately; nevertheless, it put paid to the dog's career of chasing cars and snapping at their wheels as they drove down the dusty dirt road. An ironic end.

It was that house and its environs I conjured a few years later to site the events of Edna Ferber's 1924 novel *So Big* that I read as an assigned book in an English class at North High School. I don't know why; they didn't have much of a garden, and the front and side yards came directly out of a Ma & Pa Kettle movie. I can still see the layout of the house: kitchen with door leading to the side yard and springhouse, dining room with the main entrance leading to the front porch, spare room off the dining room, living room off the dining room and bedroom off the living room. But "living room" and "dining room" give a false idea of its unfurnished spareness:

bare floors in rooms largely bare of tables and chairs. A pot-bellied stove in the dining room and a kitchen stove were the sources of heat in the winter. There was a small, cramped, low-ceilinged upstairs, unheated, containing Ralph and Audrey's bedroom and an open area where we three boys all slept in the same sagging bed.

Sex, or curiosity about its mechanics, arrives early in young men's lives. Johnny and Aubrey were startled upon discovering that I was circumcised. Apparently they had never seen such a thing. They were certain that such an abnormality could not possibly be right. Aubrey, whose authority on sexual matters resided in being two or three years older and in nothing else, told me that girls did not like that, but he did not say why. They assured me that I could return to the proper state of nature if I simply pulled down some skin—of which there was no excess—over the tip and tied it there for a few days. Then I would look like them, sort of. I thought they probably were right, but I resigned myself to my freakish condition.

My memories are fresher of staying with them when they moved to a rented house—I believe it was a duplex—in the borough of Mayfield in Lackawanna County. It was not a big move in physical distance, and only a modest step up in urban mod cons: There was running water inside, but it did not extend to a toilet, which was outside in the back yard. Johnny and Aubrey and I played pick-up baseball with other kids. I was lucky to avoid broken ribs when I was standing too close to Aubrey as he swung and missed and the follow-through with his bat hit me in the left side. I fell to the ground, doubled up in pain. Aubrey dropped the bat, bending over me and muttering anxiously, "Honey, honey." After a few minutes of excruciating pain I was OK. An inch or so higher and I would have had a broken rib or two.

Once Johnny and I and a couple other kids stole some lumber and other materials from a lumber yard and hauled them up into the hills to build a kind of fort or bunker. It was coal company land, or perhaps some other company's, which we knew, and so weren't entirely surprised when a man walking through the woods spied us and began hurrying toward us, hollering, "Hey, you kids! What do you think you're doing?" We took off like, as we used to say, a big-ass bird, with the man in hot pursuit. We laughed our heads off as, propelled by thrill and fear of being caught, we ran down the hill and out of his clutches. I wouldn't be surprised if, after reaching the road and slowing down to a ramble, we then decided, as we sometimes did when bored, to go past the house of a mean guy we didn't like and chant, "Old man Fantana with his big black banana!" And run like hell again.

It was at this time that I developed my extreme dislike of picking berries. The source of income in Ralph's house was not something I paid much attention to except to discern that it did not seem steady. Though later on he worked for a casket company, at this point money appeared to be catch-as-catch-can. The family sometimes picked berries and sold them to a cannery or packer or some other produce handler. The one occasion I went along we stayed the whole day, in blanketing heat and humidity, filling every container they had brought, and when those were exhausted, resorted to filling a pair of boots that happened to be in the car. The day seemed endless and my arms to be aching, red-hot leaden ingots.

For a short time Aubrey had a delivery route for the Scranton *Tribune*. Or was it the Scranton *Times*? No matter, there was a reason his tenure was short, or at any rate I imagine it was the reason. Johnny and I went with him to deliver. I don't know what it was, whether we didn't stop and think or were simply clueless, but for some reason on a Sunday while delivering the morning newspaper Aubrey decided to collect his money. It may be that he had just taken on the route and felt it was time to reap the fruit of his labors. Whatever, the result was, after ringing the first doorbell many times, a sleepy-eyed, tousle-haired, pajama'd, and extremely angry householder appeared at the door expressing amazement, in no uncertain and vulgar terms, at our complete idiocy in waking up decent people at that hour. He did not pay us.

Ralph's family was a little solicitous of and cautious toward me. I was used to citified ways—circumcision and other such fripperies, you know—and, compared with Johnny and Aubrey, pampered, which they knew. One night in the Gunn Hill house we three boys were giggling and talking in our communal bed. When we did not let up after repeated warnings from Ralph in the other room, he came out in the dark and larruped us once or twice with a belt. We all yelped—we were not badly hurt—and when Ralph saw that I was one of the yelpers, he apologized again and again.

Ma and I went down to Ralph's on a Shortline bus out of the Greyhound terminal on Chenango Street. It comes to me now that she went there, just as later she (taking me along) went up to Louise's future in-laws' north of Syracuse, to drink and have a good time. Drinking and having a good time was best accomplished in the company of men in taverns. I have only a shadowy recollection of the men, partly, I believe, because I blocked them or the thought of them out of my mind, knowing that such behavior was not typical of most mothers. Also, she did not bring them to the apartment, at least not until I was an older teen and she had one steady boyfriend, who in any case never stayed overnight when I was there. I only became aware of the pattern of her behavior years after the behavior had largely ceased—again, possibly because I mentally denied it. None of the men ever hurt me or, indeed, had much to do with me as I rarely saw them. There was one snaggle-toothed fellow in Mayfield named Myron who got it in his head to teach me a thing or two because I adamantly refused to eat something on my plate. I stormed out the door to the back porch, where he told me I would sit until I ate what was put before me. He was an oaf; none of my mother's suitors were mental giants, or even of average intellectual stature, but he was uncommonly thick. Why he even stirred up the little drama, since we meant nothing to each other, was only because he could not bear the idea of a little urban brat who thought he was better than anyone else (which I did not) defying his elders. When I read Tobias Wolff's memoir *This Boy's Life*, his mother's boyfriend Dwight Hansen reminded me of Myron. Fortunately Myron was but one of several passing fancies to Ma and not the long-term pain in the ass (and elsewhere) that Dwight was in Wolff's life.

Proof that I liked staying with the Sheridans', for all their rural or semi-rural hardscrabble life, is that I asked my father if I could go live with them. This now seems to me utterly insane: I wanted voluntarily to take on a childhood existence similar to the one that Louise had been forced to endure and that she spent her entire life bitterly hating?

You can imagine what Pa thought of my idea. When I broached it to him he was living on Pine Street in one of his series of dirty and cluttered, one- or two-room apartments. One thing he surely thought was that Ma had put me up to it so that she could enjoy a loose, tavern-hopping life unencumbered by a kid. That was why she "sent me" there in the summer—to get rid of me. I cannot believe that she put me up to it. For one thing, at the time of their legal separation she had insisted on my staying with her when the question came up about which parent would raise me. She loved me even though she could never say it. Anyway, Pa's notion of the looseness of her lifestyle was exaggerated.

Pa did not like the Sheridans. To him, in his artless uprightness, they were little more than white trash living in a rural slum, shiftless and work-shy. Whether he saw that these characteristics, which were wildly off the mark, were to some extent true of his hometown of Lopez and of some of his own family members I do not know. But the Sheridans knew what he thought of them and preferred to avoid him, which naturally was not hard to do. They did not dislike Pa; they thought him . . . peculiar. Once he came down to Gunn Hill. He had to travel by bus, since he had no car or, indeed, driver's license. What the purpose of his trip was I no longer know, other than that it had to do with me. There was some heated discussion. Ralph and Audrey seemed more intent on placating him than on arguing. After a while he stomped back up the hill to catch the return bus at its stop at the little Ma-and-Pa convenience store on Route 106. He left behind several comic books, which for me were the highlight of his visit.

I doubt that Ma's motives were self-serving. It may have been nice to get shut of me for a while, but honestly I think she was content to have me enjoy myself. After all, I spent most of my summers and holidays (and often weekends during the rest of the year) in Lopez with her ex-husband's family. She was not mean. She did not seek revenge or harbor other base emotions. She was generous, writing a brief note to me every week or so and enclosing a few dollars of spending money. Like Pa, she wanted me to get away from the city during summer's "polio season."

§

Poliomyelitis, or infantile paralysis. The disease frightened parents to an extent that no one who has not lived through the period of fear can fully understand. While statistics alone can't tell the story, there was an epidemic of crippling polio somewhere in the United States almost every year from 1900 to 1956. When it came into its strength, from 1942 to 1953, it felled up to 60,000 Americans a year.

The fear of getting it was compounded by the uncertainty over how you got it. We didn't know. Was it from peaches? ice cream? public drinking fountains? Why was it associated with summer? Why did it affect boys more severely than girls? What was the role of stress in contracting it? Even today, not all of these questions have answers.

There were relatively "lighter" cases that patients survived with varying degrees of disability, such as President Franklin D. Roosevelt, that left them able to function in society. Extreme cases turned patients into quadriplegics, leaving them totally dependent on others, unable to breathe without an iron lung or other respiratory assistance.

The patients weren't the only victims. Polio caused families terrible anguish. Parents desperate for even the most minimal contact with their stricken children being held in isolation climbed ladders propped against hospital walls to peer into windows.

In April 1955 came the news of federal approval of a vaccine developed by Dr. Jonas Salk and his team at the University of Pittsburgh School of Medicine, for which he sought no patent. "There is no patent," he told an interviewer. "Could you patent the sun?" A few years later came Dr. Albert Sabin's oral vaccine, which had been in development during the same years. Within a decade polio cases in the United States dropped from an annual rate of 38,000 annually to 570.

§

One of those less severely stricken was my cousin Donald Noldy, younger son of Ma's older sister Anna. One summer, it must have been my twelfth or thirteenth, I stayed for a couple of weeks on the dairy farm that Anna and her husband Charlie Noldy ran outside of Meshoppen in Wyoming County. I caused two minor disasters. I burned out the brakes on Charlie's small Ford tractor by forgetting to unlock them when I drove it, and I wrecked a fence gate and a portion of the fence by letting the gate catch on the back of the hay wagon after I had opened it for him. He did not get terribly angry. He used to go around the barnyard crooning, "There's a rainbow 'round my asshole" after the Al Jolson song, "There's a Rainbow 'Round My Shoulder."

Donald, a student at Lycoming College in Williamsport, was a cheerful chap little incommoded by the leg brace and limp that were the legacy of a childhood bout with polio. There was a young woman staying with Anna and Charlie at the same time I was there, a Binghamton friend of Louise's around the age of twenty. Had she possessed blond hair and more than average good looks, she could have been the stereotypical Dumb Blonde. Still, she was if possible even more cheerful than Donald and apparently agreeable, for I observed that they would ascend the haymow together. I had a pretty good idea what ascending the haymow together involved, though to be completely objective they may have been up there discussing animal husbandry and admiring the scenery from the advantage of height. But I thrilled at my imaginings, which were heightened when I overheard Anna warn her son, "You watch yourself, young man!" I knew, or suspected, enough to be surprised that his parents countenanced such goings-on, but, as I say, it may be that boy and girl were totally innocent. Or it may be that everyone was consoled by the fact, as I later heard Louise tell Ma, that the woman could not conceive children. That I understood.

I was sad when I had to leave the farm. Aunt Anna said, "You can take the boy out of the country, but you can't take the country out of the boy." Actually, you can, but there's no denying that I had fun there. Anna's sister Viola was married to Charlie's brother Art. That's not all. Ralph's brother Roscoe was married to Audrey's sister Isabel. A curious family, but no more curious than Pa's family, only differently.

§

The great fear of later generations, that someone was going to snatch and abuse your child, was not in the atmosphere to the extent it is today. Adults generally assumed it was safe to play without their supervision (or interference), and indeed probably were glad to be shut of the need to supervise; their lives were busy enough anyway without having to play with kids.

There were some dangers. For a short time I was the preferred victim of a slightly older boy, last name Stark, who bullied and harassed me whenever I came into his sight, which I tried not to do. We didn't even really know each other; I must have looked vulnerable and he must have been looking for anyone with signs of that. Whenever I see that bully, Skut Farkus, with braces in *A Christmas Story* grinning his fierce grin I think of Stark, except his teeth were bad, not braced.

There is a British legal/crime term, "demanding with menaces." Once another kid tried to hold me up with a knife on the Viaduct, demanding my money, but he was a wimpy-looking, pudgy guy not older than me and, as a menace, a pure joke. I told him, "Go to hell, you crazy, demented bastard," and scampered away. For years after that my high school friend Tom and I would gleefully shout out that phrase whenever we walked together over the Viaduct into town.

Non-human dangers lurked, too. There was a "kid"—a young man, really, or certainly an older teen—occasionally seen walking about the North Side whom adults used as a cautionary tale. He had two metal prosthetic arms, the result of having climbed, as we were told, a "high-tension pole" on State Street down by the "bus barns" of Triple Cities Traction and grabbed on to the wires. Let that be a lesson to you, we were told. We tried not to look at him, but, for myself, I never succeeded. He knew you were looking at him, too, and why.

Whatever was being talked about in America was being talked about on the North Side. I and every other pre-teen boy had a Davy Crockett coonskin cap. I was curious, along with Ma and our friends and neighbors, about what might be the "real truth" behind *The Search for Bridey Murphy*, a book written by an amateur hypnotist, Morey Bernstein. In 1952 he put a Colorado housewife, known as Ruth Simmons, into a trance. While under she stated that she was Bridey Murphy, a woman in nineteenth-century Ireland, and began to talk in an Irish brogue and dance a jig. The book became a bestseller and the object of intense scrutiny by news organizations and researchers, which did not completely dismiss the phenomenon but found that it could be explained by long-forgotten memories rather than as "reincarnation." Meanwhile, during the height of the craze, songs were written about it, people held "come as you were" parties, Stan Freberg had fun with it in one of his many satire records, and Teresa Wright played Ruth Simmons in a movie bearing the book's title.

While still in elementary school I went often to the Boys Club on Washington Street near the corner of Clinton Street. It was a pretty neat place with lots to do. There were occasional screenings of cartoons—Heckle and Jeckle, Mighty Mouse. You could play pool or Ping Pong and other games. There were classes in various skills, such as printing, which I liked. You could even box, which I did not want to do, but this kid slightly older than I suggested one day that we go down to the Boys Club and put on the ol' mitts. I said, Sure, why not? Once there he proceeded to paste me silly, which had been his intention all along, for I hadn't a clue how to defend myself. This was the kid who brought his drums over to our apartment to play until Ma came home and told him where he could put his drum set. At Thanksgiving the club held a raffle of a live turkey kept right there in a cage in the lobby, bobbing its head and making turkey noises. You know, in case you might have doubts that there actually was such a prize. When you left the Boys Club you walked down two or three steps underneath a large painting of Bing Crosby and his four sons—Gary, Lindsay, and the twins Philip and Dennis—representing the American Family Ideal of Intergenerational Male Bonding, or some such worthy sentiment. That was a cruel irony given what later was revealed about life in the Crosby household; I probably was better off living in a "broken home" with my mother. When you left the club, if you turned right and crossed Clinton Street you came to the Assembly of God church, to which a friend took me one weekday evening to view some cool nature film, advising me beforehand that I didn't have to pay attention to the religious blather that would precede and follow it, which embarrassed him and was the true purpose of the screening. I have been stalked by religious pitchmen all my life.

§

I slept with Ma a lot, until, oh, I don't know, the age of twelve or so. Not continually, not for great stretches, but oftener and for a longer time than was healthy, I am sure. One of the chief reasons must have been emotional, psychological. I was, frankly, a bit of a wuss, a Mama's boy, and Ma did little to discourage it. It made Louise angry, for it was a sign that Ma favored me over her, which truthfully she did.

But it was not the only reason. We had no room. When we lived at 289 Chenango in the no-bedroom apartment with the Murphy bed, I must have slept with Ma most of the time, or else one or the other of us slept on the couch in the living room. I cannot recall, probably on orders of my subconscious. Besides that, we periodically had people come to stay with us. For instance: By this time Ma had become friendly with the family who would become Louise's future in-laws up near Central Square, New York. This had come about in the usual way, through Ma's "friendship" with a man, the uncle of Louise's future husband Richard. Richard's brother was married to a nursing student, and she needed to come to Binghamton for training or something. So they stayed with us, three big people and one little in a two-room-plus-bath-and kitchenette apartment. Where did we put everybody?

I go into detail not to criticize this couple, but to illustrate how typical it would prove to be. A couple of years later one of Ma's nephews, the older son of Charlie and Anna Noldy, came up from Pennsylvania to stay with us, accompanied by his wife and baby daughter. We lived then in a slightly larger apartment on the first floor at 289 Chenango—one bedroom, kitchen, living room and entranceway—but it was nevertheless cramped. Not many months after that, when we had moved (don't ask me why) directly across the hall into an apartment the exact mirror of that one, Ma's perennially ne'er-do-well brother, Russell, dropped in from somewhere up near Buffalo for a couple months' (unemployed) stay. And a few years later still, when we lived in a larger place on the third floor at 250 Chenango (forever after enshrined in our consciousness as Van Horn's, after the owner), Ma's uncle, Hank Race, surfaced out of the cold, looking for a place to hole up until he could again hit the road that he had been traveling all his life. Ever since, he said, he had served as an Army cook with Black Jack Pershing in Mexico. Maybe yes, maybe no, but he certainly was the right age. He worked as a kind of tramp cook, or more likely dishwasher, for one restaurant after another. He remained a few weeks, then was gone.

Why was Ma such a pushover? Her relatives thought she was weak-minded and vulnerable. Not that any of them showed signs of genius. Second, she worked steadily and thus had money. Only a little, but more than they had, so why not tap it? Maybe they thought she was weak-minded for going to work every day for decades. Beyond occasional room and board, more than once she lent money that she did not have, particularly to Russell and Walter. I think she must have had almost a permanent account at HFC, Household Finance Corporation, a high-interest lender, paying back money she borrowed to hand over to her brothers and others. Perhaps they paid her back, but I doubt it.

And she was gullible. Chain letters were common then (for that matter, so were *any* letters). Ma got enthused over one in which you got a list of ten names and addresses. You copied the list, but leaving off the name at the top and adding your own name at the bottom. Then you sent your revised list and a dime to ten friends, who were supposed to copy the list in the same manner and send it with dimes to ten of their friends. And so on and so on. At some point when your name got to the top of the list you would receive millions. But don't ask me how. Someone must have broken the chain because Ma never got any money.

If I seem unwarrantedly hard on my mother, I can only say that I do not mean to be. I mean only to recount what happened as I remember it. I do believe that my youthful life with Ma, experiencing how she had to make her way, loaded me with insight into the difficulties that all girls and women face in making their way. "Loaded," I say, because the insight came not then, but later, and only gradually. Years and decades of mulling over what Ma had to put up with added immeasurably to whatever insight has come to me. The Book of Genesis—written by men—surely has it wrong in making a male the ur-human, for the female is the better—emotionally and psychologically stronger, more stable, and probably more intelligent—of the species. She has had to be, to endure in the wilderness that the deadlier male has created for her.

§

Interlude for a rant:
 We used to pay for things that we needed and thought were good for us in that era. We paid for them through taxes. "I like paying taxes," Justice Oliver Wendell Holmes said. "With them I buy civilization." So with our—by "our" I mean the city and community at large—taxes we bought the equipment and materials that schoolchildren needed to prepare for reaching a civilized state. There were twenty-one students, including me, in my sixth-grade class; an optimum number for teaching, as I understand pedagogical matters. How did our governmental masters manage to provide that for children in one of the poorer parts of the city, when today, in suburbs of mini-mansions all across the nation, citizens rail at increased taxes to pay for the increased costs of educating children? I cannot recall having to put out money for any school necessities beyond my own pens, pencils, and notebooks, and possibly My Weekly Reader. It's a good thing, too. I don't know that Ma could have borne the extra freight, nor could many of the families on the North Side. It's not that Ma didn't work; she worked harder than most women and many men. They just didn't pay her very much.

 But this was the past where things were done differently. Now we say taxes are bad and try to avoid paying for what we need. Recently Nancy and I forked out eighty-one dollars to two of our grandchildren's schools to buy magazines that we could have bought for one-third the cost through normal channels. But this was a way for the schools, which are in a different community from ours, to bring in money it needed and that its own community would not provide through taxes. The schools got forty percent of the money, the company running the scheme got sixty percent, and we paid three times the cost for magazines we did not want. This scam is not limited to our grandchildren's schools; it occurs everywhere. Sometimes it is magazines that are sold, sometimes it is overpriced chocolate bars or kitschy "gift" items that the purchasers throw out almost immediately. It is maddeningly ironic: *Taxing bodies under the sway of a political philosophy that says it is an unspeakable breach of liberty to be forced to pay for other people's undertakings (i.e., children not their own) succeed in pushing the cost of their own undertakings (i.e., their own children) on other people—and in a highly inefficient manner.*

§

On October 4, 1955, the Brooklyn Dodgers won the World Series, four games to three, over the New York Yankees. It was their first championship and would be the Dodgers' only championship as a Brooklyn franchise, for after the 1957 season they moved to Los Angeles and the world has never been the same. The Dodgers, affectionately known as the Brooklyn Bums, were much admired for being, first, not the Yankees, and second, the underdogs, so their victory caused much joy in our little Mudville. A big sign appeared in the window of a small grocery store near the corner of Doubleday Street and Chenango, run by the Libous family, screaming, DEM BUMS DOOD IT!

The North Side was a village of sorts. Not the sort that reputedly it takes to raise a child, for this village's children largely raised themselves. But it had all kinds of shops and businesses, including, until the mid-1950s, a small department store (Wilber's), at 227 Chenango and an A&P "supermarket" (laughably small compared to today's behemoth emporiums) at the corner of Chenango and Robinson. Little mom-and-pop groceries abounded, whether operated by a mom and pop or not. The one nearest us was run by a stocky bald guy with a rim of black hair around his pate and a dirty white apron around his middle. Friends, cronies would hang about, jawing with him. Once they set up a little trick. They placed a wallet out on the sidewalk with a string attached to it, and when a pedestrian fell upon it they jerked it back to the doorway, laughing their heads off. I watched it performed once at night. Again like a Hopper painting, light from the plate-glass window fell in a large white trapezoid onto the sidewalk. Within that brightened area lay the seductive wallet, pounced upon—unsuccessfully—by an unsuspecting passerby. Laughter from inside the store as the pedestrian scuttled away, humiliated and angry. A real knee-slapper, but I thought it cool. I wanted to snatch the wallet myself, but I knew the men would holler at me. Curious to think now that I could run down there in the evening to pick up a quart of milk. A quart, yes, a *quart*: That was the usual size we bought then, and in a glass bottle, imagine. Nobody in the apartments, in that high noon of the milkman, had milk delivered. Someone would have stolen it.

§

The golden, gritty dust of memory is all well and good, but at the time an actual layer of palpable grit overlay the physical world of the North Side. For me this is represented by the fact that on garbage-collection days we—the apartment dwellers, certainly—placed our garbage out on the curb in paper grocery bags, which often tipped over and spilled out their contents into the gutter or were attacked by passing dogs, with the same result.

It is a world lost to us and perhaps in many of its aspects deserves to be—a world of Saturday afternoon movies with serials, of traveling by passenger train, of women (my mother and many others excepted) whose primary work was in the home and of men who came home from work to read the newspaper—and of casually heavy drinking and smoking by both. A world of ordinary people living through ordinary days.

CHAPTER 6

Raggedy Man

"Parents are sometimes a bit of a disappointment to their children. They don't fulfill the promise of their early years."

—Anthony Powell

It being close to Father's Day one recent year, a friend asked me in an e-mail, during an exchange of comments about our families, what my father's "station in life" was. A nicely archaic way of expressing her question, but I appreciated it, as it allowed me to respond, "Oh, Pat, at my father's station in life the trains did not stop."

That was less accurate than it was clever, and admittedly it isn't all that clever. The most accurate answer as to station in life would be: essentially, none. I liked Pa, he was a nice guy, but he was pretty ineffectual. Professionally he was, in the grandest term I can summon, a "construction worker," but more honestly expressed, a day laborer. At that, he seems to have skipped a lot of days of labor. Not so much out of laziness, I think, as out of cluelessness about life and how to get along. In the manner of Lord Byron's Manfred, another chap who couldn't figure out life's mysteries, I'd like to say, but there was nothing either Faustian or tragic about Keith Miller (nor, for that matter, about his son, who inherited his share of cluelessness).

This was in the late 1940s and the 1950s. He was a member of the hod carriers union and would go to the union hall looking for work but would rarely be called. I have been told that he just pissed people off, that he went in expecting aggravation and rejection and was rarely disappointed. This is entirely possible. He was an odd combination of decent, genial fellow and suspicious paranoid. Then again, I was told this by people who didn't particularly want to speak well of him—my mother and her relatives.

His being in the union is interesting because I think he did not like unions. This was when union membership was at an all-time high of 35 percent of the national workforce. He did not rant about the issue with me, but for some reason he grew terribly exercised over the merger of the AFL (American Federation of Labor) and the CIO (Congress of Industrial Organizations) in 1955. The attack in the next year on Victor Riesel, a columnist specializing in racketeering and mob corruption in labor unions, angered him beyond words. Riesel was blinded on a New York street when someone, identified later as gangster-connected, threw sulfuric acid in Riesel's face as he was coming out of a restaurant.

Pa provided no money for my support—he rarely had any to provide—aside from pocket change, a movie now and then when I was younger, and the occasional splurge on a necessity: When I was in high school he paid for a series of dental appointments for my long-neglected teeth.

How he existed I do not know. That we go through life knowing so little about our parents is a scandal (one doubtless being perpetuated by my own children). I do know there were periods of employment, because I would see him once or twice a week, and sometimes he would be tired and dirty from work. My parents' separation was, if not amicable, then not poisonous, and I used to walk over to his wretched apartments (he had a long sequence of them, none less dingy than the previous) in the evening to read magazines. A typical posture for Keith Miller was stretched out on his unmade and unsavory looking bed, his head of tousled dark hair propped on a yellowish pillow jammed up against the headboard, reading a magazine. He bought a ton of them—*Saturday Evening Post* and *Collier's* were his (and my) favorites, but there were also *Reader's Digest* and *True* and *Argosy* and *Life* and *Look* and many, many others, especially "detective" magazines that detailed true crimes.

One magazine he did not read, as far as I know, was *Confidential*, but millions of others did, including myself when I could do it unnoticed. The prototype gossip and scandal magazine, a bimonthly with a lurid red-and-yellow cover, was immediately so successful when it hit the newsstands in 1952 that it spawned a dozen imitators. Today's "entertainment" magazines, whether in print or on television, descend directly from it. The most surprising thing, which we didn't know then, is that practically all of its stories were true, carefully fact-checked. But truth was not a defense, and Hollywood forced its suppression. Its fate presents an interesting ethical contrast: *Confidential* was condemned for telling the truth about actors while the studios profited handsomely from the actors by making up lies about them and largely getting away with it.

Pa read a lot and derived little from it; it was a way to push the days by. But then, a harmless way; other men drank. He bought the magazines singly, on the newsstand, rather than subscribing, which would have been far more economical considering that he rarely skipped an issue. I think he was not penny wise and I know he was certainly pound foolish. Perhaps that is where I came by my own passion for reading (and my lack of financial sense). Now, when I am considerably older than he was then, I wonder about my reading. Is it really as focused and purposeful as I like to believe, or is it really just a way of passing time? Often I catch myself in the same recumbent reading posture as his. Or I will realize during one of my exercise walks around my neighborhood, sporting a goofy-looking cap to ward off the cold, that decades earlier Keith Miller could have been spotted perambulating the streets of Binghamton in like fashion. The apple does not fall so very far from the tree.

The apartments he lived in were all depressingly shabby and he did nothing to improve them. In fact, under his occupancy they came out the loser. To the domestic arts he was a complete stranger; to their Sweeping and Cleaning Subdivision he was passively opposed. In a word, the apartments were dirty. Extremely. Yet in his person he was clean, though his appearance typically was disheveled. He did not believe that God gave man pants just so that they could be pressed. My Uncle Clark, his younger brother, used to tell a story about Pa's fashion sense. Pa was going into town—this was when Lopez still had a semblance of a town—when Clark alerted him that his belt was twisted in the back. Pa ignored it, saying, "I'm not trying to impress anybody." Clark told us, with a wry grin, that he replied, "Well, then you're succeeding in that."

§

Late in his life, long after his brother had died and his own death was not far off, Clark told other curious stories about Pa. He said he never told them before because he did not want me to think ill of my father or to think that he, Clark, thought ill of him. He was a good, decent, kind man, in Clark's estimation, but in some not-quite-definable way he was off-kilter.

For instance, did I know that Pa once shot a man? What! No, of course I didn't. Yes, Clark said, he and this other fellow were out hunting. Clark could not remember when it was; it could have been sometime in either the 1920s or 1930s. The two hunters had sat down to rest, perhaps to have lunch, and somehow Pa's gun went off, hitting the man's leg. The man survived, but his foot had to be amputated. Yet Pa and the man remained friends, as did their families. There was no lawsuit. As Clark said, who had any money to be sued for in those days? Besides, each admitted that they both had been careless.

Carelessness, then, appears to have been a key factor in Pa's makeup. Or was it absentmindedness? Clark told of one cold winter night in the Millers' uninsulated, central-heatingless house in Lopez when Pa walked through the dining room to the living room, lighting a cigar. He flipped the match away, as he was accustomed to do in his apartments, where dead matches formed a chief ingredient of the grit on the floors. The match landed in a small spill of kerosene underneath the space heater the family used in its losing battle to keep the place warm. Had the match not happened to go out before landing, the house would have been very warm indeed. That is similar to another incident of absentmindedness that I have carried in my head for decades: Someone told me that as a boy Pa once lit a firecracker and, instead of throwing the firecracker from his hand, threw away the match. He got painfully burned.

If absentmindedness was a key factor in his makeup, then artlessness or cluelessness, assisted by bullheadedness, was not far behind. This was exemplified by his scheme, concocted in the late 1940s, for building houses in Lopez. Now, there were many, many, many things wrong with such a scheme—too many to list. For starters, there was no market for new houses—or anything else—in Lopez. It had started as a lumber-industry town in the late nineteenth century, had never risen to anything like prosperity, and began its decline almost from its beginning. Every year more and more people departed Lopez for the cities, leaving behind a plenitude of housing, largely rundown. Even had there been a market for new houses, Pa did not know how to build them. He knew construction labor, but that barely. He did not own nor had he contracted to buy the land on which he proposed to build. For he had no capital. Likewise he had no truck or other vehicle—nor, for that matter, did he have a driver's license.

What he had was a cement mixer and a machine for making cinder blocks, though not a complete grasp of how to make them. Cinder blocks require a period of curing to harden, but Pa, Clark said, grew impatient with the curing time and decided to place them in the oven of his mother's kitchen coal-and-wood stove to speed up the process. What Grandma had to say about using her kitchen as a work site has not been recorded. Clark warned him that this would not work, but Pa forged ahead. Alas, he did not also forge cinder blocks, for the first (and only) blocks he took from the oven broke apart into their constituent cinders on the kitchen floor. So he went back to nature's way and made enough cinder blocks to replace the stone foundation of the family house and construct a front-yard fence. The latter was knocked down a few years later because no one liked it. The foundation remained until it was replaced during a top-to-bottom refurbishing of the house—done by Clark.

A like cluelessness guided Pa's passion for patents. He spent too much of the money he did not have on acquiring patents for items for which apparently he had not researched the market. There was a patent for a form-fitting yoke that must have been envisaged for peasants in the rice fields of the Far East, since few American laborers were still using yokes as they had during his youth. But who knows? You couldn't tell Pa, any more than you could advise him on the housing needs of a dying northeast Pennsylvania town. He also had a patent for a kind of extension device for ceiling light fixtures, but for fixtures that had last been in use in the 1920s. I picture this idea entering his imagination from years of staring upward in his bed at the bare light bulbs that dangled over his head by a thin electrical cord from the high ceilings of his apartments. Sort of like the lights that swing ominously, creating alternating brightness and shadow, over tied-up, interrogated, and battered private eyes or hostages in *film noir* movies.

§

During my boyhood Pa's apartments, almost all complete with dangling light cords, were mostly on the north or east sides of Binghamton or toward its central business district—Pine Street, Carroll Street, Chenango. This was when Binghamton had a strong and vibrant central business district.

Roger K. Miller

The apartment buildings were tired, distressed candidates for demolition (though one is still standing and occupied). Rarely were there three rooms, usually just two and sometimes one. Almost always the bathroom was down the hall, shared with other members of the submerged population inhabiting these warrens for the dispirited, the luckless, the feckless, and the hopeless. Not to mention the jobless.

My Aunt Frances, his younger sister, said he once asked her why I rarely brought his granddaughters (our son Ian was not yet born) to visit him on trips back to Binghamton. Frances said she told him in frank terms: You never dust, clean, or vacuum. Indeed, he owned neither mop nor vacuum nor, most possibly, a cleaning cloth. Dust overlay everything and grit overlay the floor. Pots and pans sat in filthy, gummy water in the kitchen sink (when there was one) for days or weeks. Cans emptied of their contents remained where he had opened them or last ate from them. Magazines and newspapers and paperback books minus their covers (they were bought at second-hand stores) were scattered everywhere, especially on the unmade bed. Bits of clothing, too, were strewn about the few chairs, depriving any visitors of a place to sit. But since he rarely had visitors—including his granddaughters—this presented few problems. The crowning symbol of this mess was the makeshift spittoon he kept on the floor next to his bed, an empty tin can encrusted with thick streaks of coagulated mahogany-colored chewing tobacco.

He listened to Gabriel Heatter ("There's good news tonight!") and Edward R. Murrow ("Listen to Murrow tomorrow") on their weeknight news-and-commentary programs on the radio. He never owned a television set. I offered to get him one, but he said no. Yet he watched television avidly when he was in Lopez. I should have given him the TV anyway.

He played solitaire over and over and over. The decks of cards were limp and soft and their spots and figures faded with use. He taught me cribbage and canasta—the latter game enjoyed a surge of popularity in the early 1950s—and checkers. Invariably he won. When I expressed exasperation over yet another loss, he simply smiled knowingly and shuffled the deck again.

On my way out of his apartment, after he had gone back to lying down on his bed, I would shout out to him that I was taking fifty cents or seventy-five cents from the accumulating pile of pocket change that he left lying on the table. He would reply, "All right," since that was one of the reasons he left it there. Sometimes I took a quarter or two more than I said.

§

Consider this, if you are one of those who think that "fiction isn't real" and "movies should be more like life." There is a movie from 1981, *Raggedy Man*, that makes me think of my father. It is set during World War II and stars Sissy Spacek and Eric Roberts. She is a poor single mother of two little boys in a nowhere town in Texas and earns their keep as the local telephone operator. Roberts is a sailor who happens to come through, a nice guy who gets caught up in her life. It is better-than-average filmmaking, but the reason it is meaningful to me is the occasional appearance of a strange bummy-looking guy who shambles through the dusty streets, dragging a decrepit wagon, the "Raggedy Man" of the title. At the end, when Sissy is threatened at night by two perverty rednecks, the Raggedy Man comes to the rescue, saving her and the kids—but is killed. Turns out that the "Raggedy Man" was her ex-husband, who patrolled in tattered anonymity to make sure she and his sons were safe.

Critics praised the movie, save for its ending, calling it ill-advised. To me, however, it, minus the violence, is reminiscent of my father. He was not raggedy (admittedly disheveled most of the time), but he kept an eye on me. He did not trust Ma to take care of me. He was wrong; she did, after her fashion. So he would follow us around. As we moved, so would he, nearly as frequently, to small apartments or single rooms never far from ours. It could be that he thought we were getting too far away. Maybe his need to keep an eye on me accounts for his life to some extent; maybe it took up too much of his limited personal resources for him to otherwise make a "success" of his life. There is another thing: Pa's middle name, which is his mother's maiden name, is Geist. In German that means "ghost" or "spirit." Though it has been said there is no such thing as coincidences, I nevertheless like to think of it as a literally nominal coincidence that my father hovered over me as a kind of ghost or spirit.

There is a further aspect to his need to keep an eye on me. In my preteen years he did not trust my mother to feed me. This, again, was unwarranted. She was no great cook—after all, she worked hard every day in the Endicott-Johnson shoe factory and had little time to prepare meals—but I never went hungry. There was little he could do about breakfast or supper, so he concentrated on lunch. The calories and nutrients I failed to get in those two meals could be compensated for at noontime. He arranged to run a tab for me at a restaurant where I could go for lunch without paying. There were four places at four different times. Why four? Maybe a restaurant got tired of doing it, or more likely another fit of paranoia or suspicion overcame Pa and he decided that that particular place was no longer fitting. One of them was a restaurant-bar run by his boyhood friend, Andy Kooch from Lopez, located north of the Greyhound bus station on Chenango Street. Another place was the Skat bar and grill on the corner of Chenango and Eldredge streets. And then there was Chris's hot dog stand. A moveable feast, it occupied more than one site along Chenango Street at different times, but when I ate there it was north of the Viaduct. I can distinctly see myself sitting apart, a nine-or-ten-year-old, innocent and wide-eyed among all the stool-sitters, eating my lunch.

At the two restaurant-bars I sat in booths. At Kooch's I heard a patron tell a joke that I didn't understand but that, for the first time in my experience of jokes, I somehow realized was "dirty." The joke teller said, "I heard on the news that a woman was shot and the bullet's in her yet." Pause. "What I want to know is, what's a woman's yet?" Laughter, and assurances to the teller that "that was a good one." At the Skat I sat in a booth one noontime with a public library copy of *Adventures of Huckleberry Finn* propped on the table, reading over and over again the "Notice" at the front:

> Persons attempting to find a Motive in this narrative will be prosecuted; persons attempting to find a Moral in it will be banished; persons attempting to find a Plot in it will be shot.
>
> By Order of the Author
> Per G.G., Chief of Ordnance

That troubled me, made me uneasy. Really, could "they" do that, the author or whoever? I had a vague idea what a plot was and a moral. What if I found one or the other or both? What would happen to me? And what was prosecution and what was ordnance? I did not go on to read *Huck Finn*. I did not understand the dialect, much less the point—a problem that bedevils many grown-up readers still.

The fourth place was not a restaurant but my Aunt Florence's. She was my aunt by marriage, the wife of Pa's younger brother Howard. They had an apartment downtown, at 109 Court Street near the corner with Chenango. Both Howard and Flo were champion topers, but they were nice, Flo especially. As my mother put it, Flo would say shit if she had a mouthful, unlike the Millers, who would just shut up and swallow. One day her baby grandson peed on me while I held him on my lap and I didn't want to go back to school after the lunch hour because of it, though Flo did her best to clean me up. Her grandson was the son of her child from a previous—and apparently extremely youthful—marriage. Or perhaps non-marriage. Compared to our apartment, Flo and Howard's was chic Fifties Moderne. I was much taken with the gray plastic shell that fit over their telephone. Colored plastic shells were a way to get around limitations placed by AT & T, which then legally owned every telephone in the country and would let you have one in any color as long as it was black. Flo and I ate our lunch listening to the radio soap opera *Wendy Warren and the News*.

§

You can learn a lot, and speculate more, from looking through city directories. I searched editions of the Binghamton City Directory from 1939 through 1961, seeking information about Ma and Pa and my relatives and trying to ascertain where we lived at particular times. The information in the directories is sparse, telling where a person lived and what he or she worked at. It gives either a little "h," indicating a house or apartment for which the person paid taxes or rent, or a little "r," meaning that is where the person resided as a tenant of someone else. Around those bare facts it is possible to spin credible speculations.

My parents make their first appearances in 1939. Keith Miller is a shoeworker living as an "r" at 98 Washington Street. Interesting; who is the "h" there? Mae E. Sheridan is a saleslady at Dennison Bros. living as an "r" at 24 Chenango. What is interesting is that also living there as an "r" is her younger brother, Walter C. Sheridan, no occupation given. Hmm. So did brother and sister come up together from the country to the city to seek work?

By the next year Keith, still a shoeworker, has moved to 104 Court Street and Mae (employment not reported) to 20 Chenango, both "r."

Roger K. Miller

Walter is not with her or anywhere else, but I happen to know that he got caught in the peacetime draft so he may be in the first steps of a journey that will take him to Schofield Barracks, Hawaii, and eventually the South Pacific. All of these addresses are fairly close to one another, around the corner and up the street in most cases. Keith disappears from the pages in 1941, but Mae is there as an operator at Binghamton Knitting, having moved to 166 Water Street. Things must be looking up financially, for she is an "h."

But, aha, 1942! This is what I'm looking for: Keith Miller (Mae) shoeworker h 17 Prospect Ave, meaning that they are now married and living together in their own apartment at 17 Prospect Avenue. He is again a shoeworker, but no employment is given for her. This could mean that she does not work outside the home, as little Roger is now on the scene, or more likely it reflects the assumption of the time that wives did not work and if they did it was not worth noticing.

In 1943 the Millers again display the characteristic that has distinguished them so far and will distinguish them for the next twenty years (and Roger for the rest of his life): moving domicile. They live as "h" at 4 Court Street. Keith is still a shoeworker.

Then, in 1944, the Big Move, to 135 Chenango Street—the Moon Block, the site of the future fire. They remain there at 135 Chenango as "h" through the 1949 directory. Keith is now a "felt worker" (there was a company, Faatz Brush and Felting but locally known as "the Felters," in Johnson City that manufactured felt products), an occupation he retains until 1946, when he is a laborer at Binghamton Brick. But next year no occupation is given, a blank that remains until 1949, the year of the fire.

Two reasons are possible for the blank. One is that throughout his future life Keith would go through spells of unemployment. This is the least likely reason, because three years of joblessness at that point in his life is not credible.

More likely is that, though the directory continued to list them as "Miller Keith G (Mae E)" through 1949, indicating marriage and cohabitation, by 1947 he had flown the coop. And why? It has to do with what I detailed in Chapter 3 about Louise claiming Mae had deceived Keith about her—Louise's—identity, and when he learned the truth he abandoned the domestic hearth.

Buttressing this theory is the possibility that Keith began to feel invaded by members of Ma's Sheridan family, whom, as we have seen, he did not like, for also listed at 135 Chenango in 1947 are "Sheridan Russell D (Rose J)." Russell is listed as "shoeworker." After getting out of the Army he had married a woman from their home area in Pennsylvania. It is not inconceivable that they had moved in with Mae—thus driving Keith out, if he had not already bolted?—for this is a pattern that reappears in Mae's future. But the listing has Russell and Rose as "h," so they could be renting a separate apartment at the same address.

Russell and Rose are still there in 1948. Making a reappearance is Walter, who has been absent for the duration of the war and longer. He is a "shoeworker" living as "r" at 39 Susquehanna. Now that is curious. Susquehanna Street was long known as the "Negro section," and Sheridan men abhorred Negroes even more than they did temperance. But then again, nearly everybody did. With whom was he residing?

In 1949 Russell, now a "laborer," remains at 135 Chenango, but Rose disappears (I know that their marriage did not last long after the birth of a daughter). He could be a boarder with Mae, for he is given as "r."

The Moon Block fire of that year ends the ménage à strangeness and scatters its members. In 1950 Keith (no occupation) ends up an "r" at 28 Court Street and Russell (no occupation) an "h" at 289 Chenango. The latter is an address that figures in our several lives for several years. It is, in fact, the address that "Sheridan Walter (Lena)" occupy as "h" the next year, 1951. There is no way of knowing for certain whether it is the same apartment or another one at that address, but given the Miller-Sheridan history at the time it probably is the same one.

Keith was nowhere to be found in 1951, apparently, but in 1952 he is back as "r" at 29 Pine Street. Walter and Lena have split, for she is an "h" at 83 Liberty Street while he is an "h" at 289 Chenango, which must be a delay in reported information because Ma and I had taken it over by then.

Oddly, there are no entries for Mae in 1950, '51 or '52, but she shows up again in 1953 and she has definitively shed Keith, or vice versa, for she is now "Miller Mae Mrs shoeworker h 285 Chenango." Also at 285 Chenango as "r" is "Sheridan Louise D clerk Fowler's." (Fowler's, or, formally, Fowler, Dick, and Walker, was a leading department store. It disappeared, along with hundreds of other local downtown department stores across the nation in the Malling of America that destroyed the downtowns in the 1970s and '80s.) Louise has moved in with Mae and Roger in their new digs just spitting distance from their old after having been released from her incarceration or reformation or whatever it was. I remember it with pleasure now for I greeted it with pleasure then. Keith, for his part, has moved to 219 Chenango, not more than two blocks from 285, beginning his regimen of beneficent stalking of Mae and his son.

The next year, 1954, Keith has moved even closer, to 289 Chenango. Yes, 289, our once and future address. Not the very same apartment, but one on the first floor in the front toward the north side. I visited him there. It was as untended and untidy as any of his others. No sign of Walter Sheridan, but "Sheridan Lena Mrs waitress" has moved to an "h" at 52 North Street way over on the near West Side. Louise, "clerk," is still "r" at 285 Chenango.

In 1955 Keith moves farther north to 365 Chenango. Mae, it says, has moved to 291 Chenango, but this is wrong. It should read 289; in reality, Mae and Roger had moved again to that apartment house, to an apartment on the first floor in the back. Lena Sheridan, a "waitress," has moved a block away from her North Street apartment to an "h" at 30 Thorp Street. Louise supposedly is an "r" at 289 Chenango, but this too is an error because the previous June she had married Richard Rogers and moved way upstate to his home area, Hastings, New York, twenty miles north of Syracuse.

From 1956 through 1959 there are no separate listings for Mae, but, weirdly, there are for Roger: "Miller Roger (Mae S) h 250 Chenango." What that signifies I have no idea. Perhaps that, being the male in the house Roger is the breadwinner and Mae is his wife? Nevertheless it does record accurately that we had moved across the street to the even-numbered side and a bit south. Keith, a "laborer," has also moved southward, to h 223 Chenango. No Sheridan raises his or her head during this span except Lena, who in 1958 lands as an "r" relatively far north at 478 Chenango.

The Miller-Sheridan tribe, shadowing the nation, begins to shift west; 1959 records the westward move Ma and I actually had made the year before. "Miller Roger (Mae S)" are now "h" at 82 Walnut Street, just off Main Street and behind the American Legion building. Keith remains behind as "laborer" at 223 Chenango, but not for long as we shall see.

In 1960 Keith is, shorn of occupation, "h" at 154 Oak Street, just a hop-skip-and-a-jump from "Miller Roger K (Mae S)" at 82 Walnut. Roger is now a "bookkeeper" at First-City National Bank. Even closer to Keith, for no reason at all, are "Sheridan Russell (Rose) h 120 Oak." No, Russell has not remarried his divorced wife. He has married another Rose, a very nice small mountain of a woman. Walter, too, has married again, a woman named Margaret, a beautician who operates her own shop in the house (hers) where they live at 78 Leroy Street, not terribly far from Walnut or Oak. Russell's occupation is "quarry worker" and Walter's "stone cutter," a reflection of their not terribly successful attempt to run their own quarry or stone-cutting business. They would not have been able to even make the attempt had Walter not hitched up with Margaret, who provided him with a spanking new pickup truck (as well as many other things) that he never would have afforded on his own, but I get ahead of myself.

I end my directory researches in 1961, when Mae comes back into her own as "Miller Mae S employee EJ Corp." Roger splits off to a separate listing, "Miller Roger K student." Both live at 82 Walnut. Keith continues to keep an eye on his now-grown son from 154 Oak, but Russell and Rose are no longer his neighbors, and Walter and Margaret remain at home at 78 Leroy.

§

As I said earlier, I think I know more about why my parents broke up than about how they got together. Since their marriage turned out not to be the romance of the ages, it's not something you would expect either of them to reminisce about, and I never asked them. I suspect that they met in a bar. My father was not a drinker and went to bars only infrequently. In my imagination he was a bachelor prowling for female companionship, and where better to find compliant females than in a bar?

Well, as I am here in living testimony, it would seem that Keith and Mae got together at some point in late 1940, for nine months later, on July 9, 1941, I graced this planet. Two months after that they got married. I do not understand why my mother married the father of her third child (me) but not the fathers of her two previous children. The answer may be as simple as that the other two never asked her. He was like that, whatever else he may have lacked. My mother used to say, "Keith Miller is as honest as the day is long." I got the impression it was not entirely a compliment. She also called him "Grampa Grunt."

Louise always liked my father, said he was nice to her and our sister. But he moved out of the house when I was still a small child, and the formal, legal separation came when I was ten. I sat in the judge's chambers and he asked me which parent I wanted to live with. I said my mother.

Roger K. Miller

She told me beforehand to say that. By that point neither of my two half-sisters was living with us and we were not living in the Moon Block.

When Louise got married in June 1954, she invited Pa to the wedding and he went, even though he had not had any contact with her for a decade. It was not a simple chore, for the wedding was in Central Square, New York, some ninety miles north of Binghamton, and Pa did not drive. So he took the Greyhound bus up and back. He did not make it to the wedding ceremony itself, but I can still see him striding into the reception hall that night, surprising everyone. He handed his gift—an electric percolator—to Louise, and turned around and strode out of the hall to the bus stop to await the next bus back to Binghamton, though many people implored him to stay. Clearly he wanted to avoid lengthy contact with his former wife, but he also wanted to show his support of Louise. It was sort of a grandstanding gesture—he could simply have mailed the gift, after all—but it was one that she remembered for fifty years.

Louise also remembered it as the night "my mother" got falling-down drunk. That's how she always phrased it—"my mother"—every time I heard her recount the episode. What *I* remember is that it was the night one of *my* mother's sometime boyfriends tried to crawl into bed with her, not realizing, in his drunken state, that I was in there with her. Because of crowded conditions in the house of Louise's brand-new in-laws, where we were staying overnight after the wedding and reception, I was bunked in with my mother (not a new situation). I was relieved when she told her desperate, boozy swain to buzz off.

Neither Ma nor Pa married again. My mother subsequently had a number of boyfriends. One—the last, as far as I know—she stuck with for many years As for my father's romantic life I know nothing, other than once having caught him in a semi-compromising situation with a woman when I stopped by on one of my unannounced visits to his apartment.

I have given Ma credit for not letting her boyfriends stay overnight, but perhaps she did in the summer or on weekends when I was not there. I spent every summer since I can remember, up through my seventeenth, at my grandparents' place in Lopez. I also spent many weekends there. My Miller relatives were good to me. It was a child's paradise in that we—my cousins and I—could play and do whatever we wanted, within restrictions. I think the Millers—grandparents, aunts, and uncles—looked out for me because of my "broken home," then a term redolent enough of scandal that it had to be whispered.

The Chenango Kid

I return to the succinct answer I gave to my friend in the e-mail. In the years I can remember Pa best, the 1950s, which hummed and thrummed with economic prosperity for most people, so long as they were white, what lingers with me is his being out of work a lot. I never thought about it at that time. I didn't hate him then and I don't hate him now. He died in 1980, and I never think about him much, but when I do, I feel a little sad for him. Or is it me I feel sad for? I do know he loved me and was proud of me—for going to college on my own dime (he never got past eighth grade), for serving my country in the Army (he tried to enlist at the time of Pearl Harbor but was, at 37, too old), for working in a profession that paid decent wages, and for marrying and giving him grandchildren. A realization of love and pride—that's more than a lot of sons get from their fathers. Thanks for asking, Pat. It was a good thing to think about on Father's Day.

CHAPTER 7

East Junior

"From now until the end of time no one else will ever see life with my eyes, and I mean to make the best of my chance."

—Christopher Morley

Whenever I think of school, invariably the time setting is late summer or early fall, either the bright golden haze of September or the crisp chill of October. As I set this down what comes to me, besides the pleasant weather, is that my most vivid and lasting memories of school are of East Junior High School. "Is there life after high school?" the wise man asked. I am not a wise man, but I will return to the question later. The point here is that there was life *in* junior high and I enjoyed it, partly because it was a refuge from the instability of home.

Long gone now, East Junior, grades seven through nine, was a three-story brick structure that took up much of a block bounded by Robinson and Ely streets and Broad Avenue. On its fourth side was its playground and beyond that houses and buildings down to Court Street. When I began there in September 1953, we lived at 285 Chenango.

Though similar in size and shape, 285, a three-story wooden structure, was different from 289 Chenango, which we had just left. It had fewer but larger apartments. On each floor there was one apartment on each side of the central stairwell. Our apartment on the top floor ran from the back porch to the front porch facing Chenango Street. Compared with what we had inhabited before, and would later, it was enormous. In the front was a living room, then a dining room (though we used it as a bedroom), then the kitchen. Then, off to the stairwell side, a series of smaller rooms that paralleled those three: a bedroom in the back, the bathroom, and another bedroom. The bedroom and bathroom shared an airshaft.

The reason we used the living room as a bedroom (my mother's) must have been that the back bedroom was too cold in the winter. This is because our heating system was straight out of the nineteenth century—or Lopez. We heated with coal in a pot-bellied stove in the living room and a big stove in the kitchen. That was it. (The coal had to be humped up the back stairs in bags on the backs of deliverymen.) Viewed from today, this seems crazy. Individual stoves in apartments? Was every apartment heated this way? They must have been. Given the age and condition of the building and the unknown mental and physical capabilities of its tenants, it is a miracle one of us didn't burn the place down or coal-gas ourselves to death. The tenants on the second floor of our side of the building were a family of strange, secretive, and apparently not terribly well-nourished adherents of some extreme religious sect. None of them would speak when you passed them on the stairs; the paterfamilias, the palest of this tribe of palefaces, looked at you as if he were contemplating with pleasure the torments that your hedonistic life doomed you to suffer in hell.

Oddly, despite this primitive and inefficient heating system, it was not cold other than in that back bedroom. Or it could be that I have forgotten, since I have fond memories of the place though we lived there only one year and thus one winter. We moved there because Louise had joined us and the previous apartment was too small. One thing I can say about my sister, she, like our mother, was a hard worker. A *hard* worker, and she never slackened. And she spent what she earned. Ma and I had stuff we never had before. New furniture, knickknacks, appliances. The grandest was a Bendix combination radio-record player, one of those kind that played multiple 78-rpm records. It was neat to watch: When a record was over, the tone arm swung back to the starting point, throwing a switch that caused the record-grabbing doohickey to grab the next record from the stack, move it over the turntable and drop it into playing position. I played a Stan Freberg parody record—"St. George and the Dragonet" (a spoof of *Dragnet*) and on the other side "Little Blue Riding Hood"—over and over. Years later I would do the same when I bought Freberg's parody of Lawrence Welk's music, which is still hilarious but you have to be familiar with Welk and his 1950s television program to know why. It probably was

Louise who bought "Secret Love," but I played that constantly, too, as I had seen *Calamity Jane*, the movie in which Doris Day sings it, and loved it and her.

Probably the reason for our short stay there was that Louise left and Ma could not afford to keep it. At the time Louise was engaged to Richard and in June 1954 they married, not long after he was discharged from the Air Force. He had been stationed at a U.S. base in either Bermuda or the Bahamas, I forget which, but either one would have been the best military posting I've ever heard of.

Naturally, Louise and Richard wrote letters to each other. Just as naturally, Louise and I did not always get along. Somewhat further down the line of naturalness, these two characteristics collided. One day Louise asked me to drop a letter she had written into the mailbox on the corner when I went out. I was ticked at her for something, so I wrote on the back of the envelope, "Louise is going out with . . ." and added the name of a young man who worked in his Greek family's restaurant there on Chenango Street. It's true, she was, or she did once go out with him—but, oh, that we would contemplate the consequences of the actions we are about to commit! More naturally than anything, Richard wrote back immediately, enclosing the envelope and demanding to know what was going on. When Louise confronted me with the envelope, her demands were even hotter and her eyes were blazing. I began backing away as she came after me. She chased me all around that third-floor real estate, hollering, "You little son-of-a-bitch, if I catch you I'll kill you." She never did. I was too little and too fast. I was out the door, down the stairs, and out on the street before she could get traction. Whatever breach I caused between her and Richard must have healed, for they married and remained so for fifty years, until her death November 20, 2004.

§

SOB or not, I *was* little. I weighed no more than eighty pounds in seventh grade. I know this because they used to weigh us occasionally. This astounds me that the state—the *state!*—took such extensive concern for its schoolchildren. Checking for head lice, annual physical exams. I wonder now, in our increasingly libertarian and conspiratorial age, would it be considered not concern, but interference? *Why* does the state want to know how much the children weigh? To fatten them up for making into sausages? At the time I worried about fattening *me* up. When I saw the latest results of the scale, I thought, Well, I'll be going to Lopez this weekend, I'll eat a lot there. *Why* I thought this mystifies me. I got plenty to eat, all I wanted or needed, at home.

But I digress. Ninety percent, or surely no less than eighty-five percent, of school is two things: teachers and students. Of the former, the best and worst remain forever memorable. None of mine is quite as memorable as the woman Nancy says she had in grade school in Troy, New York. Throughout the day this teacher took hits of alcohol—hard liquor—via a throat sprayer. I asked Nancy if the students could tell what it was and what she was doing. Oh yes: The teacher smelled of alcohol and her face was red. She cleared her throat frequently, each time medicating her throat with a hit from her sprayer.

As for me and my East Junior schoolmates, we had a wood-shop teacher who, I kid you not, was missing most of one thumb. Whether it was from getting it too close to a power saw or to a German or Japanese bullet I never knew. He used to run the stub along an edge of our corner shelves or cutting boards or other projects to judge their finish and if it was acceptable say, "Slick as a hair on a toad." Yes, I made a corner shelf. Everyone did. Somewhere within the deepest layers of the landfills of America must be the rotting remains of millions of junior-high corner shelves. Ma kept mine and actually put stuff on it long after I left home.

In electrical shop I made a hotdog cooker. Not being a thing of beauty and a joy forever, it did not remain outside the dump nearly as long as the corner shelf. Basically it consisted of four or five long, heavy nails hammered in vertical rows along each side of a finished board. The points of the nails in each row were bent to face each other, then connected to some attached heating device that could be plugged into a socket. You placed a hotdog between a set of facing nail points, plugged it in, and—*voila!*—you had an object so ugly it was out of place even on the North Side of Binghamton in the 1950s.

The shop teacher was a nice fellow. One day we managed to get him to waste an entire class period discussing color television, which no one could imagine coming about for decades (although, in fact, a couple of working systems had already been developed). He married another teacher in the school. That tickled us. Two teachers marrying—imagine! I forget what his wife taught, but I must have been in one of her classes for one day she stopped by my desk and picked up the copy of *The Revolt of Gunner*

Asch that I had brought to school. She looked at it disapprovingly and asked if I thought it was appropriate for me. I replied that it was good.

My eighth grade history teacher was from West Virginia but told us with high enthusiasm that it was called "West By-God" and why. She it was who explained, for the first and last times in our lives, what the "XYZ Affair" was all about. She liked patriotic history. Her first allegiance may have been to West By-God, but all the rest was for the U.S. of A. Americans were the good guys and then there was everybody else, as World War II had so recently proved. High along one wall of her classroom hung oblong placards bearing historical mottos like "Millions for defense, but not one cent for tribute." She had us enter an essay contest on the Revolutionary War sponsored by the VFW or some such likely organization. I entered and thought I had a pretty good chance with my snappy opening, "In Boston they knew their beans about revolution." Ha ha. Too bad I didn't have anything substantial to follow, for I did not win. A girl won, naturally.

It was in this class that we debated whether Alaska and Hawaii should be admitted to the Union. None of us had a clue or wanted one, but we had to have some answer when Mrs. West By-God asked, because it had been the issue of the week in *My Weekly Reader*. In lieu of thought, the default answer among us was, "No, because it would be too easy for communists to get in." It made sense to us because we heard everywhere, as well as took it in with every breath, that communists were infiltrating us at every nook and cranny. The paranoid fringe, like the John Birch Society, warned that communists were behind the fluoridation of public water supplies in an attempt to poison our precious bodily fluids. That countries with communist governments were also fluoridating their water supplies did not come up in their pamphlets. Why Alaska and Hawaii were more vulnerable to communist infiltration than, say, Iowa was logical to us: They were "outside" the forty-eight contiguous states and thus communists could foregather there and patiently wait until statehood, and then they would be "in." On the other hand, Iowa, wherever that might be, was already "in" and thus communists could not get . . . well, the logic began to peter out. I want to believe that *My Weekly Reader* had a little bird that used its beak to point out to us the important facts in its stories, but I think I must be remembering "This is a watchbird watching you" created by Munro Leaf.

We employed a number of default remarks in lieu of thought. Another was, "And if you want to know how it turns out, you'll have to read the book." This was used by students giving oral book reports desperate to bring their rambling oration to a close. It continued to be used despite the teacher's repeated warnings not to but to think of a more creative ending that "told something about the book." It continued to be used because few bothered to think about the book report until sitting down at their desks on the day it was to be given. I am sure I cannot have used it more than once because I did what I was told, mostly, and anyway I loved books. Indeed, it was around the time of eighth grade that I began reading adult novels in earnest. Since I liked English, it is strange that I cannot recall much about this eighth-grade English class other than that I liked it because the teacher, an upholstered lady of Helen Hokinson proportions, ran a book-buying club run through some publication or publisher. Every so often she would pass out a flyer listing the latest offerings of twenty-five- and thirty-five-cent paperbacks, which I pored over avidly. I bought and enjoyed Harry Leon Wilson's *Ruggles of Red Gap*. Giovannino Guareschi's *The Little World of Don Camillo* seems like a strange book to make available to early adolescents, but I ordered and read it. I did not understand much of it, but I was amused by the idea of a talking Jesus and by the neat little illustrations by the author.

Helen Eustis's gothic frightener *The Fool Killer* would have been a still stranger offering. But it was too recently published to be in paperback, so the copy I read must have been from the Binghamton Public Library. Its eerie cover bore the silhouette of a tall humanoid figure holding an ax in both hands, looming over the silhouette in the lower left corner of a much smaller man or boy looking up at it. The reason it still resides in my mind may be an assignment of the teacher's to make a poster illustrating a book we had read. I simply copied the cover, not, I think, because that was easy but because the cover was so striking. Did I give an oral book report on *The Fool Killer*? If so did the teacher cluck at its inappropriateness?

In the second semester of eighth-grade English or possibly in ninth grade—in any case, it was a different woman teacher—that I first discovered James Thurber. It seems to me a quite imaginative pedagogy for a time when the typical junior-high or high school reading fare was mossy old things like O. Henry or "The Monkey's Paw," she had us read from *My Life and Hard Times* about Thurber's late grandmother who feared that electricity dripped invisibly and dangerously from empty light sockets and his great-uncle Zenas who caught the same disease that was killing off the chestnut trees. I thought Thurber's tales were very funny. I still do.

Roger K. Miller

For an assignment for her I wrote a story probably two loose-leaf pages long, if that, in which the comedies and dramas on the radio were performed by tiny people in the radio. She thought that was terribly clever. It was the first class I ever had in which the seats were not facing front but were arranged in three sides of a square of which the fourth side was her desk. That too seems rather advanced thinking for the mid-1950s.

Seventh-grade English has barely faded from my mind in six decades. My teacher—for both semesters, I think—was Mr. Bernstein, a nice, pleasant man with a fringe of black hair encircling an otherwise bald pate. Few details remain of that year, mostly a sense of an atmosphere that must have been more relaxed than was probably good for his retaining control over a gaggle of twelve- and thirteen-year-olds. Not unruly, but looser than we had lived through in grade school. Maybe he was trying to make school fun, English fun. I wonder if I got a bit too smart-alecky for him? He had to pull me aside and "talk" to me a few times. He told us stories from his personal experience—how, for example, food could be heated on the engine of an automobile.

Two incidents stick out. We had little white class cards bearing our personal information and class schedule. One bit of information you had to put down was your religion. As I had none, the decision what to put down made me nervous (but then, didn't everything?). If I didn't put something down, what would "they" think of me? So I put down First Church of the Nazarene, the Smith family's church. That embarrassed me too, for I was pretty sure that few others—Baptists and Catholics and Methodists—had anything that exotic-sounding.

The other was when a black girl—she had been in my sixth-grade class at Thomas Edison—had to read the word "nigger" out loud during oral recitation of *The Adventures of Tom Sawyer*. She giggled to cover her discomfiture. Why did Mr. Bernstein make her do that? Was he clueless? A meanie? Or did it just happen to be her turn to read aloud and to skip her would only highlight the encroaching awkwardness? Why were we reading that book, anyway? Now the school district could choose the edition by NewSouth Books that replaces "nigger" with "slave." Not that it should. Actually, it shouldn't—and like most school districts probably doesn't—choose *any* edition. The novel is, unlike *Huckleberry Finn*, a "boy's book" meant for children, but the children of the nineteenth century were much different from those of the twenty-first, and the word "nigger" is just too big a hurdle for today's kids to get past. For their parents, too, but they should know better.

9/30/55. Many people my age will recognize with little hesitation what those numerals refer to: the death of actor James Dean on September 30, 1955, behind the wheel of his Porsche Spyder near Cholame, California. Dean is as good an example as you can find of the fatalistic injunction to live fast, die young, and leave a good-looking corpse—though since he died in a horrible automobile crash, we can't be sure of the last part. But while alive he certainly was good-looking, in that androgynous way of so many great stars (Marlene Dietrich, Gary Cooper); he lived (and drove) very fast in the short time he was a celebrity; and he died young, at age twenty-four. His death affected a lot of teenagers noticeably. An "instant" paperback biography came out within months and could be seen among the books being toted around the halls.

Around that time—it had to be eighth or ninth grade, for that is when the big-money quiz shows such as *The $64,000 Question* and *Twenty-One* burst onto television screens—I had a history or social science teacher who used the shows in class. It was an effective teaching or at any rate attention-getting gimmick that you would not expect from a guy sporting a ratty little mustache to go with his Uriah Heepish manner. A publisher had brought out another of those "instant" paperbacks to cash in on the quiz-show craze. It contained questions and answers in subjects featured on the shows—history, sports, literature, and the like. He had us up in front of the class as questioner and answerer, just as if on a TV show. We enjoyed it and we may actually have learned something. One of the subject categories was one that I never remember seeing used on any of the shows but in which I was knowledgeable: comic strips and cartooning. I surprised everyone with my knowledge; it took several questions before I was bested.

The quiz shows were really popular. It was probably *The $64,000 Question* that inspired my teacher, because it was the first one on the air, in 1955, but we—Ma and I—liked *Twenty-One*, which came along a year later. The sight of Charles Van Doren, the "big professor," as we thought of him, sweating away with headphones on in the "isolation booth" as he groped for the answer to a question on some obscure subject—now *that* was intelligence as intelligence was measured on Chenango Street! *Pretending* to grope, I should say, for two years later the "quiz show scandals" broke, revealing that Van Doren and others had been given answers as part of the shows' strategy to keep excitement at a high level.

On the first day of class, a bright, sunny day in September, his first chore after striding into the room was to order a girl to get off my lap *this instant!* This was not an occurrence common to me—I was as surprised to find her there as he was—but to the girl, a saucy lass transferred from somewhere in the Deep South, it may well have been. She had an accent as broad as the Chattahoochee and the sort of advanced-for-her-age figure and personality that has landed many a hapless male eighth- and ninth-grade teacher in the slammer over the decades. Before the teacher came into the classroom we had all—well, the boys, anyway—been mesmerized by this charming new creature and hanging on to every honeyed, accented word bubbling from her lips. Clearly, in whatever Confederate region she hailed from she had learned ways of Winning Friends and Influencing People that were not taught in the frozen North. Why it was my lap she chose to favor that day I have forgotten, if I ever knew, but one thing I do know: It cannot have been the first lap and even more certainly it was not the last.

Later in the year this teacher announced to us one day that he had written to Vice President Richard Nixon to invite him to our class, explaining that it would be a good lesson in civics and beaming as if he actually thought that such a visit might come to pass. It did not. Then it was a matter of total indifference to me, but now the thought of a Nixon visit is appalling. The thought of *Nixon* is appalling.

§

All through my school years I paid no more attention to the news than did my classmates. Ma subscribed to the *Binghamton Press* and read it or parts of it. I read only the comic strips. I was aware now and then of the ongoing Korean War. Probably the national fear of communism, which I had heard we had fought there, impressed it on me. For some reason that war always has held an interest for me, to the extent that in my sixties I wrote a novel (*Invisible Hero*) dealing with it. For the most part, however, I was unaware of what was happening in the world.

Still, a world-shaking event occasionally would burst the bubble I walked around in. Oddly, a number of those events clustered in and around the summer of 1953, the year I entered seventh grade. There was the armistice on July 27 that ended the fighting in Korea, albeit not the state of war itself. Another happening that stirred up anti-communist fever was the arrest in September of Cardinal Wyszynski in Warsaw for protesting the Soviet presence in Poland. Whatever that was about, it didn't sound good to me. More understandable to my mind was the execution of Julius Rosenberg and his wife Ethel on June 19 for being—more communism—spies for the Soviet Union. On May 29 Edmund Hillary and Tenzing Norgay succeeded in reaching the top of Mt. Everest. And shortly after that, in the biggest story of the season if not the year, came even greater glory for the fading British Empire with the coronation of Queen Elizabeth II on June 2.

§

Most East Junior teachers I associate with eighth grade, but not all. Mr. Bernstein, of course. And there was Mr. Ellison, my math teacher, in whose estimation, as in Mr. Bernstein's, I must have been too . . . enthusiastic . . . on occasion—occasions that then required an adjustment of my attitude and behavior. One such was when he caught me making a silly doodlish cartoon I had labeled "aerial attack Ellison." Where did that come from? Had he told us some anecdote of his military service? I marvel at how innocent were the infractions of those days compared with today's.

Our seventh-grade art teacher was a big fat lady who taught us perspective. Not on life—in drawing. Perspective on life would have done us more good, if she could have taught that and we could have grasped it. So perspective in drawing it was. And little else. Boy, we got perspective down 'til hell wouldn't have it. We spent most of a semester placing our vanishing point on the lower left side of a large piece of paper and, with the aid of a ruler, drawing from it a series of upward-tending, widely separating lines toward a vertical line right of center on the paper. This became the corner of what would be a sharply angular, multistoried, many-windowed, plain-faced building that looked like, if it looked like anything, the soulless insurance offices Franz Kafka would unhappily have entered each day if he had happened to survive and come to America. If nothing else the exercise gave me a perspective on perspective. As well as a view of the people going into and coming out of Perhach's pharmacy on Robinson Street below me, for my desk was next to a window out of which I could gaze and daydream while the teacher nattered on about how terrific the Cary Grant movie *Dream Wife* was.

And seventh grade introduced us to . . . da-*DUM* . . . formal physical education classes, aka gym. Taking showers with other guys. And buying our first jockstraps. Looking them over in their boxes inside the glass case of the store: Hmm, I don't know. How do you choose? That one there—wonder if it's big enough?

§

Selling encyclopedias as Mrs. Tice did or kitchen appliances as Mr. Bernstein did was not the only way teachers moonlighted for extra money. My eighth-grade math teacher, whom I will call simply Ben, was a part-time bartender at either Dud & Tom's or the Wales Hotel on Chenango Street. I assume that is where he met Ma, for she was a frequenter of those establishments, and where, I further assume, that he hit on her, for one day he said to me, "Your mother is a very beautiful lady."

I didn't know how to respond. A short, grinning, roly-poly Italian who might have been Danny DeVito's father, he spoke to me as I stood at the head of a line of fidgeting classmates at the classroom doorway, waiting for the bell to break us for lunch. It was a complete surprise to me, his knowing Ma. I suppose his comment was intended as a way of ingratiating himself with the mother through the son, hoping that it would get back to her. Anyway, my mind and the minds of everyone behind me were concentrated on bolting out of the gate as fast as possible so as to get down to the basement lunchroom and into the lunch line early. If you got there late you wasted a lot of the lunch period standing in line. It wasn't a matter of running. The entire school was admonished: *Walk, don't run*! Going down the hall we resembled a gaggle of waddling penguins or Charlie Chaplin Little Tramps attempting to race without running. All of us, as soon as we got out of range of our teachers, abandoned this absurd power walking and broke hell-for-leather for the lunchroom.

You could buy a hot lunch or bring your own lunch and buy milk, white or chocolate. Most of the time I brought mine; ring bologna was the usual sandwich du jour. You could get a free lunch if you worked in the kitchen, washing trays and so forth. A friend, whose face but not whose name stays with me, worked there. He was pretty poor, I think, and wasn't long for the life of a junior high scholar, seeing greater opportunities in the life of a drop-out. It is amazing to me the number of kids who quit school. At what age could they do that then? Sixteen? At his instigation I worked in the kitchen, but only for a short while. With my habit of situating scenes from books in venues I have known, when I read in George Orwell's *Down and Out in Paris and London* about the *plongeurs* in the Paris hotel I thought of the East Junior kitchen.

As for whether any romance, for lack of a more accurate word, sprang up between Ma and Ben I cannot say. If so she kept it hidden.

§

Where did my interests and enthusiasms come from? Some were decidedly eccentric for a kid my age. In the eighth grade I subscribed to *Punch* magazine. (Another question: Where did I get the money for it?) I had seen a copy or two and was terribly taken with it, particularly the old-style covers with the nineteenth-century representation of the figure Punch that graced nearly every issue. I can scarcely have understood the articles, humor, or cartoons no matter how intensely I scoured it; I didn't even know who or what Punch was nor the subtitle *The London Charivari*. I sent it a cartoon I had drawn showing a very tall man standing next to a very small car (thinking of the relatively new Volkswagen) with the caption, "Mr. Six-Foot-Five buys a four-foot auto." Ha ha. I thought "auto" was the word one needed to use for British audiences who might not know the word "car." I guess they already had enough cartoons because I never heard from them. Perhaps I should have included return postage. I badgered Ma into getting me a thick collection of *Punch* cartoons for Christmas. I read it and subsequently thumbed through it hundreds of times, studying drawing styles. I was particularly taken by the spare, quirky style of the cartoonist who drew under the pen name Fougasse. I retained the book in my ever-expanding-and-contracting personal library for years and wish I had it still.

It was about this time that I became mad for the work of another British illustrator and cartoonist and *Punch* contributor, Rowland Emett, of whom I learned through a spread in *Life* magazine. What fanciful mechanics and inventions and odd contraptions he dreamed up, and his railroad, the Far Tottering and Oyster Creek Railway—magnificent! The closest comparison in American cartooning is Rube Goldberg, but it is not very close, for their drawing styles were poles apart. Furthermore, Emett's eccentric creations often were part of a whimsical little world of the British countryside. He designed the inventions for the film *Chitty Chitty Bang Bang*.

I know where one enthusiasm came from: my Uncle Will Miller, Pa's youngest brother. He had earned a bachelor's degree from Syracuse University on the GI Bill and was an accountant. In the very early 1950s he moved from Binghamton to Manhattan where jobs for accountants were better and so was the cultural life. Will was always getting enthusiasms. Once it was cooking beans in pots, another time it was refinishing and caning old chairs. And another it was painting on glass. That was cool, so I took up painting on glass also, except, since I absolutely loved comic strips, I copied panels from Sunday color strips. There was a glazier just up the street who must have wondered what this nutty kid was doing with all the pieces of glass he kept coming in to buy.

Earlier than that I painted-by-numbers, which I had discovered on a visit we made to Ma's sister Romayne in Batavia, New York. As a fad it was perhaps the biggest hobby breakthrough of the decade, to the point of becoming a national mania. Somewhere I read that one painting won a prize at a San Francisco art show, to the judges' embarrassment.

Fads and manias. In eighth or ninth grade there was a fad among boys of wearing metal cleats on the heels of our shoes, the better to make noise as we clattered down the halls and up the stairs. Around this time I, along with every other American male between the ages of twelve and twenty, rich or poor, owned a pink shirt to go with charcoal gray slacks and sport jacket. The pink shirt was a startling chromatic breakout from the universal, standard white dress shirt. Decades later I read that the fashion shift was due to Mamie Eisenhower, a clotheshorse whose favorite livery color was "shocking" or "hot" pink. Maybe her preference derived—if so, certainly unwittingly—from the source from which many of our fashion, cultural, musical, and entertainment tastes flow: African Americans. There was a vogue in the black community for hot pink, including Cadillacs; black boxer Sugar Ray Robinson had one, with suit to match. Pink Cadillacs didn't become respectable until white ladies began winning them for selling mountains of Mary Kay cosmetics. Not to mention pink flamingo lawn ornaments made of polyethylene, which became, if not respectable, fashionable.

I cannot count or even estimate the number of mail-in offers on cereal boxes that hooked me, but one of the oddest was reproductions of Confederate currency. Confederate currency? What marketing geniuses thought that was a come-on, and what in the zeitgeist sparked it? They must have had Roger Miller in mind, for I couldn't send off for enough of the stuff. I had stacks of it.

In East Junior I had my last real physical fight with anyone. The cause of the fight is gone but not the sight of us rolling around in the cindery dirt of the playground within a circle of gawking schoolmates.

In seventh grade I and another fellow tried out for a stage show that was being prepared for the whole school. Our entire act was a plagiarizing from *Pogo*, my favorite comic strip, literally spouting the content that I had typed out. Hard enough for the average citizen to get as comic art, it made absolutely no sense as theater. We were given the hook not long into our "act."

Walter and Russell had decided to try their hand at their own stone-quarrying business. This actually made some sense, for both had worked in quarries and neither was noticeably good at working for others for very long. I went with them; it was a good time and I may actually have helped them a bit by scoring with a hammer and chisel flagstone for them to break. Or more likely they gave me useless scraps of stone to keep me occupied but that would not be a loss if I messed up. Surprisingly, they did not stop off in a tavern.

Though I had an eye for a pretty face or ankle—bosoms were not an issue in sixth or seventh grade—I thought my yearnings were entirely secret. They were not, as I discovered when a gaggle of girls, giggling and laughing as they marched past St. Paul's Church, opposite our place, chanted "Roger loves Linda! Roger loves Linda!" Which I did at the time; she was a lovely thing with soft blue eyes and perfect blond hair, much like Doris Day, in my estimation, with whom I was also currently in love. The Ray Noble/Buddy Clark rendition of the song "Linda" was still in the national songbook then. The chanting probably was done more to tease Linda, who was in the midst of the gaggle, walking along with head bowed in embarrassment, than me. Nothing comes of pre-teen infatuations, thank goodness. Anyway, I was too timid and shy to press any suit. In fact, later I sprained my ankle running away from a girl named Ann who lived in an apartment on the third floor. I had to get about on crutches for several days. I milked that not-very-serious injury for all it was worth.

§

I received a certificate, dated June 1956 and signed by James H. Hogan, counselor, and stamped with the signature of Willard C. Hamlin, principal, for "faithful and continued service to fellow students and school" as a member of the East Junior Honor Traffic Squad. We were the guys who, as classes changed at the end of each hour, got to stand at the intersections of halls to keep foot traffic orderly, which essentially involved making kids younger than us who were acting rowdy go back to the other end of the hall and start over again. We never picked on kids larger than us, however disruptive, no matter which grade they were in. Once at a school assembly Hogan cracked a pathetic joke playing off Mindy Carson's popular recording, "Wake the Town and Tell the People." At the top of the Hit Parade in the Soviet Union, he said, was the song, "Wake the Town and Kill the People." Judging by our laughter we in the audience must have considered it hilarious.

That same month, on the 22nd, "having satisfactorily completed the requirements for promotion from Junior High School," I was awarded a diploma of promotion stamped with the signatures of the selfsame Hamlin, Martin A. Helfer, superintendent of schools, and Miller S. Gaffney, president of the board of education. Three years later I would go to work as a messenger/trainee at First-City National Bank, where Miller Gaffney, a member of the Triple Cities aristocracy, was a vice president.

A year before, June 24, 1955, a Certificate for Perfect Attendance testified that I, a pupil in the 8A grade of East Junior High School, had been neither absent nor tardy for five-and-a-half years. Stamp-signed by Helfer, Hamlin, and Mildred C. Kenyon, unidentified—perhaps the city's chief keeper of school attendance.

That was not my last association with Martin A. Helfer and education. In 1966, when Nancy and I came back from England and I was looking for a job, Helfer tried to get me to take on a class of tough-to-manage kids. I could see he was desperate to solve an intractable problem. He said they just needed love. I suspected they just needed a parole officer. I did not take the job. I was headed for the Army anyway, which was probably a kinder fate.

§

Who is this "us" and who are these "we" I write about? Didn't I have any friends? What were their names? Yes, I did have, a fair number, though the names from my earliest years have been sucked into the slipstream of time. But at North High there was Tom, my longest-serving friend other than my cousin Ken, and Bob and Paul and Jerry and Don—and Bill, a redhead to whom I was joined at the hip for nearly six years, all through junior high and high school. I am aware of a lack of detail in here about play and childhood companions. That lack does not reflect the reality of my life. I think it is a function of the way I write, observing the past from the perspective of now. That may be the wrong way to write—breaking the rule that you should show not tell—but that is the way I do it. On the other hand, it is true that playing was limited. For one thing, I was at Lopez a lot. For another, I was fully aware that some of the other kids I knew could and did "get into trouble." And I did not want trouble; I was fearful. Things loosened up in high school.

CHAPTER 8

Uncle Russell's Reckless Romance

"Everybody sets out to do something, and everybody does something, but no one does what he sets out to do."

—George Moore

How many of you can say you have ever woken up at two o'clock in the morning to see a great big, glistening, semi-erect, totally uncircumcised phallus bobbing gently in the moonlight a few inches from your nose? Actually, nowadays, probably a fair number of both ladies and gentlemen. But in the spring of 1955—a less openly naughty time than our own—it was a highly unusual situation for a lad of almost fourteen to find himself in.

To be accurate, I had not awakened to find myself eye to eye, so to speak, with the phallus in question, which belonged to my Uncle Russell, who had only moments before withdrawn it from the (perhaps even then still jiggling) bladder-like belly of a woman I shall call Winnie, a pudgy, scraggly-haired orangehead several years my uncle's senior. Continuing the accuracy, I was already awake at that point, having been awakened, not to say aroused, by the activities that preceded my uncle's crouching next to the couch on which I had been sleeping. Russell had the telephone receiver pressed to his ear, and, except for a grayish too-short T-shirt, below which his sexual member curved detumescentally down toward the floor, he was naked as a jaybird. My brain was rapidly trying to process a lot of stimulating data at that point, but somehow it was the sight of my uncle squatting by the telephone stand in the semi-darkness and mumbling into the mouthpiece that I found most difficult to fathom. I scarcely remembered the phone ringing. My attention had been elsewhere.

How I came to be sleeping on the couch in the living room of the three-and-a-half-room apartment I shared with Ma at 289 Chenango instead of in my bed happened as follows. The relationships are accurate, though some of the names I have changed to protect the guilty (or their memories, since most have gone on to their reward, justly earned as all rewards are). The dialogue, while necessarily only an approximation of what was said—I was scarcely taking notes—is a faithful representation of what was said in a farcical episode that engraved itself onto an adolescent brain, never to fade.

Ma had come home from one (or, more likely, several) of the taverns shortly after they closed, around one-thirty or so. This was neither a unique nor a common occurrence. It wasn't so much that Ma liked to drink as that she liked the raucous, laughing atmosphere of places where people got noisily drunk. And so sometimes she would go out for hours on end, and when she came home it was with a slight buzz on, but she usually was quiet about it and she usually was alone. She would slip into the apartment with the barest minimum of noise and fuss and quickly climb into the rollaway bed she slept on in the hallway that led from the door to the living room, trying not to waken me from my slumber in the small bedroom on the far side of the kitchen.

She needn't have bothered. I rarely could fall asleep until I knew my wandering guardian was home safe (and therefore, in some psychological way, so was I), and I almost always knew when she arrived, no matter how quiet she was. This night there had been no doubt about her arrival. This night I sat up in bed, startled by the sounds of people stumbling against the door and laughing and giggling at their own clumsiness. More stumblings as the door opened and they fell into the hallway, still giggling. Hoarse whispers. Then, without turning on the light, Ma appeared, swaying slightly, in the doorway of my bedroom and told me I would have to sleep on the couch tonight because Russell was sleeping over and she and Mattie would have to sleep together in the bed. That's when I first noticed Mattie, a woman of about twenty who worked with Ma at EJ, also swaying in the blue darkness framed by the blackness of the doorway. I leaned forward and peered at Mattie, who gave a little snort of laughter. Mattie was the young woman my cousin Donald had entertained in the haymow.

"I have to sleep on the couch?" I said, stalling for time to make sense of the muted voices and movements I heard coming from the hallway.

"Yes. C'mon now, hurry up. I want to get to sleep," Ma said. Usually she did not get irritated with me like this. She began pulling blankets and a pillow out of the closet. Mattie snorted again and slid down the doorjamb into a fortuitously situated kitchen chair.

I climbed out of bed and took the blanket Ma shoved into my hands and wrapped it around me. I was clad only in underpants and T-shirt, my usual bedtime attire.

"Who's in the hall?" I asked, still trying to comprehend the more that was going on than was being revealed to me.

"It's Russell," Ma said, "now c'mon. Let us get to bed."

I shuffled out of the bedroom, through the kitchen and into the living room with the blanket twisted around me. Behind me, I heard Mattie fall to the floor and swear—"Kee-rist, I broke my ass!"—as Ma struggled to get her into bed. Then the creak of the springs as the two women collapsed into bed.

I arranged the blankets and pillow on the couch and lay down. I wasn't there long before I became sure that someone besides Russell was on the narrow rollaway, something that I had suspected before, and that each was in the arms of the other rather than in those of Morpheus. My knowledge of such matters was advanced enough to conclude that what was going on was by mutual agreement ("Oh, sweetie, it's in!"), and went on with restrained violence—accompanied by staccato grunts on the part of Russell and frenzied instructions on the part of his accomplice—for a couple of minutes more.

After the metal frame of the daybed ceased banging against the wall, I recognized, from her woozy compliments to my uncle, who my uncle's partner was: a woman of about Ma's age named Winnie who also worked at EJ. She was married and lived in an apartment house not far up Chenango Street, just north of the Viaduct. She was a great devotee of the jug, as was her husband Cyril, though obviously they were keeping separate company this night.

It was at this point that, all of a sudden, I discovered my uncle squatting and talking into the phone that sat on a stand at the head of the couch. He spoke softly, as if—oblivious of the brief cacophony that he, Winnie, and the daybed had been making—he didn't want to risk waking his nephew. I lay still, giving a pretense of sleep just as genuine as my uncle's of solicitude.

"Whattaya mean, you know who this is?" Russell said. There was a pause while he listened. "Whattaya mean, you know she's here? Who's here?" (Pause) "You're crazy, Cyril. You know it's two o'clock in the morning? Some people gotta sleep." (Pause) "Aaah, you're full of it." (Pause) "Listen, I'm not gonna stand here any more talking at this hour of the night. You're drunk." (Pause) "Yeah, well, up yours."

Russell hung up the phone carefully, continuing the pretense of trying not to wake the innocent, and, hunched over, scuttled back to bed, where he was received by a Winnie both irritated and eager.

"That goddam Cyril," she said indignantly, "he's so goddam suspicious." She grunted with satisfaction. Russell said something I couldn't make out, but it must have been a request to keep her voice down, because her next remarks were in a lower voice, but still audible. "Oh, poop, Russ, it's gone all soft. Here, let's see what I can do about that." I heard them reposition themselves in bed, and Russell mumble something about the kid being awake and Winnie respond impatiently that it's not anything he don't already know. But Russell apparently wasn't having any, because Winnie let out a sigh. After a few moments she let out a fart, long and low—I knew it was Winnie because I heard Russell mutter, "Jesus, Winnie"—and soon all was quiet.

Russell was the sort of fellow who could remember being born. He said he remembered it was snowing that day, which was entirely possible, since he was born in Pennsylvania in November. The sweet fact was, though, that in lieu of intelligence he clung to a fierce obstinacy, expressed in observations he thought would reveal his unconventional brilliance but that instead revealed, to the great majority of people who couldn't remember being born, that brain surgery was not the career path for him.

Russell had, in fact, no career path. A few ambles down weed-choked trails that petered off into nowhere came closer to describing his labors ever since he got out of the Army in World War II. In his mid-thirties, Russell preferred to be supported by women, which he mostly had been since his mid-twenties, starting with the marriage in 1946 or 1947 that ended a year or so later. He worked here and there, at this and that, now and then, but usually he contrived to find a blowzy drunk working in a dead-end job who would keep him in beer and nookie. The world is not in short supply of such women. Eventually they would part—he would beat her up once too often and she would leave, or she would lose her job and, consequently, he would lose his soft berth, and he would move on.

But now the system of human economics that provides a constant supply of helpless women to hopeless men had broken down, and Russell was on his uppers. He turned to the only woman available, his older sister, who was not helpless but—an equal vulnerability when it came to Russell—kin. And so he moved downstate from Cheektowaga—where he had been shacked up with a bottle redhead, or so I had heard Ma say—to Binghamton, promising that he would stay with us only until he could find a job.

And there he sat. He was a champion sitter. He sat and watched our television for hours and hours, afternoon and evening, no matter what was on. Many years later when he was on his third and last marriage and, for lack of a more accurate word, retired, he wore a bare spot in the linoleum in front of his favorite chair in the living room of his cheap apartment. The chair directly faced the television set, on which he watched *Hogan's Heroes* and laughed at it. Which many people did, I know, but he should have known better as a wounded veteran of combat with unfunny Germans.

After several weeks of sitting he hadn't found a job but he had found Winnie. The day after the night I observed them *flagrante delicto*, Russell moved in with Winnie. This necessitated her moving out of her husband's apartment—and, not incidentally, abandoning her nine-year-old daughter, Sharon, to Cyril's care. But then, she was in love—also, during much of her non-working time, drunk. Some said Cyril was not the father of this child, but if that was true and Cyril suspected it, it seemed to make no difference to him. After Winnie's departure from his hearth, his main concern seemed to be, no matter who the other parent was, to keep Sharon away from the maternal one. Which wasn't difficult, as Winnie wasn't contesting.

Winnie had another daughter, Lila, 10 years older than Sharon, who almost certainly was Cyril's child, as she had been the precipitating cause of their wedlock. Lila, too, was in love, in her case with—and in the family way by—a thirty-two-year-old Greyhound bus driver from Massachusetts. Lila did not live at home. She and the bus driver lived as man and wife—more like man and wife, indeed, than did the bus driver and his legal spouse (and their two children) in Massachusetts. Lila did not know that. Then.

The Chenango Kid

The move was accomplished when Cyril was at work. Russell borrowed a friend's pickup and he and Winnie made a lightning raid on Cyril's apartment, taking only Winnie's clothes and personal possessions and a few small sticks of furniture.

I was not sorry to see Russell leave. It wasn't that he was any serious trouble. He was quite amiable; he played board games with me, like Fortune, a rival to Monopoly. He was more of an irritant, an amiable irritant. He acted rather obsequious toward Ma, representing as she did his meal ticket.

But then, Ma was his sister and he couldn't beat her up. Not that beating up one's sister was unknown in the social circles in which he moved. He felt no such constraint with his new meal ticket. After a brief two-week honeymoon period, Winnie showed up in public with a fat shiner on her left eye, the first of several marks of affection Russell would leave. When they came to visit, Winnie either ignored the bruises or made light of them.

"Jesus, Mae, that brother of yours's got a temper, you know that?" Winnie would say as they talked quietly in the kitchen while Russell watched television in the living room.

"Yeah, I noticed," would be Ma's laconic reply through her cigarette smoke.

"How'd he get to be like that? Otherwise you couldn't ask for a sweeter fellow."

"I dunno. Nervous from the service, I guess." That was Ma's overworked refrain: that her brother suffered from unfathomable emotional troubles as a result of his combat service in World War II, which, admittedly, had been savage.

"I mean, it's not like I gave him any grief, for God's sake. I try to make a good home for him."

That was a lie. It wasn't even within a country mile of the truth. The truth was, after a couple months of domestic not-quite-bliss, Winnie began cheating on Russell. I never could understand how any man could be attracted to her not-too-solid flesh—she made me think of an out-of-shape female troll—but overhearing Ma's conversations with her friends revealed to me that more than a couple shoe factory or stone quarry workers had succumbed.

It was inevitable that, given Winnie's amiability and Ma's sociability, she would turn up one night with one of her rough-hewn swains at our apartment. It was late September—I had been back in school for two or three weeks—and about four months after her assignation there with Russell.

Which it did not resemble in every respect. For one thing, from what I could tell from listening in my bedroom, it was just three of them—Ma, Winnie, and a Mysterious Stranger. Mattie was not with them. For another, Winnie apparently was not nearly as eager this time. Their entrance to the apartment was just as clumsy and drunken, but it was marked not by laughing and giggling but by low-voiced argumentation.

"No, goddamit, no," I heard Winnie snap. "When I say no I mean no. I'm not going home with you. I'm sleeping here at Mae's. Right, Mae?"

I didn't hear Ma respond to this plea for affirmation, and I couldn't make out the Mysterious Stranger's exact words, but it was clear he was pleading pathetically. The longer the man's conversation with Winnie went on, the softer it got, so I could hear less and less. Finally I could hear nothing at all. Ma was apparently sleeping on the couch. The one lone light that had been put on in the living room was out, and all was, for a time, quiet.

And then it wasn't. I heard the daybed creak, and a man and a woman talking low. There was silence, and the daybed began creaking rhythmically. The man was grunting, but Winnie was silent. Then the phone rang.

"Shit!" the man ejaculated, in the only way he would that night. The phone rang again, and I thought I heard Winnie say angrily, "Get off of me."

The phone rang a third time. I looked at the luminous dial of my alarm clock. Nine minutes to two. What is it with two o'clock in the morning? I got out of bed and scurried silently into the kitchen to listen. Ma was on the phone.

"Russell, what in hell are you doing calling here at this time of night? Do you know what time it is?" (Pause) "Yeah, well, for your information, it's almost two. You've been drinking." (Pause) "What business is it of yours if I have been drinking? At least I don't go around calling people in the middle of the night." (Pause) "No, Winnie's not here. Isn't she with you?" (Pause) "What do you mean, you know Cyril's here? Of course Cyril's not here." (Pause) "What? Now Russell, I don't want you coming over here the state you're in." (Pause) "Russell?"

I heard Ma slam down the phone and run to the hallway.

"Russell's drunk as a lord and he says he's coming over here and kick Cyril's ass," she said. "Jesus, how do I let myself in for these things?"

Two thumps jarred the hallway floor. I beetled back to my bed. As I pulled the covers over myself, I heard whispered curses and the sounds of hurried dressing. ("Goddam it, never mind looking for your goddam underpants!") Then hurrying, scurrying footsteps down the short hallway, followed by the door slamming, and Ma lay down on the couch with a moan.

And, for a while, all was silent as a tomb.

CHAPTER 9

The Prevalence of Linoleum

"A boy's will is the wind's will,
"And the thoughts of youth are long, long thoughts."
—Henry Wadsworth Longfellow, *My Lost Youth*

Linoleum was our floor covering, though not of choice. If I exaggerate when I say every floor of every room of every apartment we inhabited was covered by linoleum, the exaggeration is it not by much and only by failure of complete remembrance. The linoleum was cheap or cracked or ugly or buckled and sometimes all of them. In the corners and where the walls met the floor was lodged dirt and food particles and bits of dead cockroaches and other bugs left behind by generations of previous tenants, despite Ma's best efforts at cleaning, and she was a champion house cleaner.

People say, "We were poor, but we didn't *know* we were poor." Not me. That may work in small towns and rural areas where nearly everyone is much the same, or used to be, but I don't think it works in urban areas with diverse populations. I knew we were poor and I was ashamed of it. Years and years later as a grown man I read or heard the comment, "It's no crime to be poor but it might as well be," and I couldn't agree more.

Recalling his working-class upbringing in Nottingham, central England, the late Alan Sillitoe, famous for the novel *Saturday Night and Sunday Morning* and the story "The Loneliness of the Long-Distance Runner," said it smelled of "leaking gas, stale fat, and layers of moldering wallpaper."

Layers of moldering wallpaper: There is one point where the British working class meets the American. I wonder how many times Ma repapered rooms in the successive apartments we inhabited? Impossible to know now. Think of the Kramdens' apartment in *The Honeymooners* in all of its black-and-white cheapness and plainness. That is how we lived. Not the sort of places one would think of holding Tupperware parties, which were becoming popular about the time the Kramdens were. Ma furnished our domiciles, and clothed our bodies, with items from the Volunteers of America (there was a store on Eldredge Street) and from Philadelphia Sales, a discount store on Clinton Street that can best be described as (a) a rummage sale run as a retail commercial business and (b) messy. Over the years a number of small tables, lamps to put on them, and assorted knick-knacks were obtained by cashing in painfully saved S&H Green Stamps. I know it is nothing like the deprivation of the Great Depression, but to a boy who felt like a trespasser when he entered any house with carpets it was severe enough.

§

On weekends Ma cleaned houses for people with more money than we had. One of them was a fat single woman named Sara who had, in that hallowed phrase of Our Kind, "a good government job" with the city, some sort of low-level clerk. She desperately needed a cleaning woman because her apartment was filthy because she was, actually, not simply fat but a blob of suet. I think she must have done no domestic work at all. On top of that, she had a dog—one of those small, short-haired, pug-faced breeds—that she allowed to shit in the apartment when she was too lazy to take it outside for a walk. I know this because I went with Ma once when she cleaned the apartment, which was on Chenango between Henry and Court streets, second floor overlooking the busy street below, across from the Presbyterian church where I had once buried my stolen loot. Sara, though a dullard, had lots of books in a large, glass-fronted case, books by authors popular in previous decades, such as H. Allen Smith's *Life in a Putty Knife Factory*. She let me borrow it. I found it terribly funny and went on to seek out other Smith works at the public library, *Low Man on the Totem Pole* and *People Named Smith*.

Ma cleaned houses for many other people. One job was for a pair of elderly drunks on the West Side. They had their liquor delivered to their house. They were childless, well-off, and tight-fisted, so miserly that they saved tissue paper from purchases to use as toilet paper. But they paid Ma OK, knowing that they'd never get a worker as good as she, certainly not one who would listen to their alcoholic blather. Another was for a couple on Clarke Street with a daughter roughly my age who went to Harpur College at the same time I did but whom I never really met. Odd, that: We each knew who the other was when our paths crossed in places like the college library or the union, but we never spoke. Perhaps it was the mutual embarrassment of knowing that the parent of one did menial work for the parents of the other.

The cleaning jobs were in addition to her day job at EJ. The Endicott Johnson Corporation, long gone now, once employed as many as twenty thousand workers making footwear of all kinds. That was in the 1920s, when recent immigrants "just off the boat" from southern and central Europe would ask, "Which way EJ?" But even in the 1950s it employed up to eighteen thousand or so. While wages were low in what was often piece work, the company was progressive in offering medical and other benefits. The progressivism, or "Industrial Democracy" as the company called it, was to stave off unions, and it worked. George F. Johnson, one of the founders of the company and its highest profile executive, had labeled the policy the "Square Deal," a form of welfare capitalism. On Main Street at the entrances from Binghamton to Johnson City and from Johnson City to Endicott there are stone arches that read "Home of the Square Deal."

The other big employer was IBM, primarily in the nearby community of Endicott. IBM-ers, as we called them—largely white-collar-class workers—looked down on EJ workers for earning less and getting dirty while doing it, but I believe the company's practice of giving benefits was something learned from George F. Johnson. IBM had a Country Club in Endicott with all kinds of recreational facilities for the use of its employee's families, which added to its air of exclusivity compared with EJ and other employers. EJ's recreational facilities—swimming pools, parks, carousels—were more democratic, being open to all. IBM is still a viable corporation, though also long gone from the Triple Cities area and nothing like the Tight White Collar-Organization Man image that it projected in the 1950s and '60s.

§

My mother died in 1994 at age eighty-two. I think of her . . . well, I think of her a lot. I think of her sometimes as Cousin Minnie Pearl from the *Grand Ole Opry*, except Minnie Pearl was only play-acting her rube confusion and Ma, God bless her and I mean that sincerely, didn't have to do any play-acting.

I said that I do not remember Ma ever saying she loved me. That does not bother me, because I think I intuited something that I saw explained only a couple of years ago in an article in *Atlantic* magazine. They are the observations of George Vaillant, chief curator of the Harvard Study of Adult Development, who noted the risk inherent in positive emotions such as love, compassion, gratitude, forgiveness, joy, hope, and trust.

Vaillant said positive emotions make us more vulnerable than negative ones. "One reason is that they're future-oriented. Fear and sadness have immediate payoffs—protecting us from attack or attracting resources at times of distress. Gratitude and joy, over time, will yield better health and deeper connections—but in the short term actually put us at risk. That's because, while negative emotions tend to be insulating, positive emotions expose us to the common elements of rejection and heartbreak."

To illustrate his point, he told a story about one of the men in his Harvard study, a beloved physician. On his seventieth birthday his wife asked many of his longest-running patients to write letters of appreciation. She received one hundred, most of them long and heart-felt. She put them in a presentation box covered with silk and gave it to him.

Eight years later Vaillant interviewed the man, who took the box down from the shelf. "George, I don't know what you're going to make of this," the man said, as he began to cry, "but I've never read them."

"It's very hard," Vaillant said, "for most of us to tolerate being loved."

I should add that I never remember telling my mother I loved her until I was much older and she was very ill.

§

If I walked down the street toward the center of town from Van Horn's at 250 Chenango in the mid-to-late 1950s I would pass on the right side, among other establishments, Wilber's Department Store at Number 227. Roughly across from Wilber's was Carbon's Bakery, where we could buy delicious big "half-moon" cookies, half the icing white, the other half chocolate. Next to it was a little store, always rather dark inside, that sold comic books, candy, and notions. The store was tended by a man with a white cloth wrapped around his neck who couldn't talk. That and the gloom made the place a little spooky. I bought my very first *Mad* comic there, and I mean the very first issue of all, when it was a comic book, not a magazine. Continuing a bit further I passed two taverns, the Wales Hotel and Dud & Tom's.

Back on the right side, Williams Cigar Store was at 217 and then the Skat bar and grill. When I reached the Viaduct there was an apartment house on the right at the corner of Eldredge that was the former abode of Winnie, Uncle Russell's main-squeeze-for-a-time. Continuing up the Viaduct I came to the Iroquois tavern and the offices of George Q. Moon. There were no buildings at all on the left side. On the right there were no more buildings after George Q. Moon, because I was passing over the railroad tracks, until the Lander perfume factory at the end of the Viaduct on the corner of Chenango and Lewis streets. This originally was the Kilmer Building, built by Willis Sharpe Kilmer for the manufacture of Swamp Root, the elixir invented by his father and that the son ballyhooed into a fortune. It was also the first home of the *Binghamton Press*, the newspaper Willis started in 1903, until he built the Press Building further down Chenango.

Directly across Lewis from Lander was the site of my former home, the Moon Block, but I cannot recollect what if anything took its place after it burned down. Across Chenango Street on the left was the Carlton Hotel.

Skipping along on the left, cherry-picking the spots I can remember, we have Chenango Studios, the photographers that took our school photos. Not too many steps from there was a cigar store just north of Henry Street that was reputed to be a Mafia hangout. There did seem to be a lot of men hanging about most of the time. I liked it because it had lots of comics and paperback books. Over on the right, just before getting to Henry, was (and still is) the Greyhound terminal at 81 Chenango, from which Ma and I departed on trips to Ralph's and later Louise and Richard's and once, in the early '50s, Aunt Romayne's in Batavia. They lived in a house trailer. That was cool. Romayne's husband Johnny worked in construction and the family had to move around from time to time. Across the Greyhound lot from the bus stalls, up against the wall of a building, was a taxi stand for Yellow Cab, whose phone number, 22-3-22, was emblazoned in black on the cabs, with the "3" larger than the other numbers. Five numbers only; this was before phone exchanges in the Triple Cities.

From the Greyhound station could be seen the building that housed the *Binghamton Sun* at 60 Henry, not far from the corner with Chenango on the left side. Down a ways, still on the left, I passed the office of New York State Electric & Gas, then the WKOP radio studio and the Weeks & Dickinson music store at 34 Chenango. At one time—the time of 78 rpm records—it had wooden booths with glass upper walls that customers could use to sample recordings before buying. Then came the Mohican Market at 26 Chenango. Rexall Drug and the Busy Bee, a discount "notions" store sort of like today's "dollar" stores, were there somewhere, but I don't know which side of the street they were on. The *Binghamton Press*, with its huge plate glass window offering a look at the whirling presses, was on the right at 19 Chenango. Quickly after that I came to, at the corner of Chenango and Court streets, Hills, McLean & Haskins, one of the city's three big department stores. The others were Sisson's and Fowler, Dick & Walker.

And so, in the manner of the Four Lads standing on the corner, watching all the girls go by, my pal Tom and I would head off for downtown most Thursday evenings. Stopping off first at the library on Exchange Street and then standing around in front of Kresge's store on Court Street or the City National Bank on the corner of Court and Washington Street. Just hanging out, doing nothing, sometimes meeting other kids just hanging out, doing nothing.

The convenience of stores open around the clock is, well, convenient, but it was kind of pleasant when stores were open late only one day a week, and not at all on Sunday. And by "late" I mean nine o'clock. That happened on Thursdays; otherwise, department and most other stores closed between five and six o'clock. Banks were open between nine and three and until six on Thursday. "Banker's hours." When I went to work for First-City National Bank I learned that banker's hours applied only to customers. Employees went to work at seven and worked until four, with an hour for lunch. Regular employees, that is; Miller Gaffney kept less strict hours. Interesting name, Miller Gaffney. What is it they used to say? A WASP is someone who has a last name for a first name?

Both W.T. Grant and F.W. Woolworth on Court Street had nice lunch counters. For that matter so did Fowler's, though I think I did not patronize it much; a bit more upscale (and therefore more expensive). Grover's Pig Stand on upper Court was a hangout, but I rarely hung out there because it was mainly a drive-in and who had a car? My Uncle Bob, Pa's younger brother, worked there as a cook before the war. After I acquired a car (a 1958 VW Beetle) and met Nancy, in the early 1960s, we often stopped at the Pig Stand on Main Street in Endicott. They are all gone now, as are the Carrolls and Henry's hamburger chains, both early competitors of McDonald's, though they came along after my high school days.

§

What a daydreamer I was. Walking over the Viaduct I used to pretend I was small enough to fit into the plastic toy space ship that I had and could zoom about here and there.

I lived my entire boyhood and youth in a bubble of unreality, of fiction. Tell you the truth, I don't believe I've ever fully gotten out of it, even now. In my head I was always someplace else, someplace I had just read about in a book or seen in the movies or on television or heard on the radio. For decades I held on to a *Momma* comic strip from the mid-1960s in which someone asks Arthur why he spends so much time in dreamland and he replies, "Because the opportunities are better there." That seems about right to me.

The long, long thoughts of youth . . .

Every month the insurance man would come to the door, collecting the tiny premium on the small policy Ma had to ensure that she would have a decent burial. When you have little control or choice in your life, at least you can exercise some control over how you go out of it.

Apparently there was a universal ceiling light for schools throughout the district: Pure white and vaguely like an upside-down mushroom, with the stem in the ceiling, from which bulged the main part of the globe, which had beveled sides and ended in a blunt pimple.

The standard desk for grade school and junior high had a seat that could swivel slightly, a top that slanted toward the seat, and a glass inkwell in the upper right corner. Every once in a while a janitor would come by with a large bottle of blue ink and refill the wells. Left of the inkwell at the top of the desk was a groove for holding pens and pencils. The desk top lifted to store books and papers and sometimes lunch items that were then forgotten.

In eighth or ninth grade I dropped pieces of chalk into a classroom aquarium. I don't know why I did it, but immediately afterward I began to fear that it would kill the fish and somehow their deaths would be traced back to me. I called up a pet store asking if chalk would kill fish. It was no help as they asked what kind of chalk and what kind of fish? I hung up, fearing that if I stayed on the line too long they would have this suspicious call traced and I would be apprehended even before the fish turned belly-up. But they must never have, because the Fish Police never turned up at our door.

It was supposedly a demonstrable fact—though no one that I know of ever demonstrated it—that if you saw a girl sitting with her legs crossed and continuously rocking the upper leg on the supporting one, you could be sure she *wanted* It. Also, if you very delicately and sensually ran your index finger slowly over the palm of her hand, it would drive her into paroxysms of sexual desire. Again, if any boy ever managed to get a girl to submit to such a bizarre maneuver, the girl surely had to be wondering what in hell was going on?

In high school a girl died because of naughty goings-on, but they probably weren't her fault. She was a very nice, plainly pretty girl with glasses. The story I recall is that some guy got her drunk and took photos of her. Whether he did anything else I do not know, but I saw one picture and she was definitely not dressed for church. Or anyplace else. And church was important. Her father was fiercely religious and blew the whole family up, house and all, out of shame or judgment or some other nuttily righteous reason. Whether the guy who took the photos ever got into any trouble over it I do not know.

In twelfth grade a chorus or glee club from some college came to sing at an assembly. Later they trooped into the cafeteria for lunch and some of the guys sported small chin beards. That sparked a series of exclamations from us, "Hey look, beatniks!" Beatnik: As a term of disapprobation it has not died out, though those using it now probably have little sense of its derivation. It was coined by *San Francisco Chronicle* columnist Herb Caen, borrowing the "nik" from the Soviet space satellite Sputnik and the "beat" from the "Beat generation" of writers, such as Jack Kerouac and Allen Ginsberg, who rejected the mores and restrictions of American society. A goatee, fashionable with some jazz musicians, was popularly seen as a beatnik affectation, certainly not something your average paterfamilias would sport.

I was a *Binghamton Press* carrier for about four weeks. I gave it up because it was really tough to shake the money out of my customers. They'd stiff me but I still had to pay my route man. Also, since the newspaper was seven days a week, I couldn't go to Lopez on the weekends.

For a short time Russell had a room at the Wales Hotel. I could see the window of the room from my third-floor bedroom at Van Horn's because the hotel/bar was a couple of doors down the street from us and the intervening buildings were not high. We had no storm windows and as a result in the winter much of the pane was frosted over so thickly that I could press a nickel into the ice and make a precise reverse image of it. I did that while I looked for any signs of life over there because Ma had assigned me the task of waking him up for work. Most days I had to go over and up to his room and try to roust him out. He refused to be wakened. God, his feet stank!

In tenth grade, I believe it was, or maybe the end of the ninth, I wrote a letter to Louise begging to be allowed to come up to live with her and Richard at their home in Hastings. This was out of fear of Russell, probably not long after he came to Van Horn's one night, roaring drunk, looking for Winnie. She had come to Ma for protection because she knew he was looking for her because of some slight or other; perhaps she had cheated on him or they may have broken up and she didn't want to get back together. When Ma refused to let him in he broke in the kitchen door and began chasing Winnie, squawking with panic, around the kitchen, knocking over chairs. He caught her next to a window and began hitting her. Still squawking and attempting to twist free, she bumped the pane and shattered the glass. Hanging half out the window frame, she was saved from falling three stories only by his unsteady, drunken grip. Things quieted down immediately after that.

§

There used to be record hops. I never went to any. I wish I had. Nancy did; she went with her constant pals Connie and Clara. They were held in Binghamton, Johnson City, and Endicott. Nancy remembers that in addition to disc jockeys, popular singers of the time like Bobby Rydell and Bobby Vinton made appearances.

For this book to give a proper notion of its subject—my life and that of the 1950s—it should really have a sound track, a computer chip built into it to play the appropriate songs for each chapter and section. Second best would be to put down a few lines of lyrics for each song, but copyright restrictions (and the cost to get around them) prohibit that. The best I can do, and it is nowhere good enough, is to mention song titles here and there and hope that they will trigger in readers of my vintage a similar emotion or personal remembrance. Readers of younger years will not have a clue. Their loss, I feel bound to add, but that's how old folk always feel about things the generations coming up behind them cannot know.

In 1990 John Waters released *Cry-Baby*, a movie starring Johnny Depp set in 1954 at the dawn of rock 'n' roll. Outrageous, as all Waters' movies are, it is a parody of teen musicals and, at one and the same time, a mocking of and nostalgia for 1950s teen culture and music. Two camps clash: on the one side the "drapes," led by Depp as Wade ("Cry-Baby") Walker, who loudly espouse Elvis-style rockabilly music, and on the other the "squares," who favor mellower songs like "Sh-Boom" and "Mr. Sandman." There is more to it, but the central matter is the battle over music. There is no doubt that Waters champions Depp's music for many reasons but mostly for its revolutionary challenge to society, but the confession I must make is that, while I liked a range of music, including much rock 'n' roll, I probably would have felt more at home among Waters' squares.

To this day songs, or rather bits of lyrics of songs, from the 1940s and 1950s fill my head and often, to the dismay of others, escape my head through my mouth. I loved and love the big band/swing music of the first decade and the popular ballads (and novelty songs) of the second. Music is fluid and types of music flow back and forth and interconnect, each influencing what comes next. But the 1950s were the heyday of the pop singer, supplanting the dominance of the band in the 1930s and 1940s. There are few that I do not like, male or female, single or groups.

Aside from giants like Frank Sinatra and Nat "King" Cole, even the most prominent singers of that vanished time are at best vaguely remembered or more usually completely unknown now except to ever-dwindling bands of diehard fans. Johnny Ray is one ("Cry," "The Little White Cloud That Cried," on each side of a hit single). Considered a precursor of rock 'n' roll, he was known as the "Prince of Wails" for his sobbing, histrionic singing style that involved tearing his hair and crying. Stan Freberg parodied him neatly on one of his records. Nevertheless, some of the most obscure were very, very good vocal musicians. Don Cornell, for one. I happened to be lucky enough to see and hear Cornell sing at the end of his career on one of the side stages of Milwaukee's Summerfest. He sang, among other songs, "Hold My Hand," a song from the 1954 movie *Susan Slept Here*.

Roger K. Miller

Guy Mitchell (born Albert George Cernik) had a genial manner, laid-back outlook (on some of his records you can catch him laughing lightly), solid stage presence (including a couple of movies and TV series), and a respectable string of hit records. His "My Heart Cries for You" is a quintessential song of love's yearning. "Heartaches by the Number" and "Singing the Blues" were two more of his romantic hits. His style had more than a touch of country and Western, and not even Perry Como did silly or novelty songs with such evident delight ("Sparrow in the Treetop," "Pittsburgh, Pennsylvania"). Mitch Miller at Columbia Records, famous in the 1960s for his television show *Sing Along With Mitch*, gave him both his stage name and his big start. It is said that when Sinatra refused to record "My Heart Cries for You" and "The Roving Kind," Miller replaced him on those songs with the new kid, Al Cernik.

Sentimental, schmaltzy songs easily pull me back in time, songs like the Ames Brothers' "You, You, You" and Margaret Whiting's "The Tree in the Meadow." When I hear the Tempos' "See You in September," which came out the month I graduated from high school, it still sends me back to thoughts of September's crisp fall days, heading back to school.

I liked and still like the guy quartets: the Four Lads ("No, Not Much," "Moments to Remember," "The Bus Stop Song"), the Four Preps ("26 Miles," "Big Man"), and the Four Freshmen ("It's a Blue World," "Poinciana") and many others. And the girl trios and quartets: the Chordettes from Sheboygan, Wisconsin ("Mr. Sandman," "Born to Be With You," "Lollipop") and the McGuire Sisters ("Goodnight, Sweetheart, Goodnight," "Sugartime") and many more.

If it was popular, in any style or category (except country), I liked it. Roger Williams' "Autumn Leaves"; Cozy Cole's "Topsy, Part II"; "Moonlight in Vermont" by any number of singers and performers; Moe Koffman's "Swingin' Shepherd Blues"; Harry Belafonte's "Day-O (The Banana Boat Song)"; the list is endless. And at the end of it comes rock 'n' roll (the 1950s was its establishing decade). That list is endless, too.

Much of our music came out of jukeboxes. They are all but passé now, but then there was scarcely a restaurant, diner, or other popular eatery that did not have one. Songs were five cents each or six for a quarter and you could play from the jukebox itself or from a remote device at your booth or in front of you if you were sitting at the counter. The typical image of jukeboxes is of the old curved-top Wurlitzer with the glowing, shifting colors, but what was common then was the sort of futuristic-looking

Seeburg with a large glass or plastic dome and long "dashboard" of buttons. Hmmm, quarter's dropped, what to play, what to play? After you had made your choices and the music was playing, inevitably you would ask your companions, "Hey, I didn't play that one. How come that one's playing now, ahead of mine? How do they program the choices, anyway?"

In 1955 I saw *Blackboard Jungle* and was nearly jolted out of my seat by Bill Haley and His Comets' "Rock Around the Clock" playing over the opening credits. No movie, certainly no major movie, had had music like that before. It is ironic that it became a rock 'n' roll anthem because Decca, which recorded it in 1954, had no great hopes for the song, whose original title was "We're Gonna Rock Around the Clock Tonight!" Decca chose it as the less-important "B" side to the main "A" side, "Thirteen Women (and Only One Man in Town)." The story of how it was picked up for *Blackboard Jungle* is that Peter Ford, 10-year-old son of actor Glenn Ford, was so excited upon hearing the song that he urged it upon his father, who was scheduled to begin acting in the film.

"Thirteen Women (and Only One Man in Town)," long forgotten, is also commentary on the decade. It was a novelty song about a lone man and thirteen women left after everyone else on the planet is annihilated by an atomic bomb. It was one of the many small ways Americans laughed nervously at the prospect of nuclear destruction.

Blackboard Jungle came out at a time of another national hysteria: juvenile delinquency. Based on the novel of the same title by Evan Hunter (aka Ed McBain, aka Salvatore Lombino), it is an A-movie version of a B-movie genre (*High School Hellcats*, for example, though it came along later in the decade) that exploited the fear that American teenagers were running wild in dungarees and low-cut blouses and sweaters, wielding switchblade knives, listening to "Negro" music, and menacing the citizenry. The novel, in turn, was a superior reflection of a mostly paperback genre of novels—with, as they always say, "lurid covers"—on a similar theme, reaching back to Irving Shulman's *The Amboy Dukes* of the late 1940s. As with the comic-book "scare," there was considerable posturing by members of Congress determined to get their names in front of the public if not actually to do anything concrete about the problem, if there was one.

§

Roger K. Miller

I never felt adequate to do anything that middle-class youngsters were encouraged to aspire to. I absorbed the notion that I was no good. I wish I could find a more precise, clinical, exacting word or term than "no good," but I cannot. "No good" fits. It was a notion fed by two sources. One was the evangelical, near-fundamentalist outlook that percolated through the Miller side of the family. Thinking that you were good, that you could be good at something or were good for something, that you could do something in life that fulfilled you or pleased you—all were indications of pride. You were made for one thing—what God wanted, not what you wanted. What God wanted was never terribly clear, but it probably was not what you wanted, you prideful little worm. What you wanted would only lead you to traffic with the worldly, and the worldly did not give a damn what God wanted. Those who felt this way, harbored this attitude, were not always particularly religious or church-going; it was something they had absorbed from their own upbringing and passed on as a correct view of life and behavior.

Then there was the poor-boy fatalism and envy of my mother's side of the family. Who in hell did you think you were, that you wanted to aspire to something? You think you're better than us? Anyway, it takes money to do or be something, and where in hell are you going to get the money? It was futile to aspire to anything because people like us never became anything. It would be sort of uppity of me think I could aspire to anything.

More than that, a greater restraining, inhibiting element was fear, which has long been my misguiding emotion. I didn't fully realize how much it had me in a lifetime grip until way late in life, in my fifties. It has made me reluctant to change, to take on challenges or opportunities because of the prospect of failure. I think it must have a genetic element, because it is shot through the Miller side of my family. My Uncle Will, when in retirement in Lopez, was so seized by fear that during snowstorms he ran from window to window, peering out, wondering if he and others in the house were going to perish. One wonders how he ever got through military service in World War II and a successful career as an accountant. His older brother Gerald was an even worse case, certain that cars were going to routinely fall off the road in front of the Lopez homestead and into the creek if he didn't build up a berm of dirt as a kind of homemade guard rail. Which he did.

That is the way I have been all my life. If I realized it, I hid it from myself. It made me avoid challenges and opportunities because they also were risks. It made me worry "what if?"—what if this terrible thing happened, or that? It is what made me return from college at the old State University of New York at Buffalo after spending but one night there—and thereby abandon the art career I had my heart set upon from earliest boyhood (about which more later). It made me seek avenues in which I would not have to face fearsome (to me) consequences.

Lack of sufficient talent is not the only reason I did not try to become a performer or entertainer, though I devoured movies and television and was given to showing off and had some gift for mimicry and later for witticism (or so I have been told). It can only be that old bugbear, fear—fear of trying anything unusual or out of the way of the little world with close horizons in which I grew up. We just didn't do that. It was for show-offs and people with crazy ideas. Who wants to make a fool of himself like . . . well . . . like the highly paid fools we all enjoy watching on TV? If the idea ever entered my head—it did not, really, though the urge was always in my breast—it would have been put down instantly by everyone I knew. Somewhere in all of it was also that hardshell Christian wariness of show business and its cautions not to think too highly of oneself and not to show off.

CHAPTER 10

Another Damn'd, Thick, Square Book

"People say that life is the thing, but I prefer reading."
—Logan Pearsall Smith

I wish style had stopped—had frozen—in the 1940s. I wish it had frozen and everything else—medicine, dentistry, plumbing, air conditioning, automobile safety, civil rights, women's equality—had progressed as it has or preferably more. But style, ah! Men in snap-brim fedoras and ladies in big hats, brims sometimes likewise. You know, those wide-brimmed hats that were as large as platters, and the edges of their brims pulled down and shadowed the women's faces. They could look out from under them, mysteriously. Or snoods. Women in snoods, now they were nice. And those upswept hairdos. I'm thinking of Audrey Totter and Jayne Meadows in *Lady in the Lake*. Interiors were stylish, too. Aluminum and chrome and glass and big chunky couches and love seats. Telephones were classier, in that they were what they were—devices to talk great distances on—and that functionality was reflected in their design: solid, black, clunky apparata made of Bakelite or some other seemingly bomb-proof material. You could twirl their cloth-covered wire around your fingers musingly as you talked; it helped with the thinking. Just the sort of interiors that men in pinstriped suits and ladies in black-and-white outfits with huge hats to match could feel comfortable in, sipping their martinis. I can almost hear the rasping *tszzzzzzit* as the lady crosses her seamed-stockinged legs and the mustached gentleman unsuccessfully attempts to avoid noticing. The gentleman switches on the radio, which blessedly gives you the news only on the hour and no oftener, if even that, and is itself a gorgeous piece of furniture, all wood and plastic knobs and glowing dial, with thin strips of blond hardwood running across the speaker fabric and curving to blend into the side of the cabinet. Outside it could be raining a nice steady 1940s-style rain, blurring the shimmer of the red and blue and yellow and green neon signs of the stores and bars, in which fat-tired closed-up convertibles go *tszzzzzzit*-ing along the wet pavements, echoing the stylish lady in the stylish apartment five stories above. If the couple felt in the mood for a night out, they were well set and appareled for either a diner or a nightclub. If it wasn't raining and a rare night baseball game were scheduled, they might even take in the game. They would hardly be overdressed. Even the *hoi polloi* then wore ties and hats to baseball games. The lady would never think of saying "Fuck you" to a fan behind her who asked her to remove her hat, because the occasion would not arise. She would have removed her hat first thing in the stadium out of consideration for others. Also to show off her lovely flowing hair, which she had given a fetching shake. Along with the style of the time went a few manners, even if it were only a patina. Even a patina of manners is preferable to wholesale "fuck you"s.

§

Style coarsened in the 1950s, but otherwise, culturally and creatively, the decade was vibrant, contrary to the conventional summation of it as soporific and hidebound, as an island of boring stability between the Depression and war of the 1930s-40s and the protests (and war) of the 1960s. The decade was complex in areas like international relations—it had its own vicious war in Korea—economics, and housing, and revolutionary in the politics of class, gender, and race. Ben Stein has said, "Journalists have a lazy habit of dismissing the 1950s as a time when life was sterile, stuffy, and dull." Stein, whose comments otherwise on topics like economics and politics are way wide of the mark, is right on the money here. "The 1950s," said Stein, who grew up in them, "were an explosive decade, especially culturally."

This is not to deny that the decade had the problems and dubious trends and characteristics that have been associated with it. They may not have been obvious to a teenager mooning about a small industrial city in Upstate New York, but a glance back at merely one of the many black-and-white photos of regiments of men in their suits, topcoats, and fedoras trudging up the platforms of train stations in the suburbs of New York, Chicago, and other cities is anecdotal evidence of uniformity, if not conformity, the label that has stuck most persistently. We can be forgiven if we mix things up and confuse *The Man in the Gray Flannel Suit* with *The Organization Man* who, when not participating in *The Power Elite*, was part of *The Lonely Crowd*, all books touching on the decade's reputation for uprightness and uptightness. The Man in the Gray Flannel Suit is, after all, The Organization Man in many ways. The irony of *Gray Flannel Suit*, Sloan Wilson's most famous novel, is that it is used as a kind of shorthand for 1950s conformity, but that is contrary to the gist of the novel, which is a protest by its hero, Tom Rath, against conformity and the conventions of suburban life.

No, if the label of "conformity" can be traced to any source, it is, rightly or wrongly, to William H. Whyte's book, *The Organization Man*.

Whyte got his idea for his thesis and book by observing the Yale Class of 1949, which had been touted to him as one of the best and brightest ever. When he studied its graduates, however, he found they were no such thing: They didn't want challenge or excitement; they, and graduates elsewhere, wanted the safe havens of big corporations like GE and AT&T—hothouses, we might say, for conformity, shifting away from an emphasis on individual initiative and valuing a "social ethic" over the so-called Protestant Ethic.

And yet, and yet. There is the man described by Whyte "who is so completely involved in his work that he cannot distinguish between work and the rest of his life—and is happy that he cannot." Is he not still with us? The endless number of endless meetings in the modern workplace, to the extent that the "working day" seems to consist of nothing else—how different is that from Whyte's "glorification of the group?" And speaking of groups—is modern business' dependence on focus groups not simply an abandonment of individual thought and decision-making to faceless others?

Plus ça change, which is the only reason I go into the matter at any length.

And if we praise our age for no longer seeking security in the organization, perhaps we don't seek it because we know it is no longer to be found. This is making a virtue of necessity, in an age when companies "downsize" (i.e., get rid of) older workers who have too many benefits and too many illnesses and too-high salaries.

§

To return to Stein's notion of an "explosive decade": Take literature, which I do, straight up and as often as I can. Brilliant new writers came up and established writers produced exciting new works. Just for starters: J.D. Salinger, Saul Bellow, Vladimir Nabokov (he *always* maintained that he was an American writer, and he was right), James Jones, Ernest Hemingway, Isaac Bashevis Singer, Philip Roth, John Updike. At the front of that list should be, because his book was published at the beginning of the decade (1952), Ralph Ellison and *Invisible Man*. Or look at the Beats. Actually, *you* look at the Beats, I don't want to. I think they are better known for who they were than what they did and anyway what they did was pretty forgettable. But I have to admit they were anything but conventional and dull.

Beats probably also are responsible for creating "like" as a universal pause-word and modifier, though I won't hold them responsible for the astounding growth in its mindless use over sixty years to its current omnipresence and ubiquity. As teenagers we did not use it anywhere nearly as frequently—i.e., constantly—as it is used by teenagers now. We did borrow other Beat-born usages that since have largely dropped by the wayside, such as "dig" (for understand) and "pad" (for living quarters) and "bug" (for annoy). "Square" has not quite died out; as a term denoting a conventional, dull, and clueless person, it was popularized if not invented by the Beats and was also common among young folk. Other teenage lingo came from I know not where and has retreated to the same place, such as "yo-yo" (a square or nerd) and "clutch" (to panic). But "cool"—cool is forever.

Now, four things made up what might be called, for lack of a more precise description, my intellectual life as a lad: books, movies, television, and music. And of those four the greatest is books.

Indeed, my memory works best with books, movies, and television. How it works seems to be similar to what memory experts say is the technique by which nearly everyone can dramatically improve his or her memory: Facts to be memorized are converted into vivid images that are stored in "memory palaces" for recall when needed. Certain books, movies, and television programs made such an impression on me that I can summon a rough approximation of where I was and/or when it was that I experienced them. If I hear Teresa Brewer belting out "Music! Music! Music!" I am transported back to 1950 and Eldredge Street and a batch of memories created from that time and place. Reversing the process, if I want to recall when the original *Mickey Mouse Club* was first broadcast—and not many persons besides myself would care or need to know that—I think back to where we were living when I watched it and come up with 1955-56. Close enough; it debuted in 1955.

Recently I was reading a Library of America collection of Ambrose Bierce's writings and, as always happens when I encounter his name, I think about when I first learned of his mysterious disappearance into (so it is presumed) revolutionary Mexico in December 1913, never to be heard from again. It was in a short story by Gerald Kersh in *The Saturday Evening Post* when I was in high school, in 1957 or 1958. I even remember where I read it: in the bedroom at the top of the stairs in my grandparents' house in Lopez. A little quick research just now reveals that the title was "The Secret of the Bottle" (or "The Oxoxoco Bottle") and it ran in the *Post* in 1957. After reading it I was wild to learn more about this fascinating Bierce, a reaction I have had ever since to compelling information stumbled across in books, movies, magazines, and television: I *must* go out that instant and learn more.

I mentioned that the Freddy the Pig books were my real entrance into reading. I believe the first one I read was *Freddy the Detective;* it's not the first in the series but is one of the early ones. I knew nothing of how libraries worked and therefore did not know there were a couple dozen Freddy books stretching back to the 1920s. I simply went back again and again to the shelf in the children's room in the Binghamton Public Library where the Freddy books resided, hoping against hope that another one would be there. Eventually I caught on to the card catalog and realized that there were many Freddy novels that were out being read by other eager Freddy fans. Walter R. Brooks wrote a few more before his death in 1958. Whether all of the two dozen or so novels were illustrated by Kurt Wiese I do not know, but certainly his drawings added to the books' appeal. Not until middle age did I learn that Mr. Ed, the talking horse of television fame, was based on short stories that Brooks wrote.

The Chenango Kid

I gravitated early to adult novels by way of the carts in which returned books were placed for transporting back to the shelves. How early I cannot say; my confusion over the "warning" at the beginning of *Adventures of Huckleberry Finn* could indicate that, not surprisingly, I was not ready for the subtleties and sophistication of adult novels and non-fiction at such a tender age. But who knows? I may have just plunged on, reading for the sake of reading, comprehension being a secondary matter to immersing myself in different worlds.

Because that's what I did then, I read like I viewed movies and television: with my whole being, taking in greedily what was before my eyes and coming into my ears. I was happy to be entertained and informed. I did not judge, other than to drop something if it seemed too childish for my tastes or understanding. I read like that my whole life, that is, books and other materials that I read for personal pleasure or information, not reading matter that was assigned. Although the latter often surprised me by being just as enjoyable (*Silas Marner*, for example, one of the set books in high school). I read like that until I was in my mid-forties and as a book-review editor took up critical reading as profession. Something died then. It was a pleasant way to earn a living, but it killed something in reading for pleasure.

Frank Wilson, retired book-review editor of the *Philadelphia Inquirer*, and I once had an exchange of emails about similarities and differences in our youthful reading, and why did we read what we did. Who knows?, is the truest answer, but, as they say, it got me to thinking. I read everything. I read to get out of myself. Not so much the shabby domestic conditions of living with Ma in a series of flats that barely had hot water, but to get to something that was somehow more interesting than Binghamton, New York, in the 1950s. (That's how much I knew. Binghamton was and is a lot more interesting than I gave it credit for, as these pages I am writing teach me, if no one else.) I think I liked hard-edged escapism, though the term "escapist" does a disservice to some of the good novels I stumbled across by accident. I can remember being thrilled by Walter Van Tilburg Clark's *Track of the Cat*. This was after I had seen the movie. That happened a lot; I'd see a movie, then go to the public library to look up the book.

Anyway, there they were, in the great big (big to a boy not much over five feet tall) open main room of the library: wheeled carts containing books on angled shelves, making their titles easily discernible to the strolling, idly curious library patron, who, if he was young and ignorant as

Roger K. Miller

I was, might think the carts were put there by helpful librarians desiring to make him aware of the literary treats available to him rather than the actual purpose: that patrons might snatch them up and thus reduce the number of books to be reshelved.

In such serendipitous manner was I introduced to Gerald Durrell (*The Bafut Beagles*, *The Overloaded Ark*), Charles R. McDowell's *The Iron Baby Angel*, Phil Stong's *State Fair*, Robert Ruark's *Something of Value*, Nicholas Monsarrat's *The Cruel Sea*, D.J. Hollands' *Able Company* (first published in Britain as *The Dead, the Dying, and the Damned*), Jan de Hartog's *A Sailor's Life*, and countless others. They all are names overlooked if not forgotten now, but their books were good reading then and still are. I know, because some of them I have reread (and reread again) as an adult.

I always hoped that a certain librarian was not guarding the gates when I went to check the books out. She was preternatural in size and smell, a head and scandalously large bosom atop a mound of melted and mostly but not completely congealed lard or possibly cheese that had set out too long, draped in a nondescript dress and frowning censoriously from her perch behind the high checkout desk at boys wishing to take out books that were too old for them. But, however unwillingly, check them out she did, stamping each book vigorously with a pencil that was also a date stamp and closing the back cover with a slap that was also a protest. And then, with what joy did I take those books home, scarcely able to contain my eagerness to get at their promising contents.

There was a branch of the public library in East Junior. Oh for joy; I could get more books easier. That is where I discovered Douglass Wallop's *The Year the Yankees Lost the Pennant* with its wonderful cover by Willard Mullin, the brilliant sports cartoonist for the *New York World-Telegram and Sun* and other Scripps-Howard newspapers. I must have come across the book before it was made into the movie musical *Damn Yankees*, perhaps at the time the musical was on Broadway.

When E.L. Doctorow's novel *Homer & Langley*, about the crazy, hoarding Collyer brothers, who died in 1947 in a fantastically cluttered, rat-infested New York brownstone, was published, the CBS program *Sunday Morning* jumped on it in the best tradition of the media jumping on the latest book by a name even editors and producers recognize. I don't mind that; it's the way the world works. But don't you think they could have mentioned a quite nice earlier novel (1954) on the same subject, *My*

Brother's Keeper, by Marcia Davenport? I remember it because it was one of the first novels I read in the Reader's Digest Condensed Books.

I matured as a reader on Reader's Digest Condensed Books, which my father subscribed to. Even then I knew that condensing, taking something out of the book that an author had put in there for a reason, was less than ideal. If the condensed version interested me, after reading it in whole or in part, I went to the library and looked up the complete book. Titles continue to come back to me of books I read that slid into obscurity within, I imagine, two years of publication. *This Is Goggle*; *Good Morning, Miss Dove*; *Sun in the Hunter's Eyes*. A few years ago I came across a copy of the last-named novel and reread it. It did not take long, thank goodness; for a supposed thriller it is pretty vapid. The author was wise to hide behind the pseudonym Mark Derby.

The lives and working habits of authors have always interested me as much as their books. I do not want to stalk them or pester them or make them my friends, but merely to find out about them. Such information helps connect me to their books. Literary biographies and autobiographies are among my favorite reading. To this day stray, irrelevant questions and wonderments about authors will pop into my head. Is Rosemary Thurber, James Thurber's only child, still alive? Apparently, as of this writing, she is.

§

Books have been so integrated into my life that often I can remember where and sometimes when I read many of them. Not necessarily great works of literature, rather, obscure or once best-selling but now mostly forgotten novels. I confess to being not so much well-read (that is, in respected, acclaimed Works of Great Literature) as widely read, which I believe was also true of a well-known writing Miller—Henry. Books such as James Michener's *Sayonara*, John Masters' *Bugles and a Tiger* (a memoir that made me want to run away and join Britain's Indian Army of twenty years earlier), and *The Trouble With Gumballs*, by a fellow named James Nelson, a neat title about a gumball-vending venture in 1950s California that stuck in my head for decades until I had to look it up on abebooks. com, buy it, and reread it. Fortunately, this rereading proved satisfying.

Those books and dozens of others were read at Van Horn's, 250 Chenango. My first of several readings of *The Catcher in the Rye* was

Roger K. Miller

there. I went through one title after another by Fredric Brown: *What Mad Universe, Martians, Go Home, The Lights in the Sky Are Stars, Night of the Jabberwock*. I did not realize at the time how ingenious an innovator and satirist he was; I just thought the books were funny and *different*. Or maybe instinctively if not cognitively I did appreciate his skill, since I sped through them so greedily. Nor did I realize until long after I went to work for *The Milwaukee Journal* that he once had worked there, too—in the late 1940s, I believe. I wasn't the only one; when I asked about him no one remembered him or indeed knew who he was. Admittedly, that would have been quite a while back, as much as thirty years then.

Usually I plopped the newly acquired books on the top of the cheap chest of drawers painted a milky gray in my room or on its companion cheap, milky gray nightstand next to my metal-framed bed. The reason I associate so many books with Van Horn's could be that I was then, at ages fifteen to seventeen, coming into my own as a reader, becoming old enough to appreciate a good book even if I didn't understand why it was good.

Earlier places, other books. In the first half of eighth grade I made the happy discovery of the 817 (humor) section of the Dewey Decimal System in the public library and thereby the works of the amazing Will Cuppy—*The Decline and Fall of Practically Everybody, How to Tell Your Friends From the Apes*. Other humorists, too, most notably Don Marquis and his Archy and Mehitabel, which I surely could not have understood; I think I must have been attracted by George Herriman's drawings as much as anything. It was nice up there on the second level where 817 was, cozy-like. Was the ceiling low and the floor made of opaque glass tiles, or was that another second floor in a different public library?

In the second half of eighth grade, when we had moved across the hall to another apartment on the first floor of 289 Chenango, I came across a paperback copy of Thorne Smith's *The Bishop's Jaegers*. I didn't get it, other than that it was sort of sexy, but it led me to *Topper*, of which I had heard through the film version. I liked the supernatural element, but I didn't really get it, either. Well, I was thirteen or fourteen.

Not all books are associated with one or the other of our downscale domiciles. William Brinkley's *Don't Go Near the Water*, a funny World War II service comedy, I learned about through an illustrated article in either *Life* or *Look* magazine—probably the former, since that's where the author worked when he wrote it. Published in 1956, it was made into a movie a year later. It's an interesting minor genre, the military service comedy, one that we no longer have. For twenty years or so during and after World War II (and Korea) one after the other came out: Marion Hargrove's *See Here, Private Hargrove* (actually a kind of novelized autobiography), Mac Hyman's *No Time for Sergeants*, Weldon Hill's *Onionhead*, William Goldman's *Soldier in the Rain*, and *Something About a Soldier* by Mark Harris (author of the incomparable baseball novels featuring Henry Wiggen). There are many others (from Britain, too), but they are all from a time when our military and their families were integrated into our national life. We didn't have to say "thank you for your service" out of embarrassment for avoiding that service ourselves.

But it was not until my thirties that I came across John P. Marquand, popular but critically scorned author of about a dozen middlebrow novels of the 1940s and 1950s. His *Wickford Point* has been my favorite, and most often reread, novel since I first discovered him forty years ago.

§

Before that, and sometimes after, were countless children's books. Freddy the Pig, of course, but many, many, many others. The incredibly prolific Rutherford G. Montgomery's *Ghost Town Adventure*. Two noted author-illustrators, Robert Lawson and Robert McCloskey. The former is best known for *Make Way for Ducklings* and *Blueberries for Sal*, but *Homer Price* and *Centerburg Tales*, his two books about the boy Homer Price, are closest to my heart. I still like to read the stories in them and study his cheery drawings. Lawson's *Rabbit Hill* won the Newbery Prize, but *Ben and Me*, showing Benjamin Franklin through the eyes of a mouse, tickles me the most. William Pène du Bois' *Squirrel Hotel* I must have discovered at the time of its publication (1952), as I read it in the second-floor apartment at 289 Chenango. A delightfully imaginative story about a man who builds a hotel for squirrels, it is illustrated by the author with drawings of the squirrels living and playing, even generating electricity for lighting by running in a squirrel cage, in the elaborate dollhouse-like hotel. Like many works of fiction, whether film, television or print, it made me want to enter its world.

I'm tempted to say that books destined for obscurity seem to have drawn me like a magnet, but the harsh truth is that almost all books are destined for obscurity. One of them I first read at the age of twelve or thirteen on the third floor of 285 Chenango, John Burgan's *Martin Butterfield*. As a young person I read it a couple of times and from then on carried the title in my head, where it intermittently would call me to reread. Never able to find a copy in various libraries, I finally sought the book from used-book sellers thirty-some years later and reread it when I was book-review editor at *The Milwaukee Journal*. Not surprisingly, that rereading showed it not to be the literary wonder my youthful enthusiasm must have assumed it to be. Which isn't the point when you're a kid. A thrilling book is a thrilling book, and ideas of literature go out the window. Maybe that means we should become as children again.

Martin Butterfield calls up the sense of openness, of wonder, that a child has and that Virginia Stem Owens has celebrated in her book, *A Feast of Families*. "No one is depending on me to do anything today," she writes. "All I have to do is be. Have you forgotten? This is the way life was when you were very young."

That's the way life is for 11-year-old Martin Butterfield and his buddy, Sparky Roberts, in leafy, drowsy Fern Township. For Martin and Sparky, "time seemed to move slowly; it seemed to be in inexhaustible supply." If there is a *Leave It to Beaver* quality about the boys' gentle scrapes, well, there's nothing really wrong with that.

Here is some of what I said in my *Journal* column on the book:

> *"As adults or children, we don't normally read fiction for moral improvement, though we sometimes get it nonetheless. So it is with Martin Butterfield. Martin learns lessons about the arbitrariness and unfairness of the world, the book shows how mutual hardships can make friends out of adversaries, and the author's attitude of wry detachment and mild sarcasm probably can be appreciated by even young minds."*

The book closes, as Martin and Sparky sneak a ride on a wagon, with this perfect snapshot:

"With their feet dangling, they rolled away into the long, pure, perfectly unpredictable pleasures of Saturday, a day that was put into the calendar for small boys alone."

§

The Chenango Kid

I have confessed that my desire for comic books was so strong that I was driven to appropriate them without payment; i.e., I stole them. Fortunately, that anti-social behavior did not last long. And, on the plus side, comic books, along with Freddy the Pig, made me into a reader.

I read comics of all kinds all the time until about the age of fourteen. I read them closely, examining the artwork, studying not only the words but the speech balloons that contained them. If in the world of children's books I wanted to check in to Squirrel Hotel, in the world of comic books I wanted to be Archie Andrews; if a rich kid in *Archie* had a neat sports car (like the MG-T models), that's the kind of car I imagined myself driving, with Betty (not Veronica) by my side.

Today graphic novels, the expensive modern incarnation of comic books, are given a measure of respect; then, comic books were given the back of the hand. The same with comic strips and comic strip collections.

Finally, there were all those magazines that my father got. I read them, I liked them. I miss them. I especially miss *Life* and *Look*. *Look*, a biweekly, in one way was the better magazine in that it had feature articles that sometimes tackled controversial subjects. But *Life* with its great photo spreads was meant for everyone, meant to cut across class, ethnicity, race, religion, political preferences. It didn't succeed completely, but what does? It was really the middle class or those who aspired to the middle class or somehow shared its values that got it. But *Life* was amiable. It *liked*. It tried to show that shared values unify. At its best it tried to show things, people, scenery, places that all readers could like. And the photographs were terrific. At that time I did not know or care that Henry R. Luce, its publisher, was dropping his little bombs of Republican thought—you should only pardon the oxymoron—into my brain with each issue.

As much as I miss *Life*, I miss the old *Saturday Evening Post* more. It is still extant in name, but it is a puerile nothing. Like *Life*, the *Post*, under the four-decades-long editorship of George Horace Lorimer, and then his successor for two more decades, Ben Hibbs, was conservative, but again I did not know or care. I cared only for its cartoons (Ted Key's "Hazel," always on the last page, was a highlight, though its humor was rather pallid) and regular features, such as "Post Scripts," a humor page, and "The Perfect Squelch," which offered examples of exactly what its title says And, last but not least, its wonderful, kitschy covers by such artists as Steven Dohanos and John Philip Falter and Amos Sewell. And the incomparable Norman Rockwell.

Roger K. Miller

Most of all I enjoyed its short stories and serializations of novels. All of the popular writers—the above-mentioned John P. Marquand is a perfect example—and many of the critically acclaimed wrote for it, from the beginning of the century right up to its demise as a weekly in 1969. The image that pushes to the front of my cortex when I think of the *Post* is of lying stretched out on the porch swing at my grandparents' in Lopez, a pile of *Post*s on the floor next to me, and flipping through them looking for something good to read. And I always found something. The thought that usually follows that image is one of envy of a time when a writer could actually make a living at freelancing. Short stories at the Post could fetch as much as four thousand dollars and more, a princely sum in the 1930s, '40s, and '50s and a sum not to be sneezed at today, when opportunities to sneeze are few and far between. All of that talent for writing middlebrow stories for magazines has been channeled into writing middlebrow sitcoms for television. It could be argued that it's a horse apiece, as we say in Wisconsin (or six-of-one, half-a-dozen of the other, as you say), but reading is more engaging.

Further like *Life*, and like all the great general-interest magazines, the *Post* died of an acute case of television. What does this tell us? That in this country there no longer is a general interest? Or did it, too, go to television?

Pa did not buy or read sports magazines, but Clark and his sportsmen friends did. Copies of *Sports Afield* and *Field & Stream* could always be found lying around the Lopez house. I did not and do not care for hunting or fishing, but Ed Zern's column, "Exit Laughing," in *Field & Stream* was not about engaging in those sports so much as about making fun of trying to engage in them. Zern also illustrated the column with his own cartoons. Also in that magazine worth reading by the resolute non-hunter was Corey Ford's column, "The Lower Forty Hunting, Shooting and Inside Straight Club," about a group of misadventurous sportsmen in the town of Hardscrabble, Vermont. I think I believed that it was an account of an actual hunting club that just happened to be made up of delightful characters. Proof that out there, somewhere, people were living interesting lives.

Corey Ford, by the way, coined the name "Eustace Tilley" that was given to the figure of a dandy, drawn by Rea Irvin, that appeared on the cover of the first issue of *The New Yorker* in 1925 and that has appeared on the cover of nearly every anniversary issue since. I did not know that when

The Chenango Kid

I read the magazine in high school (when its cover price was twenty-five cents; now it is twenty-four times that). I did not know much of anything. I only knew that the magazine was considered literary and sophisticated and had neat cartoons (and lots of them) and advertisements so luscious you could eat them. Even the small ads running down the sides of pages were worth exploring. Some were for items that were, to an Upstate teenager's mind, also sophisticated, such as the walking stick I burned to buy that had a hollow core in which drinks—sophisticated ones—could be stored in case the owner got thirsty while on the go. I think it cost something like seventy-five dollars.

My affection for *The Saturday Evening Post* notwithstanding, *The New Yorker* is and long has been my favorite magazine. Though I could wish that it had a bit more of the humor it once had in abundance, and though the declining fortunes of the printed word have caused it to decline in page count, it is still a great magazine. Years ago television commercials for it used to suggest that it was "maybe the best magazine that ever was," a statement that is as true as anything that can be made about journalism. Early on I fell under the spell of S.J. Perelman, whose dazzling wordplay I now and then return to in the same well-worn volume of *The Most of S.J. Perelman* that fell out of top shelf of my North High locker when I yanked it open in a hurry to grab my gym bag and head to gym class. Why I was in a hurry I do not know because gym class was one of the few things I did not like about high school.

§

I came across the following—by accident, as I come across most things—by the Hungarian writer Antal Szerb (his *The Pendragon Legend* is a comical if confusing murder mystery/ghost story)—who died at the hands of the Nazis in 1945:

> *"I expected something from literature, my redemption, let's say, because everyone's redemption is individually tailored and mine ought to have come from literature. It did not; nevertheless, I spent my entire youth in a happy purgatory, because I always felt that within minutes I would understand what I hadn't understood before, and then Beatrice would cast off her veil and the eternal city of Jerusalem would reveal itself to me."*

Roger K. Miller

That has me nailed pretty well, but what about all this rereading? What is the impulse behind that? One impulse is, naturally, to enjoy again a pleasure that I had before. But behind that, deeper than that, is an attempt to experience not just the reading pleasure, but the situation and emotions and time and place when I did the reading. In short, to recapture the past. More than that, to relive the past. To a lesser extent I do it also with movies and television. It is an attempt doomed to failure—a poignant admission, for I realize it is very close to what I am attempting with this book.

CHAPTER 11

The Silver Screen

"People say that movies should be more like life. The wise man said life should be more like the movies."
—*Red Garters*, 1954 movie, epigraph

There I am hurrying up the aisle of the Riviera or Strand theater, moving as fast as my nine-or-ten-year-old corduroy-clad legs can carry me while glancing back fearfully a couple of times at the screen. The movie I am walking out in the middle of is Howard Hawks' *The Thing (From Another World)*. It scared the bejeesus out of me, increasingly so to the point that I could bear it no longer: The "Thing," played by James Arness, after having been accidentally thawed out of his block of ice and fled the Arctic scientific station, breaks his way back in with a roar, is set on fire, and then takes a flaming header out of a window into the snow among the howling and snapping sled dogs. That's all, brother: Little Roger's going home to Mama.

§

Jeet Heer, a writer on comics, cartooning, and popular culture, has said this about film, both motion and still, which is a distinctively twentieth-century, not twenty-first, process and medium:

> "Film has this much in common with memory: both take time to develop . . . . [T]he very slowness of film has the advantage

of mimicking our thought process, with memorable events not being immediately lodged in our minds, but rather gaining solidity and force over time as we process our experiences. Our personal memories aren't like computer databases where items are easily accessed with a quick search engine. Rather, private recollections are more like a closet full of home movie canisters and photo albums, a heap of disorganized images of varying quality, some crisp and bright, others fuzzy and of uncertain provenance. Just as old photos and films fade and take on an odd coloration, our memories have the fragility and changeability of physical things."

Just so. I didn't realize it at the time, being just a kid interested in exciting movies, but it was said (and continues to be said) that *The Thing* and other movies in which beings from outer space invade Earth were a sublimated reflection of the nation's fear of a communist takeover—movies like *Invasion of the Body Snatchers* (my favorite, after *The Thing*), *The Day the Earth Stood Still, Invaders From Mars,* and *It Came From Outer Space.*

"Red paranoia" *was* widespread. One of the worst things you could call a person was "communist." Once when I and a friend wanted to go to a movie and his mother wouldn't give him money to go, he could think of no more extreme way to express his anger than to spit out at her, "Communist!" In the 1951 comedy *The Lemon Drop Kid* Bob Hope flings the same one-word epithet at someone who thwarts one of his larcenous schemes. But I don't know. Sometimes it seems a stretch to me, connecting outer space to the international communist conspiracy. Plenty of films dealt with the latter, and with internal sabotage and subversion, in a less figurative or metaphorical manner, such as *I Married a Communist, My Son John,* and *I Was a Communist for the F.B.I.* I am inclined to think the fear reflected in the "sci-fi" or outer-space movies was that of an atomic science we did not understand except to know that it could have deadly properties.

Movies could frighten me, but they also could make me happy, especially musicals. I had never seen *Red Garters* since its initial release, but I remembered it all through the years, particularly that epigraph among the opening credits. How true. In the 1950s when I went to two or three movies a week it probably sounded to me like shamanic wisdom. So a few years ago when I saw that it was out on DVD, I lost no time in requesting it from Netflix. What a strange movie, and what a treat. It is a musical spoof of Westerns (with a particular eye on *High Noon*) and possibly of musicals. The sets are stylized and spare, not to say skeletal, such as you normally see in a production of *Our Town*, and the costumes are bright and vivid, just this side of fluorescent. Something like that was done in 1959 with *Li'l Abner*, the movie version of the Broadway version of the Al Capp comic strip. *Red Garters* stars two of my favorite 1950s singers, Rosemary Clooney and Guy Mitchell. Gene Barry (né Eugene Klass) is outrageous playing a Mexican gunslinger and Cass Daley an Indian in makeup dark enough for an India Indian. Perhaps the filmmakers thought there was some commercial value in reuniting Barry and Mitchell from the previous year's *Those Redheads From Seattle*, though I doubt that it had much commercial value of its own. Most of the songs are quite lovely, creations of a time when popular music was often a combination of clever, inspired writing and excellent musicianship. I wonder what I thought of it as a teenager? What did I think I was seeing?

It doesn't matter. Happy, scared, exhilarated, sad, patriotic, fighting mad—whichever emotion they pulled out of me, movies had the power to pull me out of the bland, everyday existence I shared with everybody else. This, if truth were told, and I am sure my wife Nancy would be the first to impart the truth to you, is the figurative itch I have scratched all my life. When I left the theater, more than likely I did not step out into the boring reality of Chenango Street but rather into, say, the life raft occupied by Richard Burton and Joan Collins in *Sea Wife*, which I had just seen, and with them set sail for anywhere but home. Immaterial that, viewed critically and objectively, *Sea Wife* is a dud movie (it is sort of a cross between *Lifeboat* and *Heaven Knows, Mr. Allison*), for I did not view critically and objectively; to me it represented anywhere but here. The magical make-believe effects of a really good movie—and despite my youthful callowness I must have intuited when I was viewing something more sophisticated than a Pete Smith Specialty—might linger for days. It was more than imagination. I wanted it to *be* real. I wanted the world I inhabited to be that of *The Pajama Game*, where people in bright-colored clothes sang and danced and were happy and even when they weren't happy it was never for very long. I wanted to hang out with the interesting and comically dangerous characters of *Guys and Dolls* and converse with them in their creator Damon Runyon's eternal present tense.

Roger K. Miller

Those three films are good examples of one of my movie-viewing habits. As the film began I readied myself to scan the opening credits for the fleeting mention of the title and author of the book, if any, that the movie was based on. (Then and now and for all eternity past and future, writers have always received the fleetingest of mentions.) Afterward I looked for the book in the Binghamton Public Library, where I learned that *Sea Wife* was from J.M. Scott's *Sea-Wyf and Biscuit*, *The Pajama Game* from Richard Bissell's *7 ½ Cents*, and *Guys and Dolls* from a collection of Runyon stories that simply enchanted me when I read them in my mid-teens. Every year I re-read a handful of them. They enchant me all over again but also leave me chastened by their reminder that, as Edward Bulwer-Lytton said, genius does what it must, talent does what it can.

Since that first frightened partial viewing I have seen *The Thing*—all the way through—many, many times, for it has been a staple of television for sixty years. It is a terrific example of a scary black-and-white film made on the cheap, much better than John Carpenter's expensive 1982 color effort, *The Thing*, based on the same John W. Campbell story, "Who Goes There?" A curious coincidence is that Phil Harris, the popular singer, comedian, and band leader, had a best-selling novelty song titled "The Thing" almost contemporaneous with the movie. It had nothing to do with the movie's theme—in fact, the words "the thing" occur nowhere but in the song's title—and was produced independently of the movie, though I wouldn't be surprised if it was somehow used to promote the movie.

The movies might be scary, but going to them was not. It was not uncommon then for kids as young as nine or ten—boys, mostly, but girls, also—to go to the movies by themselves or in small groups without being accompanied by an adult. I went often by myself or with a friend or two, walking there and back or taking the bus. We were in little or no danger. I have to ask myself, though, whether that was only the case for those of us on the North Side, living relatively close to the main concentration of movie theaters, and not for kids from the West Side and other more well-off sections.

That is to say, it was *mostly* safe. Nancy once asked, after we had heard of yet another story of child enticement and/or sexual abuse, if anything like that ever happened to me. No, it did not. The closest was when a bunch of us went to the movies and an older boy, a teenager, sat with us. We probably knew him, otherwise I can't think why we would have sat with him. I was next to him and he offered me some of his popcorn.

When I reached into the box to get some, my hand came upon a rigid penis aimed straight at the ceiling. I snatched my hand back. He coaxed me to put it back in, but I wouldn't. I remained rigid in my seat, my face flushed and staring at the screen but not seeing the movie, reluctant to move away out of some weird sense that it would be embarrassing to the miscreant. The popcorn was in a white box with red lettering. I did not have any more.

When we went to the movies, we went no matter what time it might be. The phrase "This is where I came in" might have been made for us. We never checked what the starting times were. If we happened to arrive in the middle of the film, we stayed until it ran again and saw the first part that we had missed. That's different from today, that we were allowed to sit and wait for the next showing to start. It did not occur to us that that was an odd way to see a movie. In one of their "Road" movies Bob Hope and Bing Crosby made a reference to the practice.

CROSBY: The audience already knows that.
HOPE: Not the ones who came in the middle.
CROSBY: What? They missed my song?

Maybe our movie-going practice was a function of the movies we saw: cowboys, serials, sub-moronic comedies like the Bowery Boys (how we loved them!), and the cheapo sci-fi and horror (*I Was a Teenage Werewolf*) flicks that American International Pictures churned out toward the end of the decade. There was usually a double feature, so we viewed one of the movies in the orthodox beginning-to-end manner, and a cartoon and a newsreel and a "short subject," such as a Pete Smith Specialty. What did it matter when you came in? On the other hand, we would have done the same with Olivier in *Hamlet*, if that improbable occasion had ever arrived. It was just a place to eat popcorn from the Karamel Korn shop and be entertained.

Had we watched Olivier in *Hamlet* we would have been, besides utterly confused and looking around for the nearest exit, most probably in either the Strand or Riviera Theater (originally the Stone Opera House), for they showed feature films, classy films, the A-films and the better B-films from Hollywood. The two were right next to each other on Chenango Street and shared a long marquee jutting out over the sidewalk. They had huge interiors with balconies and retained some of the grandeur that was

Roger K. Miller

standard in the era they were constructed. The Star, a few doors north of them, was something different. By no means small compared with today's cineplexes, it was nevertheless considerably smaller than the Strand and Riviera. And though also built like them in the era of grand movie palaces, it had come down many notches in splendor, largely through the shabbiness-generating feet of boys and girls down the decades. The Star was the place we went to see cowboy movies, serials, brainless comedies, and other cinema of that ilk. Its name backward spelled Rats and, while I personally never saw a rat there and I doubt that those who said they had really had, to us the spelling curiosity was no mere coincidence. It rather than the Strand or Riviera seemed like the sort of theater in which rats would choose to dwell.

§

Interlude for a rant:

You know what's stupid? We're stupid, moviegoers. We pay to see advertisements, commercials. We go to the theater, pay a stiff price, sit down, and before the movie begins we are forced to watch and listen to at high decibels ten or fifteen minutes of advertising glop. Additional insult is, all that comes before the misnamed "trailers" (they don't really "trail," but precede), which are themselves nothing but too-long commercials. We used to go to the movies, pay a reasonable price, sit down, and—voilà!—the movie began (if it had not already begun). It might be preceded or followed by a cartoon, short subject, or newsreel, but they were all entertainments of a kind. The only advertisement was for "Coming Attractions" (yesteryear's term for trailers, much shorter and they didn't give away the entire movie).

What's also stupid is we television viewers. Used to be we got our television "free" over the air. We did pay a not inconsiderable price in the form of commercials, because 'way back when the first crystal sets began pulling in crackles from the ether some clever merchants twigged that there was money to be made from expropriating what were considered to be the Public Airwaves. But that's the way it was and we had to hand over no coin of the realm. Then along came cable with the lure that, for a modest expenditure, we could get televised entertainment commercial-free. You know, just like the movies.

And what do we have now? Televised entertainment with commercials for which we pay out of pocket. You know, just like the movies.

The Chenango Kid

Or is it vice versa?
Now back to our regularly scheduled programming...

§

I have a photo of myself with the comic cowboy actor and singer Smiley Burnette. He was the sidekick to Gene Autry and later to Charles Starrett, whose nickname, the "Durango Kid," gave me, through the similarity in sound and syllables, the title for this book. Winter cap dangling from my right hand, I look to be seven or eight years old, smiling and shy, toe of my right shoe jammed against the top of the other. I believe it was taken at the Binghamton Theater on State Street. There must have been a Smiley Burnette movie playing for which he made a publicity appearance. I wonder: Did I beg Ma to let me go? Did Louise take me? How else could I have gotten the photo unless someone paid for it? Burnette made dozens of movies.

Movies, oh my God, movies. Sometimes it seems that I did nothing in my waking hours but read books (including the comic variety), watch television, go to movies—and draw. The Triple Cities were well supplied with movie houses and all of them had capacious auditoriums. The biggest of all was the Capitol on Exchange Street, not far from the public library and the Binghamton Savings Bank, on or near the corner with Hawley Street. It was huge, with maybe half again the seating capacity of the Riviera. Live shows still played there occasionally. I took a girl to see a road company production of *Most Happy Fella*.

The Cameo on Robinson Street, not terribly far from East Junior or North High, was well within reach of my personal shank's mare. One Halloween, I might have been in seventh grade, it screened old scary movies like *Dracula* and *Frankenstein*. Perhaps the owners did it every year, but if so they were brave merchants indeed, because the audience of kids on the night I was there was raucous nearly to the point of being out of control. We threw Jujubes and other candy at the screen.

The Crest on Main Street I did not get to as a young kid. It was too distant from my North Side stomping grounds. Years later, however, while standing in line with friends to see *What Ever Happened to Baby Jane?* it was where I first met the girl who would become my wife. She was standing in line with her friends. She claims I gave her one of those sugar-encrusted green spearmint candies. She could be right; females

Roger K. Miller

remember that sort of thing. The Jarvis, also on Main, was not quite so far out that I could not get to it—once, at least, for one of those Saturday morning marathon cartoon festivals that theaters occasionally put on for kids. It was a madhouse of noise, even without the cartoons in which you could sing along by following the bouncing ball. The Sun on Glenwood Avenue and the Ritz on Clinton Street I rarely got to, if ever. I have the impression that they were fleatraps, but that could be North Side cultural imperialism.

Mostly I stuck to the theaters I could easily and quickly reach by foot, those around the center of downtown or my area of town: Strand, Riviera, Star, Capitol, Binghamton, and Cameo. There was also the Symphony theater, not exactly downtown but not far from it and easily reachable by me, being not many doors south of the Moon Block on Chenango. I believe it was one of the first theaters to be closed. I went there with Pa to see *Kon-Tiki* and *The Beast With Five Fingers*, the latter of which, if he had not taken me, I probably would also have walked out on in fright. The Regus was also on Chenango, but north of where I lived, up around Munsell Street or thereabouts. I did not get there often, but I did see a biblical epic there, possibly *Samson and Delilah*. (Groucho Marx on Victor Mature: "I don't like any movie where the leading man's tits are bigger than the leading lady's.") The Regus too may have been one that shuttered its doors early, a victim of television and of the slow shift in the venue in which movies were exhibited, from huge palaces to small boxes.

The confluence of the right time and a lenient parent who let me go to the movies as often as I liked and could afford meant that I saw a ton of Westerns. The late 1940s and early 1950s brought an extended blooming of quickly and inexpensively made oaters featuring a small legion of cowboy stars. I saw them all. The legion, without question led by Roy Rogers and Gene Autry, included: Johnny Mack Brown; Wild Bill Elliott (who portrayed Red Ryder, whose young sidekick Little Beaver was played by Robert Blake); Rex Allen; Monte Hale; Jimmy Wakely (one of the last of the crooning cowboys); Eddie Dean (the best of the crooning cowboys, according to two other such singers, Roy and Gene); Whip Wilson, who got his moniker because Monogram wanted a rival to go up against the much more popular Lash LaRue. But not Hopalong Cassidy, who admittedly belongs in there. For some reason I cannot recall seeing his movies. Maybe he was not making them at the time; his great popularity came with television.

None of them was ever going to come within a country mile of an Oscar. Acting styles ranged from the indifferent to the wooden to the robotic. Lash LaRue's character Marshal Cheyenne Davis could well have been the inspiration for Jack Webb and his School of Poker-Faced Thespianism.

Nor were the stories. Much time was used up in chases on horseback, guns blazing and background music galloping in time with the hoofbeats, as the good guys chased the bad guys and vice versa past rocks and boulders and clumps of trees that had stood mute witness to similar scenes in countless previous movies. The frequent shooting was rarely or possibly never fatal—now *there's* a subject for a PhD dissertation in American studies—and when someone was wounded it was usually in the shoulder, sans blood. Favorite stunt: a casually aimed shot from the hip with a fast draw out of the holster that took the gun out of the other guy's hand. Bet that stung. The Westerns were short, sometimes less than an hour, making them suitable when television came along to be shown on programs like Bill Parker's *TV Ranch Club* on WNBF. My cousin Ken was on that show and it made me terribly jealous, so jealous that I acted as if it were nothing. Oh yeah? Well, I was on *radio*!

We boys had spirited discussions as to which cowboy hero had the best sidekick. Gene Autry's Pat Buttram, who spoke in a kind of yodel? Whip Wilson's Andy Clyde with that wide-eyed, surprised stare? Lash LaRue's twisty-grinned Al "Fuzzy" St. John, also known as Fuzzy Q. Jones, was my favorite, probably because I saw more of LaRue's movies than any. We knew George "Gabby" Hayes, but his main era was slightly before ours, and Roy Rogers's goofy pal Pat Brady was popular, but from the TV show, not movies. There were several more, and they shifted allegiances, pairing up with different cowboys at different times—Gabby Hayes served Roy Rogers and Wild Bill Elliott, and, as mentioned, Smiley Burnette with Roy and the Durango Kid.

Their horses stayed loyal, however, or their names did, for, aside from Roy's Trigger and Gene's Champion, we probably couldn't have told whether a cowboy star was riding the same horse from one film to the next. But we knew their names: Lash LaRue's Rush, Monte Hale's Lightnin', Wild Bill Elliott's Thunder. I liked Rocky Lane's Black Jack.

§

Roger K. Miller

Were they all Comerford theaters? It seemed so to me at the time, but surely not; there must have been several Mom-and-Pop operations. I believe Comerford was a chain most widespread in Pennsylvania.

When there was a Bowery Boys movie, we *had* to see it. "Hey, there's a new Bowery Boys. Wanna go?" We were connoisseurs of the lads from the Bowery, all of whom were well beyond boyhood: Horace Debussy Jones, Slip Mahoney, Louie Dombrowski. Watching the Bowery Boys or a Western could sometimes wind us up so much that an usher had to come tell us to pipe down. And get your feet off the back of the seat! Once, for an infraction long forgotten, I was thrown out. Oh, was I livid! I stormed out to the lobby, trotted after by an usher or manager or some other authority, crying with rage and shouting obscenities and threatening whatever repercussions came to mind.

Dean Martin and Jerry Lewis. *Oh La-AY-deeeeeee!* I don't think I missed one of their movies. They were a big act—huge, mammoth—in radio, television, movies, and on stage. They were among the top ten box office attractions, and nearly always at the top of the top, from 1950 through 1955. In 1951 they earned more than $70,000 a week, when $4,500 was a respectable *year's* pay, from their stage appearances alone. And when they broke up, ten years to the day after they started their duo on July 25, 1946, it was news that blew all other big news off the front pages.

3-D and Cinerama were both introduced around 1952. Binghamton had no theaters that could handle the three-camera projection required for Cinerama, so I didn't see that until a few years later in New York City. It was the introductory film, *This Is Cinerama*; after that only two standard features and a handful of travelogues were made. But in 3-D I saw *Bwana Devil*, the first in that moviemaking process, and *House of Wax* (and ducked when the paddle balls came shooting out from the screen). After that 3-D sort of petered out, possibly because moviegoers were not completely comfortable wearing the special glasses, though a Paramount Pictures executive had claimed that people "will wear toilet seats around their necks if you give 'em what they want to see." Not the first or the last brave Hollywood assertion. 3-D has made something of a comeback of late, but it is no more impressive, the technological advances notwithstanding, than it was then; Nancy and I go to see the 2-D versions of the films and forgo the toilet seats.

In my teen years I went to many movies with my friend Tom. When we saw *Peyton Place*, in the row behind us were several men in clerical collar, presumably priests but I suppose they could have been clergymen of some other flavor. That surprised us, particularly Tom, who was Roman Catholic. Why did they not wear mufti? Did they mean to make a stand? A statement? To shame by their presence the audience for attending this piece of celluloid moral depravity?

I am grateful for Turner Classic Movies, for the classics it shows but also for the easily forgettable and forgotten films that it revives. I am amazed now at what we used to like, but I shouldn't be. Hollywood has always offered, besides serious drama and sophisticated comedy, bits of entertainment made quickly and on the cheap. Bright little musicals, for instance, like Debbie Reynolds' *The Affairs of Dobie Gillis*, *I Love Melvin*, and *Two Weeks With Love* (with "Aba Daba Honeymoon," a song written in 1914 that became a hit record in 1951 for Debbie Reynolds and Carleton Carpenter). I loved, and love, those bits of fluff, and, if I haven't made it obvious elsewhere, I am especially partial to Debbie Reynolds. I am inexplicably besotted with her 1954 movie, co-starring Dick Powell, *Susan Slept Here*, having seen it uncounted times, probably more than fifteen. I managed to get published an essay about my obsession, "Living, Though Not Sleeping, With Susan."

Still, knowledge can be disillusioning. For more than fifty years I had wondered about another film I saw as a kid, *The Girl He Left Behind* from 1956, with Tab Hunter and Natalie Wood (and an early screen appearance by James Garner). I had, as was my fashion, read the Marion Hargrove novel, either before or more likely after seeing the movie, and liked both. It was never shown on television, that I could find, nor was it out on tape or DVD. So when TCM finally played it I eagerly tuned in. Sadly, not every fondly remembered personal gem turns out to be a *Susan Slept Here* or even a *Red Garters*.

CHAPTER 12

The Little Screen

Woman in audience: *Do they get your program in Philadelphia?*
Steve Allen: *They see it, but they don't get it.*

The theme of the 1959 North High School yearbook, the *Wampum*, was television. Boy, did our class get that right. We were part of the television generation, indeed the first of that generation to come of age watching television.

Newton Minow also got it right, mostly. Television *was* a vast wasteland. In 1961 Minow (a Milwaukee native) as chairman of the Federal Communications Commission gave a speech to the National Association of Broadcasters so controversial it is quoted still, sometimes by critics who disagree with him (and misspell his name as the fish). The critics don't get it. Television has *always* been a vast wasteland. It is a vast wasteland today, and not just because the number of channels is so much greater. The proportion per hour of commercials to content (regardless of its quality) is greater than before Ronald Reagan began the campaign of deregulation that has devastated so many aspects of our lives. Actually, to state the case more precisely, television is and was *half*-vast. Say that three times quickly.

§

Whoever remembers test patterns raise your hands. I thought so. For the rest of you I can describe the test pattern only as a static picture or card that in the earliest days of television was broadcast by stations at various times of the day, most often at night before the station went off the air. As I understand it, engineers used it to adjust the transmitted image that frequently went wonky. Used in the United States and Canada and in a few other countries, it was known as the Indian Head Test Pattern for the American Indian in full headdress that dominated the inside of a large circle within a box the dimensions of a TV screen. At each corner of the oblong box is another, smaller circle, and inside all of the circles are bands of thin lines that resemble fasciae. To stare at it too long was to induce optical illusion. With the coming of improved transmission and color television, the test pattern went away.

In those earliest days we kids came to school in the morning and regaled each other with excited chatter about the same program that, because of Binghamton having only one channel, all of us had watched the night before. Wednesday mornings at Thomas Edison it was *The Red Buttons Show*. As if recalling something from months ago rather than the previous evening, we stepped all over each other's heated gabble of, "Remember when Red Buttons did that 'Ho ho . . . hee hee . . . ha ha . . . Strange things are happening'?" Which Buttons (born Aaron Chwatt) did on every week's program, all while cocking his palm behind one ear and rocking back and forth from one foot to another. It made no sense but it became a national craze (and a hit recording), though a shorter one than the later craze for Davy Crockett.

WNBF Channel 12 was not on the air continuously throughout the day. Didn't matter; as so many others of that period have remarked, we watched whatever was on. Television was magic, and its blue-gray glow lit up our nights. Some of the early series Ma and I liked were Ann Sothern's *Private Secretary*, *The Fred Waring Show*, and *Life With Luigi*. The last was—like many early TV shows—a rollover from a radio series, though it didn't last long on television. It was a comic celebration of the Italian immigrant experience, as *The Goldbergs*, which lasted much longer on both radio and television, was of the Jewish. We don't do that anymore concerning our immigrants, though we remain an immigrant country; I think also of Leo Rosten's hilarious but affectionate stories about the American Night Preparatory School for Adults in New York City, collected in *The Education of H*Y*M*A*N K*A*P*L*A*N*. For a while I continued to listen to radio comedy, like *Meet Corliss Archer* (CBS's answer to NBC's popular *A Date With Judy*), and drama, like *Suspense*, with its meant-to-be-chilling opening phrase, "Tales well-calculated to keep you in . . . [dramatic pause] *sus-PENSE!*" All also made the leap to television, but none as successfully as *Suspense*. It was broadcast live, like so many early 1950s television shows, and hosted by Rex Marshall, who touted the merits of Autolite spark plugs, the sponsor.

No, television did not kill radio, network or local, immediately. There was much good stuff on the air. Young as I was, I liked NBC's *Monitor*, a weekend-long magazine of the air offering, each week, a mix of news, sports, interviews, comedy, and other short items. The program, which gradually declined in length over the years from forty hours per weekend at its start in 1955 to twelve hours at its end twenty years later, was one of the several bright ideas of NBC President Sylvester J. ("Pat") Weaver (father of Sigourney). Once it had an interview with a cartoonist (either Al Capp or Walt Kelly, I forget) who described how he mugged in front of a mirror clamped to his drawing board to get the right facial expressions for his characters. That was mother's milk to a would-be cartoonist.

I even listened occasionally to radio soap operas, though far less than did their target audience—housewives—which was about one-third of the episodes. Plenty were still on: *When a Girl Marries, Young Doctor Malone, One Man's Family, Our Gal Sunday*, several others. Before World War II there were as many as sixty-five such "daytime dramas" overburdening the airwaves and the nation's ears, but by the mid-1950s that number had dropped by more than half. James Thurber once did a superb series of articles for *The New Yorker* after subjecting himself to a year's worth of soap operas, objective yet not condescending in describing their least-common-denominator emphasis on bathos and long-drawn-out pathos. Sponsors hovered over the shows, anxious to avoid controversy. A sponsor's representative explained to the writers why he wanted them to eliminate a Jewish woman from their show: "We don't want to antagonize the anti-Semites."

For that matter I miss Bob and Ray (Bob Elliott and Ray Goulding). Radio was their natural element. One of their bits was "Mary Backstage, Noble Wife," a deadpan parody of *Mary Noble, Backstage Wife*, a soap opera that ran from the mid-1930s until almost the 1960s about a small-town woman who goes to New York City and marries Larry Noble, a prominent actor and "matinee idol of a million other women."

It is too bad that radio, especially network radio, is dead. Sound was a wonderful medium. Radio's effect depended upon the use of the listener's imagination. Writers (like the great Arch Oboler), actors, and directors all have said that radio's success was due to the listeners' involvement and imagination. Radio shares that advantage with the written word.

But die radio did. Time of death can be stated with precision: 6:35 p.m. Eastern Time, September 30, 1962, when "The Tip-Off Matter," the last episode of the insurance-investigator drama, *Yours Truly, Johnny Dollar*, went off the air.

Its corpse, feasted on by the maggots of right-wing talk shows, has been stinking ever since.

§

Television came to Binghamton just in time to report the Moon Block fire. WNBF went on the air December 1, 1949, operating out of studios in the Arlington Hotel, directly across Chenango Street from the Moon Block. Six days later it got its baptism of fire, so to speak, when employees hauled the klunky old cameras up to the roof of the hotel to capture some of the conflagration for the handful of set owners in the city.

(However, a former resident of Hillcrest, a community just outside of Binghamton, informs me that the first TV signal ever received in Broome County was in 1949, when an airplane circling above transmitted a signal to the Trelease-Wolfinger appliance store on Chenango Street, opposite Fenton Avenue.)

Binghamton did not get a second television station until 1957, when on November 1 WINR Channel 40 signed on as an NBC affiliate. A third station did not come until November 9, 1962, when WBJA Channel 34, an ABC affiliate, began broadcasting. All three stations later changed their call letters.

Thus most of my muddled memories of television in the Southern Tier are from WNBF and to a lesser extent WINR. It caused quite a stir when WINR, owned (along with the *Binghamton Press*) by the Gannett newspaper chain, started up, for it doubled our TV offerings. Unlike WNBF, which was a VHF station, WINR was UHF and could not be received on most existing sets without a converter and a different kind of set-top antenna from the rabbit ears that pulled in VHF signals. That occasioned lively debates among both the television experts and the hoi polloi over just which style, brands, and designs of indoors antennas were the best to buy. It scarcely seemed to make any difference. For the

Roger K. Miller

first twenty years or so of television, reception could be a chancy affair, necessitating fiddling with the "vertical hold" and the "horizontal hold" when the picture flipped over and over or skewed to the left or the right. Sometimes it helped to climb on a chair and place the rabbit ears on the curtain rod.

Local programming was skimpier than it is today and, until the end of the decade, local programming outside the studio was skimpy to the point of nonexistence. Cameras and other equipment were simply too bulky. In 1959 or 1960 one of the TV stations broadcast live an appearance by Duane Eddy (a native of Corning, New York) racing up the Chenango River in a speedboat while allegedly playing his big "twangy" hit, "Rebel Rouser." What that was supposed to mean or symbolize, or than to show off the station's capabilities, was probably as obscure then as it is now, but I am sure the music was not played live from the boat.

Studio shows there were, naturally. Bill Parker's *TV Ranch Club* was prominent. Later he played a character called Officer Bill on a program of the same name. He also did the brief news-and-weather shows of the time. In the earliest days (Parker was with WNBF for more than fifty years) an on-air person had to do triple duty and then some. For the weather report he had the aid of little stick-on clouds and sunshines to let us know what the weather had been and would be and we were not noticeably less informed than with Doppler weather radar. Tom Cawley, star columnist of the *Binghamton Press*, made a stab at reading the news on television accompanied by the clatter of a Teletype machine but I think that fortunately for him and television it did not last long.

Ralph Carroll was a WNBF personality whose broadcasting career went back to the 1920s. He was popular—"with the housewives," as they used to say—and played several roles on several programs, one of them being a talk show called *Carroll Caravan*, a name he may have borrowed from *Camel Caravan*, a long-running musical variety program on NBC and CBS radio. Or maybe it was from *Camel News Caravan*, national television's first newscast (1949-1956), a fifteen-minute program hosted by John Cameron Swayze ("Let's go hop-scotching around the world for headlines"). Carroll was also a pitchman for hearing aids, being a hearing aid user himself. As a young pup I thought him a pompous old poop, probably because on one of his programs he used to sign off with, "If you see someone without a smile, give him one of yours." Or it may have been, "And remember: You can't spread happiness on others without getting some on yourself." Either way, no thanks, Ralph; if you don't mind I think I'll just quietly throw up here in the corner.

Another program that, if it didn't make me want to throw up, then at least laugh, was *Fashions for Milady*, a blatant half-hour commercial on Monday night for Drazen's City of Fashion, a high-end woman's clothing store in downtown Binghamton. It gives you an idea of how willing we were to watch anything in those days that we would listen to Bruce Drazen, son of the family that owned the store, oleaginously introduce a series of local young women modeling dresses and gowns from the store. But, as I said, it offered laughs. "Hey Ma," I used to holler, "Brucie's on!" On the other hand, I believe the show stayed on into the 1960s, when television offerings were much greater. What that shows I'm not sure, other than it can't be good.

In high school a girl who seemed to like me asked me if I watched *American Bandstand*, Dick Clark's live music-and-dance show out of Philadelphia that aired mid-afternoons. She said she raced home every day to catch as much of it as she could. It seemed to disappoint her when I said I didn't. Maybe that's when she lost her not-very-long-held interest in me. Women are so fickle. For a short while in the late 1950s WNBF tried a local live replica of *American Bandstand*, called *TV Party Night* or something like that, on Saturday nights. Teenagers came to the studio and danced to records. My Aunt Frances said my grandmother said, "Oh, maybe we'll see Roger." Little did Grandma know.

§

Exactly at mid-century, America turned a sharp cultural corner with one of those tiny events that later can be viewed as a defining moment of an era. On September 9, 1950, on the first episode of the now incredibly obscure half-hour sitcom, *The Hank McCune Show*, the laugh track was born. *Variety*, the entertainment trade newspaper, was quick to see the implications. "Although the show is lensed on film without a studio audience," *Variety* said in its review of the first telecast, "there are chuckles and yocks dubbed in. Whether this induces a jovial mood in home viewers is still to be determined." *The Hank McCune Show* died almost a-borning—it folded three months later, December 2—but ten zillion yocks and chuckles later, television laughter still comes in a can.

Roger K. Miller

The emergence of the laugh track at this time was no accident. At the midpoint of what Henry R. Luce called the "American Century," America turned away from the more linear-oriented culture of print and radio and toward the spatial culture of television. Anything that could serve this new culture—like the laugh track—if it did not exist, was sure to be invented. The link of the 1950 television season to the laugh track is remarkable, for television at that juncture showed the way it would go. That way was the resolutely popular one, leading to a wasteland rather than a promised one, the way that has had critics for six decades reciting variations on the remarks made by Boston University President Daniel Marsh at graduation ceremonies in June of that year: "If the television craze continues with the present level of programs, we are destined to have a nation of morons."

§

Oddities and curiosities.

Roman Catholic Bishop Fulton J. Sheen was an extremely popular TV figure in the early 1950s. God may know why, I certainly don't. I did not watch him then, but I have seen television reports of him, and bits of his DuMont program, *Life Is Worth Living*, and there isn't much there, though he was formidably educated. There wasn't much to his Tuesday night competition on NBC, Milton Berle's *Texaco Star Theater*, either, but Berle was funny, in a vaudeville sort of way. Berle said of the bishop, "He uses old material, too." In response the bishop said that since Berle was known as Uncle Miltie, people should start calling him Uncle Fultie. Oh, hell: I declare it a tie: Berle was as funny as the bishop was profound. Martin Sheen, born Ramón Antonio Gerard Estévez, chose the stage name Sheen because he admired the bishop so much, which must be one of the most curious influences in show business. Bishop Sheen later got promoted to archbishop and now the church wants to promote him all the way to saint, though the process is taking longer than it otherwise might because Pope John Paul II, though a later entry, has jumped the sainthood queue.

The blast of a factory whistle began each episode of *Industry on Parade*, a series of fifteen-minute weekly documentaries about American manufacturing and business that spanned the decade. It was produced by the National Association of Manufacturers and provided at no cost to stations to use as a public service, apparently to forestall America going over to communism under President Dwight D. Eisenhower. Looks as if it worked. Despite its propagandistic purpose, of which most adolescent and probably post-adolescent minds were in any event unaware, I ran to the television when I heard the whistle's blast. Each episode contained three or four interesting segments on inventions, research, technological developments and industrial processes.

For a time around 1953-54 I, and the rest of the country, was mad for Droodles. They were the creation of comedy writer Roger Price, who introduced them on one of Garry Moore's shows, *I've Got a Secret,* I believe it was. They were an instant hit with viewers. Droodle is a nonsense word combining "drawing" and "doodle." It is nothing more than a square box containing a few minimal lines that might inspire one or more captions. Price said a Droodle was a strange little drawing that makes no sense until the observer knows the correct title.

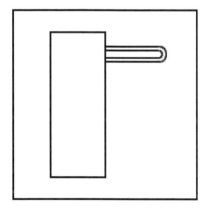

The Droodle above could be a person playing a trombone in a telephone booth or a paperclip playing hide and seek, though I feel as if I should explain what a telephone booth was. One Droodle from that time was labeled "King Farouk sitting on a barstool." If the concept of "telephone booth" is unclear to today's younger folk, King Farouk may be beyond explanation, so I'll let you imagine the Droodle if you remember him. Price went on to publish collections of Droodles and later created Mad Libs.

My cousin Ken and I liked the stories (based on real incidents) on *Navy Log.* Inspired by it, both of us were going to join the Navy when we got out of school. We even got the Navy to send us the Navy's house magazine for enlisted men. Only Ken ended up in the Navy—for twenty-one years as an officer.

I liked to watch Walter Cronkite doing the morning news on CBS because he did it with a puppet lion named Charlemagne. That was a response to Dave Garroway doing the morning news on NBC's *Today* show (its first host, starting in January 1952) with J. Fred Muggs, a (real) chimpanzee. So popular was J. Fred that later a female counterpart, Phoebe B. Beebee, was added. Garroway, bespectacled and bow-tied, always signed off by saying "Peace," something that may have been lacking in his own life, for he committed suicide at age sixty-nine.

Color TV was available to the masses if the masses went out and bought a sheet of plastic to place over the black-and-white screen. The plastic was colored in shimmery bands of green, brown, and blue and was not successful in giving the effect of color TV even in farm scenes dominated by green grass, brown dirt, and blue skies.

Obscure moments from television remain lodged in my head. Some I can date roughly by where we lived at the time I saw the programs. There was an episode of some half-hour drama or other from 1956, '57, or '58 that starred Steve Allen and wife Jayne Meadows in which they defied 1950s attitudes and convention by having their house painted some bizarre color scheme (which could only be rendered in black and white) that outraged their neighbors. Probably I remember it because they zipped about in a nifty sports car, an old MG-T model, which I loved and still love, or a Morgan or something similar. Despite extensive searching I have been unable to nail down the title of the episode or the show on which it appeared. Another I remember by star and title, David Niven and "Uncle Fred Flits By." It was on *Four Star Playhouse*; Niven was one of the four actors who originally took alternating starring roles. Later I learned it is from a short story by P.G. Wodehouse, which probably explains its power to remain lodged in my memory. I wish I could see it again.

Disneyland was a place that was also a TV show, or, rather, the other way 'round, for the show helped build (and promote) the place. Walt Disney in an act of audacious self-assurance—the construction of Disneyland—made himself, his interests, and his movies, into objective physical representations of American culture. Three decades before "If you build it, they will come" became a cliché, he thought it and did it. If I like it, the people will like it, was his reasoning. And we did. Disney broadcast periodic progress reports on *Disneyland* the show (premiered October

1954) about Disneyland the place (opened in July 1955) and I, three thousand miles away, watched the show and yearned to go to the place, knowing that I never could. (I did, though, nearly forty years later.)

In junior high I began collecting television stars' photographs. I thumbtacked them onto the wall of Van Horn's at 250 Chenango, which dates it as a hobby I must have engaged in for two years and more. I wrote to CBS regardless which network the actors appeared on for the simple reason that I was unaware there was more than one network; somehow I had come across the CBS address (485 Madison Avenue in New York) and used it exclusively. WNBF Channel 12 being for a time the lone television channel in Binghamton, until other channels came along it carried programs from all four networks, CBS (its chief affiliate), NBC, ABC, and DuMont (which folded in 1955). CBS must have sent the errant requests on to the right place for I got my photos—without having enclosed return postage, a thoughtless practice I employed later when requesting sample comic strips from cartoonists. I long ago lost or threw away all of the photographs. Ah, Imogene Coca, would that I still possessed your black-and-white eight-by-ten visage signed by you Sincerely in thick black stamp-pad ink.

§

But I don't and didn't blame you, Imogene. You were busy busy busy on *Your Show of Shows*. Who could take time out to sign eight-by-ten glossies for Upstate apple-knockers from Palookaville? How did you ever get anywhere in show business with the name Imogene, by the way, not to mention Coca? (I just looked you up on Wikipedia. You were born Imogene Fernandez de Coca in 1908 to show-biz parents, so that helps explain it. That and talent.)

Talk about Saturday Night Live—that's what *Your Show of Shows* was. Another, perhaps the most, brilliant creation of Pat Weaver of NBC, it ran live from 9:00 to 10:30 Eastern time Saturday night from 1950 to 1954. The stars were in alignment, you might say if you weren't ashamed of phrases too clever by half, especially in the conjunction of Coca with Sid Caesar. Small bits of some of their sketches still play out in my head: Their parody of the movie *From Here to Eternity* ("From Here to Obscurity"); test pilot Caesar's alarm when he's told his next assignment will be in one of the new jets ("Where's da propeller? Where's da propeller?"); the recurring sketch of the bickering couple, the Hickenloopers; and Caesar's totally confused Germanic professor in interviews with Carl Reiner. I'm not sure: We may not have seen *Your Show of Shows* live on WNBF (a CBS affiliate), but in delayed transcription via kinescope, an early-1950s version of tape, because it was not a CBS program. Alas, NBC discarded most of the kinescopes, so later generations cannot fully appreciate the comic genius of these performers.

I loved Steve Allen and Jack Paar. I never got to see much of Allen's *Tonight* show. The few times I saw it were on a Syracuse station when we went up to Hastings to Louise's future in-laws. But when Allen got his Sunday night variety show I sucked it in. Everyone else in the country was watching Ed Sullivan; I was watching Steve and Don Knotts, Louis Nye, Tom Poston, Bill Dana, Pat Harrington, and all the rest. "The Man on the Street" segment was the hilarious high spot of each broadcast: Knotts as the nervous Mr. Morrison, Harrington as the Italian golf pro Guido Panzini, Nye as the smarmy Gordon Hathaway, who, perhaps sending a secret signal from the closet, always greeted Allen with, "Hi ho, Steverino!" That became a catchphrase, as did Bill Dana's poker-faced "My name José Jiménez." If none of it could start you laughing, then Allen's out-of-sight, and sometimes out-of-control, cackling laughter would. If you ever need a laugh, go to YouTube, type in "Steve Allen laughing," click on what pops up, and you will be just as incapable of not laughing as Allen is while experiencing himself cracking up.

And then, Jack Paar. I sat in rapt reverence. Allen originated *Tonight* in 1954 and Johnny Carson became its emblem, but in between, starting in June 1957, Paar established it as a mostly-talk-and-some variety show. It has kept roughly that format ever since, though the talk went way downhill not long after Paar left the show in 1962. Maybe the chosen talkers are simply dumber, but more likely it is that witty, intelligent banter is not encouraged. Some of Paar's delightful regulars were comedian Cliff Arquette (whose introduction on every appearance was immediately followed by "as Charlie Weaver"); Genevieve, a French singer with mangled English; character actress Dody Goodman; Alexander King, a Vienna-born (as Alexander Koenig) memoirist, humorist, painter, and raconteur; and the incomparable comic genius Jonathan Winters. I stayed up much later than I should on weeknights to watch the show. The arrival of Friday night was welcomed because I could watch it up until its close at 1 a.m. Incredible to think that it ran for an hour and a half each night—an

The Chenango Kid

hour and forty-five minutes in the very beginning. In that era our minds and space and lives were not invaded every breathing second by multiple images of the Very Newest Thing, so occasional exposure to the Recently Novel was sufficiently entertaining. Bermuda shorts became a fashion statement so acceptable that business executives could be seen wearing them at work, though probably just for the momentary shock value. Paar one night added to the fashion statement, if not shock, by coming on stage attired in Bermuda shorts made of tuxedo trousers, long black socks with garters, and a serene Jack Benny-like demeanor. Did it not take much to make us laugh? Not if it was funny.

He was wry, self-deprecating, and satiric; he once nominated Elizabeth Taylor at the height of her marrying-and-unmarrying for the "Other Woman of the Year Award." When Paar died in 2004, *Time* magazine's obituary got it right in saying that talk-show history could be divided into two eras: Before Paar and Below Paar.

Lassie is a treasured program of baby boomers, but being slightly older than they I maintain that they are remembering the wrong *Lassie*, which is the version starting in 1957 with Jon Provost playing the wimpy little blond kid, Timmy Martin. Before that, in 1954, came the *real* one, in which Tommy Rettig played Jeff Miller, Jan Clayton his widowed mother Ellen, and George Cleveland Gramps ("pusillanimous polecats!").

§

Television seasons come and television seasons go—mostly go. With the explosion in numbers of cable channels, what used to be thought of as the traditional autumn start of the television season is itself gone. One thing is certain, however: Any season—fall, mid-, or partial—has to go a long way to beat or even match the season of 1955, when television was entering its Golden Age.

The fall of 1955 saw the premiere of eight programs whose renown will last probably as long as the history of television continues to be written. Some are periodically seen in re-runs to this day. Add to them a number of memorable programs that were already on the air before 1955, and then recollect that they all emerged from only three channels and not scores, and you have quite an achievement indeed. (That fall the airwaves were dominated by the three national networks that for three succeeding decades were virtually synonymous with American television—ABC, CBS, and NBC—the DuMont network having ceased operations in May.)

The eight great premieres were *Gunsmoke*, *The Lawrence Welk Show*, *The Life and Legend of Wyatt Earp*, *The Millionaire*, *The $64,000 Question*, *Alfred Hitchcock Presents*, *The Phil Silvers Show*, and *The Honeymooners*. Strictly speaking *The Honeymooners* was not born on October 1, 1955. That was its inauguration as a weekly series, the one that we see in re-runs. *The Honeymooners* had always been a pet project of Jackie Gleason's. It was first seen as a sketch on DuMont's *Cavalcade of Stars* in 1951, and when Gleason moved to CBS, he took it with him. As a weekly series it lasted only one season (39 episodes), but Gleason revived the bit again and again as part of future programs.

The Many Loves of Dobie Gillis is a more interesting program than it should be, since it was so patently silly. Perhaps that's the reason: because it was *deliberately* silly. That gave the writers freedom to engage in wordplay and absurdities that would have been out of place in a more conventional setting. The show comes outside the chronological scope of these ramblings, which end with my graduation from North High in June 1959, because it ran on CBS from September 1959 until September 1963. But considering that the 1950s lasted until about 1962-63, it is very much of the 1950s in essence and outlook. (The original Dobie Gillis of Max Shulman's short stories was a college student of the 1940s.)

Watched now, the series seems dopey, but that is because it had to work within strict conventions as to what could be said and done and we are accustomed to more daring inventiveness. Viewed in the context of its times it essayed the kind of loopiness to be found in Walt Kelly's *Pogo* or Ernie Kovacs' comedy. It sabotaged bland sitcoms. Its silliness masks another subversive element, one that ever so softly questions the domestic "American Dream" theme that the decade supposedly is all about. Dobie, played by Dwayne Hickman, talks directly to the viewers through the invisible "fourth wall," an unusual technique in itself. While he calls himself just another clean-cut American teenager looking for a pretty girlfriend, he doesn't want to mature into just another American schlep of an American male like his humorless, work-like-a-dog father. And Dobie's best friend, Maynard G. Krebs (played by Bob Denver), is the very opposite of the Solid Citizen Who Plays by the Rules. He is a beatnik, with all that that meant in non-conformism, living for jazz and hating even the sound of the word "work."

The Chenango Kid

Two other shows worth mentioning are also slightly beyond my purview, but again only chronologically; stylistically and atmospherically they are part of the Decade That Never Ends. The first is *The Twilight Zone*, created by Binghamton native Rod Serling. It began in the same year as *Dobie Gillis* and in its own oblique way was subversive of contemporary values and assumptions. It used science fiction and fantasy to criticize such things as racism, mindless greed, the arms race, and the "rat race." (The episode, "A Stop at Willoughby," starring James Daly, is a superb expression of the last subject.) Serling was a leading creative light of television before he created *The Twilight Zone*, and Binghamton is rightly very proud of him. When people ask me where I am from, most of the time they have no idea of Binghamton, but when I tell them Rod Serling was also from there, they express knowledge and interest, though he has been dead nearly forty years.

The second, less celebrated than *The Twilight Zone* and therefore less known, is *Route 66*. Created by Stirling Silliphant (love that name!), it was on CBS from 1960 to 1964. A combination of episodic drama and anthology (continuing characters and cast yet a different story each week), it centered around the travels of two young men, Martin Milner as Tod Stiles and George Maharis as Buz Murdock, in a beautiful Corvette convertible. (Maharis was sick for much of the third season, so late in that season Glenn Corbett was introduced as Lincoln Case and he stayed with the series until its end.) The open-ended format of two rootless young men roaming the country to no purpose other than to see what they can see and do what they wanted to do allowed the writers to create a wide variety of situations and dramatic (and occasionally comic) story lines. And the driving theme song by Nelson Riddle—it is as much a part of the series as anything and remains a memorable and playable piece of music.

The stories, admittedly, are slow-moving—*maddeningly* slow, even for their era. Yet the series was popular, perhaps because it gave viewers a look at their country in an entertaining setting. That is its attraction for me today: traveling around the country and seeing different places with different kinds of people. Regions of the country *were* different from one another then, when roads were fewer and fewer of them were high speed, and so were the people within them. *Route 66* is like a documentary in giving a glimpse into the scenery, infrastructure, clothing, manners, and regional styles and speech of a less speeded up time before McRestaurants and McMotels.

Roger K. Miller

Whatever road they were on, however, it was almost never Route 66 (which traversed only eight states). It was rarely mentioned in the series.

§

People often say of the past, wistfully, "It was such a time of innocence" and "We were so innocent." By now we must be guilty as hell, because each generation has been saying that about earlier generations for . . . well . . . generations. Sometimes it is expressed, wonderingly, in the phrase, "We're not in Kansas anymore," or, scornfully, as "Life is not like Ozzie and Harriet."

The program that life is not like, *The Adventures of Ozzie & Harriet*, began at 8:00 Eastern Time on a Friday night, October 3, in 1952. It would run for fourteen years on ABC, becoming the longest-running family situation comedy in television history, a distinction it would hold for decades. Technically, *The Simpsons* has overtaken it, though *The Simpsons* is animated, not live action. Those fourteen years translate into 435 episodes, forty-three more than *My Three Sons*, which ran for twelve seasons. Furthermore, *Ozzie & Harriet*, as it was commonly known, had been a weekly series on radio for eight years before it jumped to TV. (The radio show continued until 1954.)

Ozzie & Harriet did not quite invent the family TV sitcom—others were present at the creation, such as *The Stu Erwin Show*—but it formed the mold for what we once thought of, and to some extent still do, as family sitcom, from which were cast such solid ingots as *Father Knows Best* and *Leave It to Beaver*.

The other sitcom that was derided, then and later, for not being like life was *Father Knows Best*. Big revelation. When confronted with that charge, Robert Young, who played the father in the show, would reply, "No, of course, but that's how we'd *like* it to be."

Young also helped create the show, so in a very real sense "father" did know best. Television executives certainly didn't. The show almost failed to make it to a second season. The series, which debuted on CBS at 10 p.m. Eastern time Sunday, October 3, 1954, did not do well in the ratings. In March of the next year CBS announced that it was canceling the show.

A flood of viewer protests poured in, and someone got the word, but not at CBS, for NBC picked up the show and moved it in August to the more family-friendly time slot of 8:30 Eastern on Wednesday nights, where it remained until September 1958. After that it moved back to CBS and finally, in 1962, over to ABC, before finally leaving prime time in April 1963.

A durable and popular property, indeed, especially considering, again, that a series season in those days consisted of anywhere from thirty-two to thirty-nine episodes, not the twenty-two (or fewer) of today. Its final season with original episodes, 1959-60, was also its most successful, when it ranked sixth among all TV programs. Equally as impressive is that from 1960 to 1963, CBS and ABC got away with airing only reruns.

Some say the show was nothing more than an idealized version of American life, and what's wrong with that? Others say it institutionalized complacency and conformity and male dominance, and there's everything wrong with that. Young and producer Eugene B. Rodney were candid about their efforts to project moral lessons. Nothing unusual about that: So were *Leave It to Beaver* creators Bob Mosher and Joe Connelly.

So why is it that *Beaver* doesn't draw—or didn't draw; the issue crops up less and less as the years go by—the same complaints about being an unrealistic portrayal of the American nuclear family? After all, it could be argued that *FKB* was better written and better acted and had more interesting characters. Perhaps it is because *Beaver* is more jokey than *FKB*.

One thing *FKB* was not was *Ozzie and Harriet*. Nor *Leave It to Beaver*. You might say it was on its way from one to the other. Even in the radio version Jim Anderson as husband and father was a departure from the usual witless incompetents who filled that role on such shows as *The Life of Riley*, *Blondie*, and even *Ozzie and Harriet* (all of which also began on radio before moving to television). Young's Anderson was wise, kind, stable, and helpful, a forerunner of Ward Cleaver of *Beaver*, Andy Taylor of *The Andy Griffith Show* and Steve Douglas of *My Three Sons*.

The strongest charge that can be laid at the family sitcoms is that they—and *all* programs, period—were snow white. Not that I as a kid or most other (white) viewers of any age noticed anything wrong with that. In the mid-1950s 88 percent of Americans were of European descent (compared with 69 percent fifty years later), but a simple statistic such as that is no excuse for, or adequate explanation of the reasons for, television being a Caucasian preserve. The fact that almost everything else was a Caucasian preserve comes closer to an explanation.

Roger K. Miller

The struggle of blacks to win civil rights and equality, an element in the underappreciated dynamism of the 1950s, was not something, frankly, that I was aware of. "We" told ourselves we knew how bad "they" had it in the South—actually, "we" had only an inkling of how bad—but as for the North or even Binghamton's small black community, "we" turned a blind eye. Now and then news of some particularly egregious crime, like the murder of fourteen-year-old Emmett Till in Mississippi in 1955, would penetrate the shell. As the decade moved along the struggle against the offenses appeared in less-than-crispy film images more and more often on our seventeen- and twenty-one-inch, black-and-white television screens.

It is an interesting question, by the way, what members of my family thought about blacks—coloreds, Negroes, as they were then. In general it was not good. Ma was prejudiced in the "casual" way that most people were then, although she almost never had any contacts with African Americans. Talking with her friends and Sheridan relatives she would refer to them as niggers, coons, and jigaboos without fear of being contradicted. It is puzzling, then, that I could have had the "little friend," a black boy also named Roger, that she told me about more than once. My father, I don't know: I never heard him say anything prejudicial, but I assume he would just as soon not have anything to do with blacks. Among the Millers the subject rarely seemed to come up and the vile epithets even more rarely. Pa's brother Lawrence did use the terms and with relish, but their sister Frances, despite having little interaction with blacks, was almost programmatically unprejudiced; more than once she laced into me when she heard me say something intolerant.

I thought of myself as unprejudiced, with even less justification than now. Personally, I never used the word nigger, but I never protested when others did nor when I listened to godawful racial "jokes." I did not realize that as a relatively poor white boy I was better off, certainly in terms of opportunity and freedom of movement, than 100 percent of the children in the black community. One possibly telling incident: One evening I met Tom at a high school basketball game. He was already in the upper stands of the bleachers, so I worked my way through the crowd up to him. A black guy was sitting next to him. I sort of wedged my way in between and said, "Move down one beer," thinking, ha ha, that that took the edge off my intrusiveness. Apparently not. He looked at me as if he could kill me, and moved, if at all, a few millimeters. In my own defense, I think that was naïveté or insensitivity rather than white superiority, that I would have used the same lame jocularity had a white person been there. And probably received the same response, if slightly less lethal-seeming.

§

Television didn't seriously begin to discover news until Chet Huntley and David Brinkley took over from John Cameron Swayze in 1956, when everything that happened in the world could be told in fifteen minutes minus commercials. News, however, had persisted in happening well before that and occasionally it got onto television.

One of those occasions was the "crime hearings" in 1950 and '51, officially known as the Senate Special Committee to Investigate Crime in Interstate Commerce and unofficially as the Kefauver Committee for its chairman, Senator Estes Kefauver of Kentucky, who was hoping to ride the nationwide interest in the televised hearings to the Democratic nomination for the presidency. (He had to settle for being Adlai Stevenson's running mate in 1956.) They were the first great television phenomenon in the country. Hearings were held in fourteen cities. It was said that in New York City alone nearly 70 percent of sets were tuned to them. *Life* magazine said, "People had suddenly gone indoors into living rooms, taverns, and clubrooms, auditoriums and back-offices. There, in eerie half-light, looking at millions of small frosty screens, people sat as if charmed. Never before had the attention of the nation been riveted so completely on a single matter." I came home from school and turned the hearings on, not for their content or import, about which I hadn't a clue, but because I knew everybody was talking about them and about the high-profile crime figures among the witnesses, such as Frank Costello. *Ooooh*, crime bosses. Who knew we had them? Not the FBI, apparently. Its longtime director, J. Edgar Hoover, had to admit that there were crime organizations across the country and the FBI had done little about it.

Similarly gripping and creating a similar carnival atmosphere was the first televised explosion of an atomic bomb. It happened at Yucca Flat, Nevada, in April 1952. It attracted the curious who came in cars and campers, and it and other atomic-bomb tests contributed to an "atomic craze" in the country, especially in Las Vegas, the nearest large city to the test site. I cannot be sure whether I saw that first test or one of the later ones. Whichever it was, it was conducted early in the morning but not early enough for me to get to school on time. I was late because I lingered to watch it. Previous tests had not been televised. Insanely, American soldiers were made to take part as observers, sometimes as close as 2,500 yards from ground zero—way too close for their own good, as a much later study reported, because they received excessive doses of radiation. One soldier said the shock wave hit him in the chest like a 100-pound bag of sand and knocked him backward a considerable distance. He died of leukemia at age sixty-eight.

Not long after, *The Conqueror*, the worst film John Wayne ever made and a strong contender for the worst film of the decade (it was released in 1956), was filmed at St. George, Utah, 137 miles downwind from the Nevada Test Site. By 1981, ninety-one of the 221 cast and crew members had developed some form of cancer and forty-six had died of it. (Howard Hughes, its producer, had unwittingly compounded the danger by having sixty tons of dirt, most likely radioactive, shipped to Hollywood to match the Utah terrain for re-shoots.)

Memories etched in youth are longest lasting. The late writer Christopher Hitchens, a brilliant essayist who died too young at age sixty-two, was politically attuned even as a seven-year-old. In 1997 he told *The Progressive* magazine, "I was precocious enough to watch the news and read the papers, and I can remember October 1956, the simultaneous crisis in Hungary and Suez, very well. And getting a sense that the world was dangerous, a sense that the game was up, that the Empire was over."

I am eight years older than Hitchens. I was nowhere near as precocious, and have nowhere near the intellect, but I retain images of those events and others great and small, personal, national, and international. Such as the Hungarian Uprising. How angry the suppression of it made us—until refugees began to arrive on our shores and we began to perceive in them disgusting un-American habits and unscrupulous behavior. Eastern Europeans, after all. Even more vivid is my remembrance of the murderous rampage of Charles Starkweather and his fourteen-year-old girlfriend Caril Ann Fugate across Nebraska and Wyoming in late 1957. My memory didn't extend to the number he killed, which I had to look up. It was eleven, including three in Fugate's family. After they were caught a photograph showed a happily smiling Fugate and Starkweather with a grin underneath demented-looking eyes. It was a scandalous national story because so highly unusual. What was our country, what were our youth, coming to? What they were coming to, apparently, is what we have now, a nation armed, if not yet quite to the teeth then to the armpits, where youth and non-youth mow themselves and the rest of us down with alarming frequency, bringing calls for yet more personal armaments. Such deadly outbursts still shock us, but we get over it fairly easily and quickly.

But, there is news and then there is news. The wedding of actress Grace Kelly to Prince Rainier of Monaco on April 19, 1956, was news of the kind that in the intervening decades has come to dominate if not define "news": something that happens to a Hollywood figure or other celebrity. What Kelly wanted is difficult to understand with the passage of time; her married life seems to have been restricted in a way that does not fit her personality as she presented herself to the public. What Rainier demanded, and got, was a two-million-dollar dowry—and a prenuptial fertility test. He needed heirs, else his principality would be absorbed by France. She passed the test, and then gave him three children, the first, Caroline, nine months and three days after the wedding. Thirty million people around the world watched the ceremony on television. The sinking three months later of the Italian passenger liner Andrea Doria off the coast of Nantucket after colliding with the Swedish ship Stockholm, with the loss of fifty-two lives, paled in comparison.

§

The values go up up up
And the prices go down, down, down,
Robert Hall this season
Shows you the reason:
Low overhead!
Low overhead!

Commercials, having been hammered into the brain repeatedly, stick there the longest. Robert Hall was a pioneer in low-overhead, large-facility merchandising, selling inexpensive but not necessarily cheap-looking goods. Ma and I shopped there. The store was on a corner of Main Street somewhere on the near West Side if I am not mistaken.

Piels Beer was a New York brand, so people in other parts of the country may not know of the marvelous series of Piels animated commercials in the mid-to-late 1950s featuring the fictitious Bert and Harry Piel, voiced by the incomparable Bob Elliott (as Harry) and Ray Goulding (as Bert). Harry was tall, composed, and calm, Bert tubby and excitable. We used to run to watch when one came on, hoping that it would be a new one that we hadn't seen. They were terribly clever commercials, but I have heard they didn't boost beer sales. Shouted repetition is what moves product.

Another prominent New York beer was Rheingold. Both those who drank it, whose numbers were impressive (as high as a third of the state's beer market during the decade), and those who didn't knew it from its Miss Rheingold publicity campaign. Each year drinkers and non-drinkers voted their choice for the next Miss Rheingold, who would appear in the next year's advertisements, which invariably bore the slogan, "My beer is Rheingold, the DRY beer!" The contest drew aspiring models and actresses from across the country. Ballots could be found at the check-out counters of stores in every town and city.

Like Robert Hall, Rheingold had a commercial jingle. Sung to Emil Waldteufel's "Estudiantina Valse," it went something like this:

> My beer is Rheingold, the dry beer,
> Think of Rheingold whenever you buy beer,
> It's not bitter, not sweet,
> Extra dry flavor treat
> Won't you try extra dry Rheingold beer?

The Web was a high-quality, live, half-hour anthology series on CBS in the early 1950s. Actors who later became famous, such as Paul Newman and Leslie Nielsen, got their start there performing in its suspenseful stories. What I mostly remember about it is its opening. The host/narrator, Jonathan Blake, would introduce the night's presentation as the smoke from a Kent cigarette (the sponsor) drifted upward and sort of morphed into a web. It was cool, to an eleven-year-old. What wasn't cool was the much-touted "Micronite" filter on Kents. It had been added to the brand after a *Reader's Digest* article warned about the dangers of cancer from smoking. What those who thought they were protecting themselves from cancer with a filter cigarette did not know was that the Micronite filter contained blue asbestos, a carcinogen. Oops.

Cigarette advertising, long since banned from television, flourished in my youth, as did smoking. In the early 1950s about 44 percent of American adults smoked cigarettes. Dancing cigarette packages (and dancing matchboxes) somehow were meant to encourage viewers to buy Old Gold. Maybe it was the shapely female legs in white boots below the packages. Or maybe it was the manufacturer's assurance that Old Golds offered a "a treat instead of a treatment" and the assurance that they were made "by tobacco men, not medicine men." What was that supposed to mean? A slam at doctors promoting certain brands, or, on the other side, at doctors condemning smoking? Camel boasted that "more doctors smoked Camels than any other cigarette." Dr. Cary Middlecoff, a dentist turned pro golfer, plugged Viceroy cigarettes (and before that Carling's Red Cap Ale). He even smoked on the green while on golf tours. Santa also got his endorsement in, in print ads if not on television, by informing us that Pall Malls "guard against throat scratch."

How fleeting is fame! If Ipana toothpaste is still made and sold anymore, apparently it is not in the United States. But it was certainly made and sold in the 1950s. A venerable brand, it was all over radio and television in animated commercials sung by one Bucky Beaver:

> *Brusha, brusha, brusha!*
> *Get the new Ipana!*
> *With the brand new flavor*
> *It's dandy for your teeth!*

Did Ipana contain chlorophyll? Everything else did, short of motor oil: chewing gum, tooth pastes and tooth powders, deodorants, cough drops, breath tablets, even dog food. Advertisements touted chlorophyll, a green pigment found in almost all plants, as having the power to make your breath, your underarms, and apparently your dog smell fresh and sweet, though the *Journal of the American Medical Association* reminded consumers that it did not have that effect on goats. They practically live on chlorophyll and it does nothing for their legendarily bad smell.

Many products had high-profile and long-lasting spokesmen and spokeswomen. One of the most iconic, as we say now but wouldn't have then, was Betty Furness, an actress who lucked into her role flogging Westinghouse appliances. The image that may linger in the minds of viewers of that era may be that of her opening wide a refrigerator door and exclaiming, "You can be sure . . . if it's Westinghouse." That often-repeated bit created a famous television blooper when on one occasion the door refused to open, but Furness was not at the handle then—another actress had substituted for her. Later she went on to become a respected consumer advocate.

CHAPTER 13

Portrait of the Would-Be Artist as a Boy

"Every artist makes himself born. It is very much harder than the other time, and longer."

—Willa Cather

In eighth or ninth grade I wanted to take a correspondence art course. It was the one from Art Instruction Schools of Minneapolis advertised on matchbook covers, showing a drawing of a face and challenging the matchbook holder to "Draw Me!" If he did and his drawing was good enough, the ad inside the cover said, he might win a free correspondence course.

I'd like to know the percentage of entrants who won the free course. As far as that goes, I'd like to know the percentage of entrants whose drawings were deemed so unaccomplished that they were not invited to take the course by paying the fee. I'm thinking that both percentages probably did not rise far above the zero mark. Decades later I learned that Charles M. Schulz, whose *Peanuts* comic strip I have always thought was a work of brilliance and occasionally of genius, had been an instructor there. I don't like to think he would be party to anything shady; probably not, for he worked in instruction, not sales.

By return of mail I learned that—*mirabile dictu!*—I *was* good enough. Alas, I was not also rich enough. When Ma and I learned the cost—about three hundred dollars, the equivalent of more than three thousand dollars today—that put paid to that, so to speak.

But one evening some time later one of those men who did work in sales knocked on our door at 289 Chenango. He wanted to know, he said, whether I was still interested in the fine course offered by Art Instruction Schools of Minneapolis, Minnesota? He was dressed in a gray suit and a fedora and looked like that owlishly bespectacled actor, Edward Andrews, who made a career of playing unctuous businessmen in movies and on television.

I certainly was interested, I said, but we just didn't have the money. I must have pleaded with Ma one more time, Couldn't I do it, huh, Ma, please Ma? And she must have sat there, submissive, weary, beaten down by another side of life, feeling miserable that she couldn't accommodate me but knowing that three hundred dollars was nine or ten weeks' wages in the shoe factory.

Whatever Ma might have been thinking or feeling, that triggered the salesman's capitalistic sanctimony. If I wanted the art course so much, he said, astride his high horse, why didn't I go out and earn the money for it?

Boom! No denying he was right. If I wanted it, why *didn't* I go out and earn the money for it? The reasonable answer, and the one that came to mind as quickly as the question was asked, was that it would have been hard for a thirteen- or fourteen-year-old to earn three hundred dollars even in the thriving Fifties. But the truth was that I was not then or later very good at wanting to work. Unless it was work that I wanted to do, and that would involve reading, drawing, or—bringing up the rear—writing.

We represented for him a wasted call. So any form of badgering on his part was worth trying if it might rescue a disappearing sale. But sanctimony would come easy to a person who looked as if he adhered to the "root, hog, or die" school of philosophy or liked to think he did. "I had to work for everything I've got and look where it's got me," was going through his head. "And I fought my way across Hitler's Europe with the 518th Mess Kit Repair Company. It wouldn't hurt this punk kid, this Mama's Boy, to get out and do something for himself." Maybe it even occurred to him that Mama, the weak-willed walkover there in this shitbag of an apartment, might be an easy lay.

Anyway, that was one of my early failures in the field of art.

§

When did I first have a real passion for drawing, for art? I think seventh grade, though I already enjoyed drawing in sixth. Another sixth-grader named Miller, Eddie (no relation), and I decided to collaborate on a comic strip, an enthusiasm that must have lasted all of a week and a half. I don't remember the subject matter, but I'll bet it was full of talking animals like *Pogo*. Early on I was attracted to *Pogo*, not for its story line and satire, which were beyond my youthful ken, but for the clever renderings of animals with human characteristics.

I always was drawn to, no pun intended, drawing and illustration—to frankly, commercial art rather than fine art, if any such distinction is justified. I pored over illustrations in the many "slick" magazines of the time, studying the styles of artists like Austin Briggs and Jon Whitcomb to understand how they created the effects that they did. But, as my sixth-grade effort shows, almost as soon as the seed of art was planted the twig was bent in favor of cartooning, particularly comic strips. I bought paperback collections of strips, most notably *Pogo*. The *Pogo* books were not cheap for the time—one dollar each. I still have several of them, battered but not tattered. And Harry Haenigsen's *Penny*, also one dollar. Others, like *Dennis the Menace* (a panel, not a strip), were twenty-five- or thirty-five-cent mass-market paperbacks. To my small but growing library of cartooniana I added the hardcover *The Best of H. T. Webster*, which rests on a bookshelf near me as I type.

Once or twice I sent cartoons to *The Saturday Evening Post* drawn on blue-lined, loose-leaf-binder paper. I provided no stamped return envelope, being ignorant of such courtesies as well as of the unsuitability of loose-leaf paper as an artistic surface. I received a reply, cartoon enclosed and politely declined.

I sent off letters requesting samples of cartoonists' work. I did not know their addresses, so I wrote to their syndicates, finding the syndicates' addresses from some reference book in the library. Cartooning, comic books, comic strips, and comic art in general were not valued then, so I received a response from many of them. Again, without having enclosed return postage. They must have been so pleased that someone appreciated their work and wanted to encourage a budding cartoonist that they were moved to respond. I no longer have any letters that might have been enclosed. Nor do I have most of the comics. At one time I had more than a dozen or so originals, from cartoonists as varied as J.R. Williams (*Out Our Way*) to *Moon Mullins* (by either Frank Willard or his assistant/successor Ferd Johnson), but over a lifetime of too many moves a lot went missing. I still retain an *Alley Oop* (V.T. Hamlin), a *Mark Trail* (Ed Dodd), a *Heart of Juliet Jones* (Stan Drake), and a *Mutt and Jeff* (Al Smith, successor to the strip's creator, Bud Fisher), all from 1956 and signed to me by the artists.

If I ever had an original *B.C.* by Johnny Hart I have managed to lose it. By rights, as we used to say, I should have had one, because Hart was from my hometown, or as good as—he was a native of neighboring Endicott and lived all his life in Broome County. When his *B.C.* first appeared in the *Binghamton Press* in 1958 I was excited beyond any telling of it. I was too shy and insecure to go beyond thinking of contacting Hart to ask for advice. But a comic strip by a local cartoonist! So it *is* possible!

Not according to my family, it wasn't. I was discouraged from pursuing art and illustration and cartooning. "You can't make a living at it." What they were thinking was, *They* couldn't make a living at it, so what made me think that I could? When I had graduated from high school and obtained the bank-trainee job, Charlie Noldy, Ma's sister Anna's husband, advised me to stick with the bank job, never mind drawing "your scripts." Those who weren't actively discouraging were not particularly encouraging, like Ma and Pa and some of the Millers. I think they saw a youthful passion that the harsh world would soon extinguish. Aside from the "soon" part, looks as if they were right.

§

Shmoos (or shmoon; the singular is shmoo) were Al Capp's embodiment of the bountiful possibilities of human existence. They resembled large-bottomed bowling pins with two short legs, an always-grinning mouth sporting sparse whiskers, and eyes that seemed to beg for love and acceptance. Shmoos lived on air and reproduced asexually faster than rabbits. They existed, like Earth itself in a state of nature, for nothing less than to please and sustain *you*, the human being. They produced eggs and milk and butter, and if you looked upon one hungrily, it ecstatically committed suicide by means of frying pan or broiler, rendering it into a tasty meal resembling chicken or steak. And somehow its pelt could also be rendered into either leather or wood. They became a national craze upon their first (and, as it developed, brief) appearance in Capp's *Li'l Abner* in

1948, not long before I began reading comic strips in earnest. But even as a seven-year-old capable only of appreciating their lovable appearance, I loved shmoos as much as they reputedly loved me (and everyone).

Shmoos, like everything he drew or wrote, were part of Capp's grand satire. While commentators interpreted them variously as a leftist or a rightist phenomenon, my feeling is that Capp, as a liberal, used them to satirize grasping capitalism, which corrupted the planet's natural richness for capitalists' monetary enrichment. Shmoos were declared a menace because they were bad for business and for national security. On the orders of J. Roaringham Fatback, the Pork King, "Shmooicide Squads" were sent out to slaughter them with guns, and after their near-elimination they rarely appeared in *Li'l Abner* again.

That is, Capp was a liberal in the late 1940s and the 1950s. In the 1960s he was a conservative, or if not quite that, then certainly far less liberal. He might best be described as a contrarian. During the Vietnam War college and university campuses were alive with war protests, at which he was a popular speaker both because of and despite his views. He relished putting hecklers down. I attended one such talk in either 1969 or 1970 at Pennsylvania State University, where I was studying for a master's degree in journalism after getting out of the Army. One heckler grew so incensed that he stormed up the aisle, shouting and tearing up a piece of paper, something symbolic, apparently, though I forget what it was. Capp, chortling and clearly enjoying himself, shot back, "Try that with your next allowance check!"

Capp, born Alfred Gerald Caplin in 1909, was a genius of the comic strip during the heyday of the medium, from, say, the 1920s through the 1960s. Genius is not too strong a word. There were several others, my favorites among them being Walt Kelly (*Pogo*), Frank King (*Gasoline Alley*), Charles M. Schulz (*Peanuts*), and Milton Caniff (for his stellar illustrating of *Terry and the Pirates* and then *Steve Canyon*). I studied their work each day with eager gimlet eye, but none with more eagerness and the wish that I could do *that* than Walt Kelly's.

To study it I had to buy an out-of-town newspaper. The *Binghamton Press* did not carry *Pogo*. I wrote the newspaper asking why not and received a reply from the editor, Fred Stein (who became *my* editor when I went to work for the newspaper in 1970), saying it appealed only to college students and other elites. So almost every day I put out five cents to buy,

Roger K. Miller

if I remember right, the Buffalo *Courier-Express* at Art's News Stand on Chenango.

If Walt Kelly had written "regular" books, he might be recognized today as one of the finest satirists of the 20th century. As a wizard of wordplay he might well be mentioned, if not in the same breath with Lewis Carroll and Edward Lear, then in the very next. But he didn't. He drew a comic strip, which was then, as now, a low estate, and the books he produced were compilations of his strip, featuring Pogo Possum, Albert the Alligator, and a whole raft of animals inhabiting Kelly's highly imaginative rendering of Georgia's Okefenokee Swamp.

In his day—the 1950s and '60s, which his strip commented on so masterfully—he was hailed for his comedic and artistic talents. In 1951 those talents landed him on the best-seller lists with the first compilation, titled, simply, *Pogo*. That first book could be considered a forerunner of the graphic novel. More than that, the entire twenty-seven-year run of *Pogo*, from 1948 to 1975, can be considered one long novel, rather in the way that, say, the twelve novels of Anthony Powell's *A Dance to the Music of Time* series are really one long novel or John Updike's four Rabbit Angstrom novels are all of one artistic piece.

Pogo is best known for its political satire, particularly the parodying of McCarthyism and communist-hunting by the U.S. Congress. This led to the creation in 1953 of a stand-in for Republican Senator Joseph R. McCarthy of Wisconsin, a wildcat named Simple J. Malarkey whose name as well as threatening looks and manner perfectly reflect their original.

Political satire cropped up from time to time throughout the run of the strip, but none of it can be fully understood without an appreciation of what *Pogo* really was about, which was, in a word, nonsense. Kelly used elements of vaudeville, slapstick, and, especially, inventive language to create a delightfully loony world of adults masquerading as animals. T.S. Eliot used to have the Pogo books sent to him in England as they appeared. To Kelly, plots were unrealistic. In life, and so in *Pogo*, things happen higgledy-piggledy. Typically a story line goes, Kelly said, "from one exaggeration to another, and the second exaggeration is supposedly an explanation of the first."

Kelly said he used animals—"nature's screechers," he called them—"largely because you can do more with animals. They don't hurt as easily, and it's possible to make them more believable in an exaggerated pose." That is a powerful insight. As zanily creative as Al Capp was, Kelly's use of animals is what makes his satire more intellectually satisfying. He chose, not soft and cuddly animals, but oddball "critters"—possum, turtle, owl, porcupine, "mushrat." Each has its own personality. Pogo is benign, bland, and neutral, and while the strip is named for and revolves around him, the fiery Albert is the strip's true protagonist.

Kelly's fantastically fertile and creative brain was snuffed out way too early. He died of complications of diabetes at age sixty in 1973. His thoughts on that aspect of existence were in keeping with his strip's general outlook. "Don't take life so serious, son," Porky Pine once said to Albert. "It ain't nohow permanent."

Nor is renown. Kelly is little known now and his creation only slightly more, largely for the saying, "We have met the enemy, and he is us." Though actually it was Kelly, not Pogo, who said it, and in slightly different form in Kelly's foreword to a 1953 collection of strips, *The Pogo Papers*:

"Resolve then, that on this very ground, with small flags waving and tinny blasts on tiny trumpets, we shall meet the enemy, and not only may he be ours, he may be us."

Few other things in popular entertainment of the time catch and parody that time, the time in which I struggled to come of age, so well. If you want to know the 1950s, one of the pieces of evidence you have to examine is *Pogo*.

§

It does no good to have regrets, so the line goes. Not healthy. The past is past, what can you do about it? Maybe nothing, but we certainly spend enough time exploring to bring it back. I have more than a few regrets, and at the top of the list is not pursuing the interest in drawing and art far enough to see if I had the ability to make something out of the interest. As I write this I surprise myself at how agitated I get at this late date, at others for their discouraging words or for the lack of encouraging ones, but mostly at myself for not ignoring and overcoming the lack of support.

To a certain extent and for a time I did ignore and overcome. To explain this I must go slightly beyond my timeline and say that after high school I got the trainee job at the bank, but my goal was to work for a year, save money for the first year of college, and go, worrying about the financing of future years as they came along. And so I did. I really wanted to go to the Rhode Island School of Design. I applied there; the application included an art test that was mailed to me and that I completed under supervision of my old high school counselor, Mr. Brennan. But it was really a pointless dream as there was no way I could save enough money for the tuition. I also went down to New York City, staying with my Uncle Will for a weekend, to take the drawing test for admission to Cooper Union (a tuition-free institution), but did not pass that. I was not surprised. As I was taking the test in the Cooper auditorium I glanced around at the work others were doing (one segment was to draw a bucket on a ladder that was on the stage in front of us) and I could tell I was out of my league. Those people were imaginative, *creative*.

My fallback was the state university system, which at that time consisted—aside from Harpur College in Binghamton, the only liberal arts unit—of a number of teachers colleges. Each college specialized in a subject. Albany was math education and Brockport was phys ed, for instance. Buffalo was art education. I applied to Buffalo, sent a portfolio, had an interview (conducted at Harpur by a recruiter who came down from Buffalo), and was accepted.

And so one hot morn in early September 1960 I loaded myself and a large trunk onto the Greyhound bus at the station on Chenango near Henry Street and headed off for academia. I still am somewhat bitter—you can also read that as self-pity—that there was no one to take me up there in a car, for if there had been, what happened immediately thereafter might not have. Probably it would have, but maybe not.

What happened was I turned right around and came back. I lay there all night in my assigned dorm room (my roommate was from the neighboring community of Endwell) scared as hell, petrified, my heart going like a hummingbird's wings, not sleeping a wink, telling myself this was not for me, these were not my kind of people, I had to get out of there. And that is what I did the next morning. As quickly and as surreptitiously as I could (I was ashamed of my cowardly behavior) I got a taxi, loaded on my trunk, drove me to the Greyhound station, and skulked back home to Mama.

What happened after that is the future in all its messiness. I think now that what I should have done at that point was enlist in the military, probably the Air Force, for military service was a likely part of my future since the draft was still in force and I would have to face it sooner or later. In those days of the Eisenhower peace a guy who didn't know what to do with himself could do worse than join the military. But I did not.

(Wouldn't *that* have been scary, life in the barracks, for a guy who couldn't take life in the dorm room?) Facing it later is what most guys chose to do. And when I did face it six years later it wasn't so much scary as boring.

But then if art or drawing or cartooning was so important to me, I would have found a way to keep at it, wouldn't I? That reasoning is hard to refute. If it's important to you, and you live in a free society, you will find a way to do it. But I did not. In fact, at that point I all but shut down art altogether. I stopped. I ceased to do it.

So boo hoo, stop your whining. In the Army they taught me where I could find sympathy: between "shit" and "syphilis" in the dictionary. And then I have to tell myself that if I had stayed at Buffalo or joined the Air Force, I most likely never would have crashed a wedding reception on Clinton Street in November 1962 and thus never have met, for the second and conclusive time, the lovely young woman who two years later became my wife.

Now *that* would be something to regret.

CHAPTER 14

Lopez

"And yet what was it that people had in those days? A feeling of security, even when they weren't secure. More exactly, it was a feeling of continuity."

—George Orwell, *Coming Up for Air*

Anyone happening to stroll down a certain dirt road in the tiny village of Lopez in Sullivan County in northeastern Pennsylvania during a certain July in the mid-1950s would likely have come upon two scrawny boys in their early teens lying prone upon their stomachs in a field and clutching upon their sweaty heads two-and-a-half-gallon galvanized-metal buckets and peering intently into the clear blue arc of the bright summer sky.

Who these boys were and what they were looking at while wearing such unconventional headgear would be a complete puzzle to the stroller. But they were, in fact, none other than myself and my cousin Ken, two adolescent louts from Binghamton, spending, as usual, our summer at our grandparents' home in Lopez.

What we were doing with our heavenward-bent heads in buckets is the point of this little tale. (For the record, Ken claims that only I sported a bucket, that upon his noggin was a sensible German helmet that one of our uncles had brought back from the war. I say, let him write his own book.)

Now, Lopez in summer today is surpassingly lovely. But in the 1950s it was an absolute boys' paradise of swimming, hiking, bike-riding, loafing

The Chenango Kid

in the sun and general all-around having a time like you will never again have in your life.

However, even paradise can use a little shaking up now and then. Which is why, around the Fourth of July one year, Ken and I decided to make our own fireworks. We were inspired to this rash act by Ken's coming into possession of several spent, metal Crossman CO_2 cylinders, each about three inches long. In messing around with them, trying to figure out what interesting unauthorized uses they might be put to, it occurred to us that they looked a lot like rockets—or like rockets looked in the 1950s—and we should do something about that.

Then, inspired probably by some misunderstood physics information gleaned from *Watch Mr. Wizard*, it further occurred to one of us that if you took some of our grandmother's Diamond kitchen matches, clipped off their heads, stuffed them into the cylinders as fuel, and added a thin piece of kerosene-soaked yarn as a fuse, you might have the makings of an actual working rocket. That is how adolescent male brains work.

But we realized that rockets need a launcher and guidance system, else they tend to go off helter-skelter, threatening all and sundry. When we looked around our only possible source of supply, our grandparents' basement, it appeared, though chock-full of tools and interesting junk, to be lamentably lacking in rocket guidance systems.

Until our glance fell upon a rusted, broken old tire pump, minus handle. The very thing! Why, if you dropped the cylinder down the pump barrel and pulled the fuse out the bottom you'd have a perfect rocket launcher. Or maybe a homemade mortar.

Realizing that what goes up must inevitably come down, we searched for something to protect our heads. It could come down on some other part of our anatomy, but who cared? Happily, two of our grandmother's mop pails turned out to be just our head size. Or maybe also a retired German helmet—are you satisfied, Ken?

So off we marched, Penrod and Sam, to the big flat area near the Loyalsock Creek known as the ball diamond. There we set up our pint-sized Pennemünde as visions of glory danced in our heads.

Surprisingly, it worked—two or three times. We propped the pump handle up in the sand, carefully placed the cylinder inside, pulled the fuse out along the ground, lighted it gingerly, and ran back as far and as fast as we could, plopping down on our stomachs with pails/helmet on heads and hoping for spectacular results.

Most of the time the fuse fizzled, or it worked but the rocket didn't launch, which resulted in one of us daring the other to go up and see what the problem was.

But sometimes, infrequently—*WHOOSH!* The cylinder rattled out of its launcher and soared magnificently into the wild blue yonder. We could even track it for part of its flight, and occasionally retrieve it, except when it came down in the Loyalsock. It never came down anywhere near our carefully protected crania.

Our budding careers as rocket scientists ended late one sunny afternoon when we were sitting on the front steps and painstakingly poking match heads into a cylinder with a six-penny nail. Our Uncle Clark, home from work, saw us and asked what we were doing. We told him, certain that he would praise our ingenuity.

"Don't you kids realize that's dangerous?" he said. "If you struck a spark and set that thing off in your hands, you could burn yourself bad. Or put your eye out."

Decades later, whenever I watch the marathon showing of *A Christmas Story* on the TBS cable channel and listen to Ralphie pleading for an Official Red Ryder Carbine-Action Two-Hundred-Shot Range Model Air Rifle for Christmas, my uncle's warning comes back to me and I know just how Ralphie felt.

§

The only running water was from a spring on a hill above the house. It ran by gravity into two sinks, one in each kitchen of the formerly two-family house. When the spring dried up, as it not infrequently did in the summer, there was no water, period. When that happened, we hauled drinking water in jugs and bottles and cans from the "cold spring" outside of town. Ken and I were pressed into hauling water for washing clothes, etc., from the Loyalsock that ran just below the house. There was no *hot* running water at any time. We got hot water by heating water on the coal-and-wood stove in the main kitchen, either in a pot or kettle on the top of the stove or in the built-in hot-water tank on its side. There was no plumbing, hence no indoor toilet or bathtub. To take a bath you brought a long galvanized tub into the kitchen and filled it with water heated on the stove—after having secured your privacy by warning everyone and blockaded all entrances to the kitchen. The wastewater from the sinks ran out of the house in pipes into a low, open ditch along the side of the house and into a larger pipe, from there to be absorbed into the soil. That was the theory. The toilet was a two-seater in a small weathered cabana a respectable distance from the house.

Garbage collection was equally primitive. There was none. We took our trash—food waste, cans, bottles, anything that wasn't burnable—and threw it over the bank of the creek below the house. Amazingly it did not seem to grow to monstrous proportions even after years of dumping. Maybe each year's addition was carried away in the spring by the rising waters of the season. I do not remember any rats. In the spring I liked to use the dump for target practice with my Daisy Red Ryder air rifle, probably much like Ralphie's. Plenty of glass jars and bottles were to hand to throw into the rushing waters to aim at. Sometimes I even hit one. That glass remained in shards on the creek bottom, joining the jagged, rusting tin cans that we and others had thrown in over the decades.

§

That was Lopez in the 1950s, a very small part of it. Lopez was such a big part of my life as a boy—later, too, for that matter—that I cannot tell it all in one chapter. It deserves a book of its own. Perhaps someday I shall write it.

"Until that time, Eustis," as Master Sergeant Slaughter was wont to say to Sergeant Clay in William Goldman's *Soldier in the Rain*, until that time this must suffice . . . .

§

No one is certain how Lopez came by its name unusual for a section of the state that rarely sees a Hispanic person even now. It began in the late nineteenth century—its founding, according to a sign at the town's entrance, was in 1876, conveniently one hundred years after the country's—as a lumber town. After the surrounding forests were denuded, it tried coal mining, a chief industry of many areas of Pennsylvania, especially eastern Pennsylvania, which has one of only two pockets of anthracite (hard coal) in the world. That didn't last long as a major source of employment (though coal mining continued to a certain extent until the 1950s), and Lopez has been on the decline since the 1920s. At its peak it could boast of more than one thousand inhabitants. Now it has no more than two hundred and no commercial activity to speak of.

Ken, who tracks family history more than anyone, thinks that our grandparents, James Lawrence Miller and Alice Amelia (Geist) Miller, came to Lopez around 1907. Where they came from we are not sure. It might have been from Wyalusing in Bradford County, little more than twenty miles away, where Lawrence's father, George P. Miller, had lived. (My grandfather signed his name J. Lawrence Miller and was generally known by his middle name or later more commonly by the nickname "Squire.") Or they might have come from Shickshinny in Luzerne County, slightly more distant, where they had met and married. The Rev. George P. Miller, who died in 1901, had been pastor of a Methodist church there, of which my grandmother's mother, Sarah E. Geist, was a member.

Whenever they came, they brought with them three or four of what would eventually be twelve children. In order of appearance in this world they were:

Ruth Rachel Miller
Aura Porter Miller
Keith Geist Miller
James Lawrence Miller Jr.
Mima Harriet Miller
Howard Leroy Miller
Robert Ambrose Miller
Gerald Christian Miller
Reed Bosworth Miller
Clark Elmer Miller
William Ellsworth Miller
Frances Alice Miller

We are certain that the first three were born elsewhere, and possibly James Lawrence Jr. also. The remaining eight were definitely born in Lopez. Twelve children, born from 1901 to 1925. Ouch, my poor grandmother!

Poor is the word, poor literally, figuratively, metaphorically, and any way you can imagine. It was hard enough to house and feed and clothe and keep afloat a family of fourteen in a one-lung town in the center of nowhere without adding the anchor of drink, which Grandpa did. It could not be said that he was the town drunk, for there were too many contestants for that title. But his drinking, probably to the point of alcoholism, kept the family in or near poverty for decades. Not all of the children were at home at the same time, of course. They tended to head off as soon as they could to find work, usually in Binghamton.

Grandpa wasn't a bum, a ne'er-do-well, a hopeless slacker. Even his sons, none of whom had a good word to say for him otherwise, admitted that he was a steady worker when he had work. Among his employment at various times were town postmaster and justice of the peace. The last post is what earned him the nickname "Squire." It was just that he tended to pour his earnings down his throat.

I have often wondered why he drank, other than an addiction is an addiction, if that's what he had. Also, he wasn't the only one. The Ken Burns series on Prohibition on PBS showed graphically how extensive the male saloon or drink culture was throughout the nation in the three decades around the turn of the twentieth century. The drink culture *was* strong in Lopez, not least among the large Russian and Slavic population. But I wonder if it wasn't frustration, not that that excuses it. He was said to be quite smart, interested in politics and history and literature. Perhaps he was a small-town intellectual frustrated by the smothering insularity and lack of opportunities in a small town and the burden of a large family—which, to be frank, he was responsible for continually enlarging.

No, that doesn't excuse it. Nothing does. And he may not have been a nice man generally. There are many stories. A telling one comes from Uncle Lawrence via Uncle Clark. (Lawrence, being his father's namesake, also was known by his middle name or as "Squire.") Lawrence was thirteen years older than his brother. Clark said that when they were grown men Lawrence told him about when he, Lawrence, was a small boy his father gave him a few cents to go buy two eggs for breakfast. Eggs were a treat in that household. Lawrence scampered off with the pennies in his hand and came back with the two eggs.

"And he got Mom to cook those two eggs and he ate them both himself!" Clark quoted Lawrence as saying. "What kind of a father was that?"

Clark had his own stories about his father. One, told many times, was that he came up to Clark one day and out of the blue informed him, "Remember, I'm your meal ticket." Clark, incredulous, asked me what he was supposed to make of that. "I was ten or eleven years old, for Pete's sake. What did he mean by that? What did he mean by *telling* me that?" Clark added that, if he *was* a meal ticket, it didn't buy many meals.

All of the children, on the other hand, worshipped their mother, to judge by the comments of those Ruth, my father, Lawrence, Mima, Reed, Clark, William, and Frances; the others I saw only infrequently. They deplored what she had had to put up with and marveled at how she was able to create a stable hom.

We grandkids worshipped her, too. She was wonderfully loving to what she called "kidlets" of any generation. When I had contracted some sort of scabrous infection—impetigo, most likely—that was all over me, even in embarrassing areas, she nonchalantly took me off to the side of the kitchen stove where no one could see and patiently daubed medication "down there."

I wonder, too, what kind of dynamics went on in that family to cause the children to shy from marriage and children of their own. Consider: Of the twelve children, only six of them married, and those six marriages produced but five children. Five from twelve: That's a family tree in reverse. Was it something they experienced in their family that made them want to have no part of marriage and children? Yet the aunts and uncles were always kind and generous to me and my cousins, with the exception of Lawrence, who tended toward grouchiness if not meanness.

Lawrence inherited something besides his name from his father. He too was basically a low-grade alkie. One night Ken and I, aged thirteen or fourteen, saw him laid out like a snoring cross underneath the apple tree next to the grandparental house, having been unable to make it up the path to the door after a night out on the tiles. In our ignorance of his habits we thought sleep must have overcome him like a bolt of lightning. Two other brothers, Howard and Robert, were also heavy drinkers. None of the four sisters drank at all.

The family lived here and there in the village, including on what was called The Flat (now Flat Street). In the mid-1930s, when I believe only Clark, Will, and Frances, and possibly Reed, were still living at home, my grandparents bought a two-family house on a dirt road off the left side of Route 487 that parallels the Loyalsock Creek. Now it is officially designated Millers Road, with a proper sign, but when I was a boy it had no name or sign though it had been called both Pond Avenue and Stony Brook Street. The former came from the "pond" or more accurately pool that had once been formed there by a small concrete dam, long since broken, built for use in logging. The latter name came from the fact that the dirt road was the former bed of the Stony Brook Railway, a small spur line used by loggers. You will not be surprised to learn that Loyalsock Creek, a sixty-four-mile-long tributary of the West Branch Susquehanna River, is a *very* stony brook. Its name is a corruption of an Indian word supposedly meaning "middle creek." Almost everything in Sullivan County is stony, when it's not rocky.

Where a poor family got the money to buy a house in the middle of the Great Depression is a mystery. The family's rural Republicanism was taken in with the country air. Grandpa was a Republican—it was what got him his short-term posts as j.p. and postmaster—probably because his family had been Republicans as far back as the party's founding. Decent people—i.e., Anglo-Saxons in a country village filled with eastern Europeans—weren't Democrats, whose city cousins might come storming out of their festering urban redoubts and take all they possessed. Not that it was much. For an extended period the Millers stayed above water thanks to New Deal-provided "relief" and apparently never twigged the irony, then or later. Except for Uncle Will. He realized it and it made him chuckle cryptically.

The place they bought was typical of houses in Lopez, thrown up quickly around the turn of the twentieth century to house workers in the lumber industry. Built over a cellar of stone walls, most were of plank construction—that is, they had no frame; their own boards, or planking, held them up. Many, like my grandparents', were two-family, with a kitchen, dining room, and living room on the first floor and three bedrooms on the second, all tiny. Each family had its own stairway up to the second floor. They were not intended to last; Clark always maintained that they had been built with green, or uncured, lumber. Yet many still stand, remodeled and fixed up over the decades.

Grandma and Grandpa knocked the house into a one-family by removing one stairway and expanding one kitchen and making other adjustments. Clark, a teenager, did a lot of the work. Nothing terribly fancy or expensive. It still had no central heating to fight the bitter winter cold that easily penetrated a structure with no proper insulation: Clapboard siding, then some less-than-useless sawdust "insulation," then planking, then wallpaper. That's what stood between the inhabitants and the elements.

In that house and in that village I spent, beginning in infancy, some of the pleasantest hours, days, and weeks of my youth.

Roger K. Miller

§

We had, quite literally, an Ol' Swimming Hole so classic that it could have been a model for a Norman Rockwell painting. The pond that I mentioned was gone, but a third of the broken dam was still standing, jutting out into the creek and creating a relatively deep and wide spot that was perfect for swimming. And the dam itself was perfect for jumping from. All just a two-minute run from the house. On really hot days it swarmed with kids from the town. In those days car tires had inner tubes, and there was always a much-patched inner tube lying around for floating on. But beware of the valve stems. They could scratch painfully! Ken, his sister Ruth, and I, though we shied away from playing with the townies, nevertheless spent hours there. Our eyes grew bloodshot from being in the water so long and our fingers looked like pale, elongated prunes.

(It's a fact, we did not play with the local kids. That was noticed. Almost sixty years later one of those former kids said to Nancy, learning that she was married to a Miller, that townspeople thought we were stuck up. That is not *strictly* true. The line was that we were there to be company for Grandma and Grandpa, not to play with townies. That was not true, either. The truth was that, in a family ethos redolent of evangelicalism, the worldly town kids, many of them Roman Catholic or Russian Orthodox, could be a bad influence; we might learn things we were better off not learning. I guess that is being stuck up, in a way.)

And we had Uncle Clark and Aunt Frances, both of whom would do things for us and with us. Did Ken and I want to build a doghouse for Clark's beagle Snubber from a plan we saw in *Popular Mechanics*? Clark helped us, using wood lying around in the capacious, dirt-floored cellar with its many tools from the last six or seven decades. Did we want to build a thirty-foot tower to nowhere and to no purpose simply because we had seen one in *Boys' Life* or somewhere? Off we trekked with Clark to the twelve acres he owned on Dutch Mountain Road to cut down trees and bolt them together to erect a tower at the edge of the road. Did we want to go fishing? Swimming? Make homemade root beer? Clark, Clark, Clark.

Frances enabled much of it. It was she who took Ruth and Ken and me to Lopez from Binghamton and back, usually in her own car, sometimes in the car of another Lopez native returning to his roots. Weekends, Thanksgiving, Christmas, other holidays, summer vacations—endlessly making that journey, sixty-five miles each way. Making it for us because,

The Chenango Kid

I am sure, she loved us and, single all her life, as was Clark, we may have been surrogate children. But making it for herself, too, for deep, unfathomable emotional and psychological reasons that pulled her from Binghamton where she worked back to her childhood home. Just as Clark for similar unfathomable reasons was never able, aside from a few years before and during World War II, to leave it. They were not a second mother and father, more like a much older, caring, sensible brother and sister whom, unlike real brothers and sisters, you had to respect, and did. Together they contributed to a golden, even indulged—but not exactly pampered—childhood.

§

I spent more time at Lopez than my cousins did. I began going there for extended periods at an earlier age than they and I usually remained there longer during each stay. For me Lopez was a refuge from a somewhat unstable existence in the city. What my mother couldn't do for me, Lopez and the Millers did. I think Ma realized that.

When I was nine or ten years old and there by myself, I slept in my grandparents' bedroom on the first floor because to be upstairs alone frightened me. I wasn't alone, as Clark's bedroom was there, but that apparently wasn't sufficient for a little weenie. So Grandma made up a bed for me on a horsehair divan that they must have brought with them from the nineteenth century. The damn thing was slippery as an eel and humped or rounded along its length, so that I slid around when I turned over and the covers slipped off. Usually I ended up sleeping in the "trough" created between the couch's center hump and the wall.

My grandparents used a kerosene lamp with the wick set low for a night light for when they had to get up and use the chamber pot. It sat in a chair designed for that purpose, probably also from the previous century. My God did that thing stink when the lid was off! Understandably, they kept it as far from themselves as possible, which unfortunately for me was across the room at the head of my bed. Hence my strong olfactory memories. Grandma tinkled and Grandpa dribbled.

Ken and I are, as I noted, only three months apart in age. He rarely loses a chance to remind me that I am ancient compared to him. For my part I like to remark, when I am introducing him to someone or he me, that we used to sleep together. It seems to make him uncomfortable.

Roger K. Miller

For several years, from about our twelfth through our sixteenth years, the essence of Lopez was Ken and Roger having Huck and Tom adventures (albeit dialed down a few notches from river rafting, spelunking, and consorting with a runaway slave). Ruth did not go to Lopez as much in part because there was no girl her age for company. Plus, Ken and I were not very nice to her. (Though I was a little nicer. Just ask Ruth.)

What did we do, other than endangering ourselves with homemade mini-rockets? Some of it was active pursuits, some of it was done to us, some of it—really, most of it—was simply the atmosphere and ambience of Lopez.

It must have been about the summer we were fourteen that Ken and I started to go prowling late at night. Since few restrictions were placed on us, we stayed up watching television or doing other things after everyone else had gone to bed. During the week there weren't many adults there, anyway—usually just Grandma, Clark, and Clark's older unmarried sister, our Aunt Aura.

Somehow it came into our heads that it would be fun to go prowling around after midnight, seeing what we could see. Chiefly it was the frisson of scariness involved in scampering about in the dark that animated us, for we never saw much. Frankly, there wasn't much to see in the town even when it was somewhat more active. We weren't Peeping Toms; we didn't peek into people's lighted windows. Our greatest thrill was hiding behind a monument on a hill that overlooked the Hotel Lopez, which was more tavern than hotel, across the road. We watched men come staggering out, the screen door slamming behind them, shout to each other, climb unsteadily into their cars and drive off drunkenly. Pretty exciting, eh?

Aunt Aura put an end to our midnight marauding. It upset her that we were sleeping till noon. Boys our age, she said, should be up early and out in the fresh air. So that was the end of that.

Aunt Aura was the very stereotype of a spinster and is, for me, another of the personality/psychological oddities of the insular and reclusive Miller family. She was then in her early fifties and had lived and worked in Binghamton with her sister Mima. But sometime before the Second World War, perhaps when Mima got married, she moved back to Lopez and there she stayed. She had no outside employment; she received a little money now and then from her brother Gerald, another unmarried sibling, who worked for a tire company in Connecticut. She was not an unpleasant person though her manner was a bit severe. Frances, who may secretly have envied Aura's having been able to come "back home" and hide away, used to praise what she called her "wisdom," but I can't see it. She died at home of breast cancer one subzero night in 1958.

"Exploring" is what we did. Around this same time we decided to poke around in the abandoned house next door. We didn't break in for it wasn't locked. No one had inhabited it for a couple of years, but it was still full of . . . junk. Well, to be fair, furnishings of a kind—the filthy kind. We went from one to room, turning over this and that—carefully—until we came to a bedroom for which "messy" would be a kind description. What caught our glance there was something bright red on the sagging bed. Closer—and careful—inspection revealed it to be a huge Nazi flag being used as a sheet or mattress cover.

Well, now, wasn't that something? We removed it and took it down to the creek and washed it thoroughly. Then we took it up to our back yard and hung it out on the line to dry.

The next week's issue of *The Sullivan Review*, the local weekly newspaper, contained a story about the puzzling display of a Nazi flag in Lopez. This was barely a decade after the end of the war. As far as I know no one ever interviewed anyone in the family about it, but that didn't stop the newspaper from speculating. Making an Olympics-class leap, the newspaper opined that it might have something to do with the next house up the road, also unoccupied, that once had been owned by a family with a German name.

The Geiger Counter Episode is probably more interesting for the fact that I had the instrument and why I had it than for anything Ken and I did with it. I had one because my father gave it to me and he gave it to me because he was the quirky person I described in Chapter 8. This was the 1950s, the flowering of the Atomic Age, and what do you need for an Atomic Age but uranium? That's what we'd heard. Uranium was the word of the decade. Uranium emits radiation and Geiger counters detect radiation, so Pa figured there could be a golden chance to get rich by hunting for uranium in the endless rocks of Sullivan County's Endless Mountains.

Neither he nor any adult ever went prospecting, but Ken and I did. Just the clicking of the scientific-looking device as it snooped for fortune-making uranium was enough to send us up into the hills above our grandparents' house. Unfortunately we did not know, or in our excitement did not pay heed if we did know, that *everything* emits radiation. So for a couple of days we scoured the woods and underbrush, passing the device over every stone, rock, boulder, and likely looking lump of earth and getting heart palpitations whenever the ticking grew faster.

Our efforts did not last any longer than our rocket-making or other enthusiasms. We never solved, or for that matter considered, the questions of what uranium looks like or what to do with it if found. But we were probably the only household in the county with its own Geiger counter. I had wanted a typewriter.

Like Kenneth Grahame's Ratty and Mole enjoying themselves "simply messing about in boats," we could always pass a pleasant day messing about the creek. Once we did try to go rafting. We built a raft of one-gallon oil cans and boards and tried to float it in the swimming hole. It sank, quickly if not immediately, because cans nailed into boards do not a watertight craft make. We had given no thought to the fact that in our part of the Loyalsock Creek in the summer it is impossible to boat or raft any farther than a hundred yards before running into impassable rocks or low water.

Another time, some sticks and boards cast off from a closed sawmill not far from the swimming hole looked to us as if they might be made into a "Humphreymobile." This was an odd little shack-on-a-tricycle pedaled by Joe Palooka's lovable, eccentric friend, the huge blacksmith Humphrey Pennyworth, in the *Joe Palooka* comic strip and comic books. We tabled the project early, having gotten no further than laying out some sticks on the ground, until chance might cause us to come across a cast-off tricycle.

We didn't have to do many chores. Besides running down to Ortleib's grocery store in town for the occasional item and hauling water, both from the cold spring and from the creek, we were supposed to help keep the woodbox on the small side porch filled with wood that Uncle Squire had split, but we honored that more in the breach than the observance.

Life was pretty safe as well as pleasant, but once real danger threw its shadow over our paradise. Clark had built a small cinderblock "cabin" on his property on Dutch Mountain Road. All three of us kids liked to drive up there with him just to be with him when he worked on projects and to run around in the woods.

Sometimes Clark reluctantly let a friend use the cabin when the friend had no other place to hole up, which was not infrequent as he was both work-shy and perennially short of money. He was a big fat fellow about Clark's age and when he showed up at the house he was tolerated if not exactly welcomed. But not admired. My grandfather, something of an artist in creating poisonous nicknames, referred to him as "Puss Guts." Clark referred to him as "Boomerang" because he just kept coming back. Grandma was nice to him; he was the son of a deceased woman friend of hers.

One night Ken and I were allowed to sleep overnight at the cabin. Boomerang stayed with us but for some reason Clark did not. It was chilly so they had built a coal fire in the fireplace.

Early in the morning Ken and I woke up deathly ill. Thank God we woke up or we would have been not ill, but dead. We stumbled outside and threw up, again and again. Coal gas had overcome us.

I do not know how we got back to our grandparents' house. Boomerang must have had a car; I remember throwing up from a car. When we got there Frances put us to bed upstairs with the windows wide open. Today we would have been taken to a hospital, but if it looked as if you were going to be all right, families didn't do that then, and the nearest small hospital was a forty-minute drive away.

Frances was livid. I can still see her standing four-square before Boomerang, eyes blazing.

"What in the world is the matter with you? Why didn't you get the boys out of there when you knew something was wrong? Weren't you sick?"

Boomerang was abashed. "But Frances. I didn't know. I just had a little gas, that's all. You know, burping."

By the end of the day we were back to normal.

§

That was a boy's Lopez, or part of it. But the whole of Lopez was more than the sum of its parts. The unspoken, unformulated rule seemed to be that you went there to be allowed to be something that you weren't where you came from. The whole was, as I said earlier in two unsatisfactory words, its atmosphere or ambience.

Lopez was the kitchen screen door slamming shut with a frightening bang. Clark said that when he was trying to take a nap he thought the spring must be connected directly to his bedsprings in his room above on the second floor.

Roger K. Miller

It was waking up in a frigid upstairs bedroom on an arctic weekend morning in January and, after pulling on clothes so hastily that they nearly tore, clattering down the wooden, uncarpeted stairs to the kitchen, hoping that the big wooden chair between the wall and the stove was unoccupied so that you could sit there on its thin, tattered cushions, wrapped in a shawl or a blanket, as warm as the toast that you soon would make in the ancient, two-slice toaster with flop-down sides that had toasted its first slice of bread about the time Warren G. Harding first took Nan Britton into a White House closet to give her a squeeze to see what it might lead to.

It was, along with the other lacks, the lack of refrigeration, which meant that we rarely had fresh milk. Hence we kids mixed sugar into Pet or Carnation condensed milk as a very imperfect substitute to pour over our cereal, which more often than not was Nabisco shredded wheat. They came twelve to a box, four layers of three each, with pieces of gray cardboard separating the layers. On the cardboard was printed "secrets of Indian lore and knowhow" offered by Straight Arrow, a fictional Indian character from radio, comic books, and comic strip. With our shredded wheat we could have Postum, a beverage made from grain that we pretended was our coffee.

Lopez was the amber-colored flypaper hanging in the kitchen, thick with flies. Grandpa once offered me a penny for each fly I killed with a swatter. It was the excitement of ordering items from the big thick Sears, Roebuck catalog and waiting impatiently for them to arrive in the mail. It was a crowd of family and friends lounging around on the porch on a warm summer night, talking and listening to the talk with the squeak of the porch swing as a backdrop and fireflies blinking, blinking, blinking out there in the dark. It was sitting on the ratty old rug in the living room, taking the 78 rpm records from the 1930s, '40s, and '50s out of their paper slipcases and playing them over and over—Burl Ives, the Mills Brothers, Bing Crosby, Margaret Whiting.

Lopez was all that and so much more that it can be contained only in a book of its own. And most of all, most piercing of all, it was Christmas. That is another thing Ma had no problem with. She let me have Christmas in Lopez. Not that she and I did not get into a Christmas spirit at home. We always had a Christmas tree. There were tree lots within easy walking distance and we both went to pick one out, making the choice by weighing the relative beauty of the trees against what she could afford to spend. I lugged it home, usually ending up after my arms got tired by dragging it by the tip and with the end of the trunk scraping the ground. Once set up she arranged a small scene underneath, using a mirror to represent ice for tiny figures to skate upon. A sheet sprinkled with glitter did its best to mask the fakery. As I got into my middle teens I felt bad about that, abandoning my mother at Christmas. But Christmas at Lopez was just too nice.

There are many many many descriptions in literature of warm, pleasant, happy Christmas celebrations. One I have retained ever since I first came across it is in, of all unlikely places, Sinclair Lewis's *Main Street*. Carol Kennicott is reminiscing:

> *"She remembered her father's Christmas fantasies: the sacred old rag doll at the top of the tree, the score of cheap presents, the punch and carols, the roasted chestnuts by the fire, and the gravity with which the judge opened the children's scrawly notes and took cognizance of demands for sled-rides, for opinions upon the existence of Santa Claus. She remembered him reading out a long indictment of himself for being a sentimentalist, against the peace and dignity of the State of Minnesota."*

That is a far cry from the abundance, the coziness, the thickness, the contrasting dark and light heralded in *A Christmas Carol* by the master of Christmas, Charles Dickens, but I like it for the element of American rusticity that, eighty years on from Carol Kennicott's childhood, we experienced at Lopez.

And so we all bundled into, not sleighs, but cars and headed south from Upstate New York to go over the river and through the woods to grandmother's house for Christmas. Which Frances and Clark did so much to make. Clark cut the tree and always got a beautiful, perfectly proportioned one. Frances trimmed it—the most admired ornaments were glass candles filled with bubbling colored fluid—and did most of everything else. She got Clark and Will to pony up for gifts for Ruth and Ken and me, which she bought and wrapped. She was careful to get the very same thing, or things of equal cost, for Ken and me so there could be no complaining. That was not difficult in our mid-to-later teens, for we wanted additions to our train sets. We kept them at Lopez and set them up only at Christmas, combining the two into one large layout that put a strain on the house's ancient and overtaxed electric wiring. The wall socket looked like the octopus of wiring in the movie *A Christmas Story*, though without the sparks and smoke.

Soon the sun would set and we would gather together, in and near the living room, perhaps to watch our one television channel, whose weak signal brought us snow to match that whipping around outside. Perhaps to listen to Christmas programs on the radio; in my younger years Lionel Barrymore was still playing Scrooge. Or perhaps just to talk, or listen to grown-ups talk, and try to figure out just what was meant by what was being said, or—more significantly—not being said.

And then, still later, to bed, up the creaking stairs, with the night dark and the wind whistling and the unseen snow still falling. To listen, in the intervals of silence, to the night that had the power—which we had given it—to be the most magical night of the year.

CHAPTER 15

North High

"The life of every man is a diary in which he means to write one story, and writes another, and his humblest hour is when he compares the volume as it is with what he vowed to make it."

—J.M. Barrie

New York Mayor Jimmy Walker said no girl had ever been ruined by a book. Maybe not, but I can say I was made by one, for what that has been worth.

In tenth grade I was drifting along, never thinking I'd go to college because who had the money even if he had been encouraged to do so, which he had not? But I happened to read *Onionhead*, a relatively new novel by Weldon Hill, about a guy in the U.S. Coast Guard in World War II. (A couple of years later it was made into a mediocre movie with Andy Griffith.) So taken was I with the book's story that I investigated the Coast Guard and discovered you could get into the Coast Guard Academy without a congressional appointment (unlike the other military academies). I thought, hey, maybe even a kid with no political pull or money might have a shot at that, a free education. So I started taking college-prep courses. And by the time I graduated from North High I was mostly ready, academically, for college, though I never did apply to the academy. After the academic abortion I made of my artistic aspirations, I went instead to Harpur College, the state liberal arts college in my hometown, which was being beefed up by money being thrown at it by that profligate Republican, Governor Nelson A. Rockefeller, thus making it possible for poor boys and girls to get a college education. Something we no longer bother to do, but that's another story.

Some thirty years later, when I was book-review editor of the late and much-lamented *Milwaukee Journal*, I re-read the novel and looked up the author—part of that curiosity about authors' lives I mentioned earlier—and found that his real name was William R. Scott and he was living in his native Oklahoma. I called him up and thanked him. For the novel and for what it did.

Well, I digress, which is pretty much what I have done throughout my life. The question at hand, the one I raised in the chapter on East Junior, is, "Is there life after high school?" The answer is, I'm not sure. I tend to think rather of an *afterlife* after high school because most of us become so dead to the excitements of life once we are out in the real world. Some—many, actually—are dead even while in school and too bad for them. Most of us, though, live so intensely then, before we are out of our teens, we experience things so sharply and fully. Everything is brighter, clearer, more vivid. Every incident impresses itself on us strongly, so that the ones we remember a half-century later seem as if they must have been a constant part of our life, whereas they may have occurred but once or twice. But it does not matter how often they happened or even whether we remember them. They formed us so completely and in a way that few experiences, outside of military combat, can do.

Or maybe it's just me. I *liked* high school, had fun there. Many people, I have found, did not. My wife Nancy did not. My son Ian did not, and daughters Krista and Jennifer were not sorry to see twelfth grade come to an end, I believe. Still others are indifferent about the experience. But me, I liked high school.

Yet when I look at the photos of the members of my class in my copy of the 1959 *Wampum* I am struck by how few of the kids I knew. And how fewer still could be called my friends or even close acquaintances. Sometimes in looking at the photos my heart aches with knowledge of all the potential that will come to nothing, all the hopes that will go smash.

§

Truth to tell, just as I like to think that, as it says in the Western spoof *Red Garters*, life should be more like the movies, I also like to think that high school should be more like Dobie Gillis'. That is, the Dobie Gillis portrayed by Dwayne Hickman on television, not the Dobie Gillis that Max Shulman originally wrote about in his books and not Bobby Van's Dobie Gillis of the 1953 movie *The Affairs of Dobie Gillis*. You rang, good buddy?

These days if there were a storm day like the one I depicted in my prelude, nervous school authorities with an ear to television's nonstop warnings of impending doom would have canceled classes two days earlier. I do not remember school ever being called because of snow and, as we know, winters in the past have always been harsher than the ones currently being endured.

If such a day were forecast it would have been on the radio. Local television news wasn't up to doing that. In our incredibly small apartment at 82 Walnut Street the radio sat on a wobbly, oilcloth-covered shelf above the toaster in our unbelievably small kitchen. The kitchen could not have been larger than five feet by five feet. Each winter morning when I got up after Ma had gone to work I turned the radio on and listened to the morning weather roundup, which invariably reported that Boonville was the coldest spot in the entire Empire State. No matter how fierce the storm or wet the day I did not wear boots or galoshes because they were dorky. Nor did I carry my books and other school materials in a briefcase or backpack because ditto. Guys walked along carrying their books canted upon their hip by one hand; girls carried theirs cradled in front of their breasts or propped on the soft bulge of their upper stomachs with one hand or both hands. Girls might possibly carry their books on their hips, but for guys to cradle their books in front of their chest was one of the many things that were seen as *queer*. Wearing yellow on Thursday, for instance, was definitely queer.

§

Binghamton North High School on East Frederick Street on the corner with Moeller Street was, like its crosstown rival, the much older Central High School on Main Street, a three-year institution: grades ten, eleven, and twelve. It opened in 1937 to accommodate the city's expanding population and closed in 1982 as a result of its declining population. Thus my graduating class of June 1959—there were two graduating classes each year, January and June—was almost exactly in the middle of its history as a high school. The three-story building, refurbished and remodeled, is now East Middle School.

Before Ma and I moved to 82 Walnut Street on the West Side, the way I got myself to North High each day was via shank's mare. It was not a short walk, even when I went directly there from 250 Chenango. But normally I didn't. Nearly every morning I walked north up Chenango to my friend Paul's house on Moffatt Avenue where I met three other friends—Tom, Bob, and Bill—who gathered there from their homes on neighboring streets. As I think back on it, it must have been like a scene from *Leave It to Beaver*, with each of us arriving separately, ringing the doorbell and saying "hi" or "good morning" to his mother and she being very patient with all of us, day after day. In fact, Paul had a younger brother who was sort of a Beaver to Paul's Wally and whom we treated with the amused tolerance of lordly high schoolers. From there the five of us continued on, crossing the railroad tracks to school. It was a pleasant walk, talking about this and that. On Fridays the talk probably concerned the previous evening's episode of *The Real McCoys*—the earlier and better and nicer imagining of the notion of West Virginia hillbillies moving to California than *The Beverly Hillbillies*—which all of us liked. It might have had something to do with Richard Crenna, recently sprung from his role as high schooler Walter Denton on *Our Miss Brooks*, but probably more to do with pretty Kathleen Nolan, who played Crenna's wife on *McCoys*.

After we moved to Walnut Street it was too far to walk to North, twice the distance as before. I cannot remember when we moved there from 250 Chenango, but it likely was in the summer of 1958, as I have no recollection of attending twelfth grade from that address. It was an odd, small apartment. In addition to that tiny kitchen, it consisted of a small living room, where Ma slept on a fold-out couch, and a small bathroom with octagonal tiles on the floor like in a public toilet, and, across a public hall by which other residents got to their apartments, a bedroom, where I slept. That meant that I had to cross the hall to get to the bathroom or watch television or do anything else. Ma must have gotten that place cheap to put up with such an inconvenient arrangement.

Why I was allowed to continue attending a school outside my district, as I also had been allowed in fourth grade, I do not know. But I am glad I was, as twelfth grade in Central would have been difficult to endure.

So I rode to school. I either took a bus—students could buy reduced-price tokens from the school office—or I got a ride with my math teacher, Mr. McGinnis, who lived right around the corner on North Street. Infrequently I was given a ride by a schoolmate who would take the trouble to swing over my way from his home on the North Side—what was his name? He had thick eyeglasses, making his eyes look enormous—but mostly it was either the city bus or Mr. McGinnis.

When I took the bus I usually saw my cousin Ken. He attended North instead of Central, to which he should have gone, because he took a technical-electrical course that was not offered at Central. Many of his classes were held in the basement, the "Dungeon," along with technical-mechanical classes and vocational machine and auto shop and other "practical" or vocational subjects. Curious, that: When they laid out the school did they think, guided by hoary tradition, that such subjects did not belong up in the light with established academic subjects? The necessities of sound abatement and accessibility required some classes, such as auto, to be held down there, but drafting?

When I rode with Mr. McGinnis it was in his new, black Cadillac. As we went past St. Paul's Church near the corner of Chenango and Robinson he nodded his head ever so slightly and tugged respectfully on the front of the narrow brim of his fedora in lieu of crossing himself.

§

Mr. McGinnis—James J. or J.J. or Jim McGinnis—chuckled. He was a cheerful little paunchy Irishman and one of my favorite teachers. Favorite because he was an excellent teacher who could make an art-absorbed, mathematics-resistant adolescent male understand geometry and trigonometry and, moreover, enjoy the subjects and feel good about doing well in them. He chuckled winningly when he saw the light of understanding go on over a puzzled student's head. When he did not chuckle, when something had happened to arouse opposite emotions in him, you could tell it from the little gray cloud that formed on his forehead like that which Van Wyck Brooks said used to gather on the brow of Daniel Webster when he had his moods of God-Almightiness. I swear tiny lightning bolts flashed inside the cloud.

He chuckled once at seeing me with my arm around the waist of a girl in the hallway. Public Displays of Affection were little tolerated in schools during that Pleistocene Era, and when I realized he was behind me I looked back in alarm and pulled my arm away as if I had received an electric shock. That's when he chuckled—and said "I approve." That was a stunner, but I understood that he was expressing approval not of the Public Display of Affection, necessarily, but of the two particular young people who were being affectionate—and of my good sense in dropping the Public Display once caught in the act.

A nice man. Word was he had family money. There was the Cadillac, after all, which was not the usual automobile of public school teachers. If so, he may have gone into teaching because of the summers off. And, if so, both he and education gained. I believe he died relatively young. I see that he is not in the 1960 *Wampum*. Or maybe he just moved on. In his Cadillac.

Another math teacher was not so nice, either as a person or an educator. She taught algebra as if it was something to which she had been sentenced and we had to share the punishment. Word about her, a woman crowding sixty, was that she took excessive dancing lessons from the Arthur Murray studio.

My favorite teacher, since she taught English, was Genevieve Heffron, mentioned in the prelude. At the end of eleventh grade I was assigned to her twelfth-grade Honors English class. Perhaps I was asked if I wanted to be in it or perhaps I was just automatically assigned to it. If the former I surely must have said "yes," for it meant lots of reading, and lots of reading is what I did. Those of us assigned to the class received a recommended reading list for the preceding summer, titles like *The Great Gatsby* and *Main Street* and *Nostromo*. I did my best to get through it. The book that left the biggest impression on me was *Main Street*. Though it depicted an America then fifty years in the past, that depiction struck me as exactly the way things were: oafish people living a dysfunctional existence. Sinclair Lewis holds a high place in my estimation, if not in that of the professoriate. Though God knows what is going on in the minds and halls of university English departments in these benighted times.

Those departments would be better served were they headed by pedagogues the likes of Genevieve Heffron, an inspiring teacher who was North's English Department chairman. I can see her now, matronly and pretty and not quite plump, talking and intermittently chewing on the temples of her pale-gray-framed glasses. She was clever—clever and tired-looking and sad of face. Now and then she uttered a mild sarcasm directed at our lives and we sat in glazed attention, not understanding this latest shaft from a spinster of that long line of spinsters (which is an honorable estate) who corrected the grammar and behavior of the young and thereby helped make the Republic great. She smiled indulgently and chewed a bit more thoughtfully on her glasses before continuing with the lesson.

We read things that were unusual for an American high school of the time, Maxwell Anderson's *Winterset* and Henrik Ibsen's *Hedda Gabler*. She was inspiring. Even as a callow clod I caught some of the subtleties of her personality and teaching manner. She seemed both dedicated to coaxing some understanding into our heads and amused by our resistance to her efforts. I did not read Grace Metalious' 1956 novel *Peyton Place* until years later, but when I did and came upon the character Miss Elsie Thornton, a tired, dedicated teacher at Peyton Place School, I thought immediately of Miss Heffron. Miss Thornton muses while regarding her young charges, "What chance have any of these children to break out of the pattern in which they were born?" Miss Heffron, asking a pertinent question, would chew on the temple of her glasses and look at us askance, one eyebrow cocked, as if to say, "Well? Will anyone get it?"

Mostly we did not get it. We read *Macbeth* and when we got to "a tale/Told by an idiot, full of sound and fury,/Signifying nothing," she stopped and asked us what we thought that meant. Our blank stares indicating to her that none of us had a clue, she went on, wide-eyed, as if she herself could not believe that any writer would have the audacity to say what she was about to suggest he was saying: "Is he saying that God is an idiot and that his entire creation is just a lot of noise and violence that makes no sense?"

If you say so, Miss Heffron. I tried. I loved the class and was surprised, though I should not have been, to learn that others did not. They resented it, which makes me think we were assigned to the class whether we wanted to be there or not. A boy named Jerry, who sat in front of me and was the son of a man who grew up in Lopez with my father, turned around one day and said he wished he wasn't in the class because it was harder to get an A than in a regular English class. That was the problem: He and the many others who were planning to go to college wanted a good grade on their high school transcripts and to hell with the honor of Honors English. I simply gloried in the reading and did not worry about the grade—I knew I would pass the course OK—since any college plans I had were amorphous at best.

Roger K. Miller

That fall after I had gone to work as at the bank I stopped in at North to see her on my lunch hour. I guess I thought she would be pleased to see me, one of her most eager students. It took a moment or two for her to realize that I was introducing myself as a former student, one of quite recent vintage. I did not seem to make a great impression.

The only other teacher I had for English I had for both tenth and eleventh grades. Let us call her Lizzie, as in Borden. Lizzie was the polar opposite of Miss Heffron in both personality and pedagogy. She let her class know more than once, when she suspected that we were inclined to undervalue her attainments, that she was an "expert in her field," meaning that she had a master's degree. Some of us guys thought that she was, rather, not so much a master as a mistress—of the football team, because she seemed to fawn over the football players particularly and not for their knowledge of Eng Lit. I do not recall nearly as much about her in two years as I do about Miss Heffron in one and I did not seek her out on that day I paid a visit to my alma mater.

A history teacher, Mr. Lalley, demonstrated to me if not to anyone else in class the educative value of personal witness. Attempting to shake us children of relative privilege out of our apathy, he told a story to illustrate the awfulness of the Great Depression. Out of work himself in those years, he was walking along a city street one day when he saw a small crowd at a doorway encircling a man on the ground who proved to be dead. Only later, he said, did he learn that the man had died of starvation.

There was a French club so French must have been taught, though no French teacher comes to mind. Otherwise, the only foreign languages taught at North were Latin and German. I wish I could be sure of the name of my first German teacher, a little old lady in my memory. Mrs. Whitman, I believe, Margaret Whitman. Probably she was a little old lady only in the eyes of a fifteen-year-old. She had German sayings written in Gothic script on little yellowing placards—probably she had had them made back when she was a young, new teacher, long before Hitler had given the German language a bad name—high on the walls around the room. *Übung macht den Meister* ("practice makes perfect") was one. She liked to have us sing German folk songs.

We read about Nathan der Weise (Nathan the Wise) in our textbook and about Emil und die detectives in the classic Erich Kästner children's novel of that title (*Emil und die Detektive*). To this day Kästner remains one of my favorite German authors. She had an innocent enthusiasm for the language that she wished to impart to us, but, as with Miss Heffron and English, we were reluctant to receive. The most reluctant was a snotty German kid, presumably the son of immigrant parents, who refused to take part in anything, though she practically begged him to because his German pronunciation was perfect. Besides affecting a sullen truculence, he did not want to comply. I think it must have been because it emphasized his German-ness and he wanted to be an American teenager.

I had her for only tenth grade, then Mr. Sprenger, Rudy Sprenger, for eleventh and twelfth. Originally he taught history, but took over German when something happened—either retirement or death—to the little old lady. Mr. Sprenger spit as he talked—we kids spoke about getting our daily shower in his class—but otherwise was a decent enough guy. He did not always have perfect control of the classroom, but by the third year of the language we were a small, select group and not inclined to give him a hard time. One year he was coach of the tennis team, which shows his status, in that tennis had no status as a high school sport at the time.

Officially my high school course was Academic-Art. This meant that, while I specialized in what were considered, in the popular mind and probably in the educational administration, "puff" or "pipe" classes, I also took traditional academic subjects like history and English. Mrs. Adelaide Walker was my art teacher for, it must have been, all three years. The art room—two or maybe three normal-size rooms converted into one long room—was on the third floor, not far from the doors that led into the cafeteria. Mrs. Walker was a nice person and a helpful, capable teacher with, I believe, some talent of her own.

She encouraged us in inventiveness and creativity. We did all sorts of things: drawing with pen, pencil, and pastel chalks; drawing live models (students who volunteered to sit for us—clothed); woodcuts; sculpting in clay; firing items in the kiln (I made cufflinks). Once she had us design book jackets; take a favorite book and come up with your own idea of how its contents should be packaged. My passion was pen and ink drawing, especially cartooning. Each student had a large portfolio folder that was kept in a cupboard at the front of the room. On mine I wrote in my best Zaner-Bloser cursive, "Roger Miller Boy Wonder." Mrs. Walker reacted with wry amusement when she saw it. I still have that portfolio and its half-century-old contents.

It is odd, but I do not remember a boy named Jeff being in any of my art classes, but he must have been because he was active in many kinds of artistic activities. It could be that his art classes were at different times of the day. I should say that he was active in many kinds of activities, period, for he was quite popular and very much in the social swim, whereas I was not. There the difficulty may lie: Lingering jealousy that caused me to blot him out of my mind, for there was an unspoken rivalry between us as artists. My social obscurity notwithstanding, I was voted Class Artist. But the joke was on both of us, for the true artist was a shy young man named Joe, who came to North High late, perhaps in the twelfth grade. Quietly he worked away at his paintings in art class with a talent and facility neither of us could touch. I met Joe again at the only North High class reunion I ever went to, the thirty-fifth, and learned that he had gone on to a successful career in advertising and was still a painter.

No, they weren't puff courses to me, little though I made of them in later life. But they were to a guy, older than us, who sat there accumulating graduation credits while doing the absolute minimum, and that truculently. He had quit school some time before after getting his girlfriend pregnant and, realizing his error, had come back to get enough credits for a diploma. He ignored us and we him, because we didn't want to catch what he had, and so did Mrs. Walker, though with some indignation at having to accommodate what he represented.

§

I always have thought it would be neat to take a canoe trip down the Susquehanna River, but I never have done it—except for a little bit in tenth or eleventh grade in a nutty stunt undertaken by me and a North High friend that had a high potential for danger.

The potential arose right at the start in that we had no firm plan for what we were doing. Evidence of this is that we did it in the fall when it was chilly if not cold. It may even have been close to or in November. If we had a goal, a town or place on the river that we wanted to reach, I have forgotten it. Maybe, in the grand, unthought-out schemes of youth, it was the home of my Great-Aunt Frances, my grandmother's sister, in Shickshinny, Pennsylvania, which lies on the banks of the Susquehanna. Trouble is, it lies there about hundred miles from Binghamton. Great-Aunt Frances' probably was not our goal, but why it occurs to me as a possibility is that it was the goal of another expedition that I thought would be neat. This, which I had broached a couple of times to Ken, was to bicycle from

Binghamton, or perhaps from Lopez, to Shickshinny—on our balloon-tire, single-speed, coaster-braked, totally unsuitable Roadmaster and J.C. Higgins bikes. I think we must never have broached the expedition to the Miller family; if we had they would have scotched it instanter as being not neat at all, but idiotic. As for Great-Aunt Frances, had I turned up on her doorstep via either canoe or bicycle, not only would she have been startled, she would have had great difficulty recalling who I was—the little shaver brought to her house many years ago by her niece, my Aunt Frances. We were kin but not at all close. She simply happened to live on the only town on the Susquehanna I could think of besides Binghamton.

We launched the canoe—it must have been his; I certainly did not have one—one morning into the chilly waters of the Chenango River somewhere near his house around Moffatt Avenue. I think the trip was fairly incident-free until we reached the confluence with the Susquehanna near Front Street and Riverside Drive. We had to portage or wrestle the canoe past low areas, which got our feet and legs wet. Then it began to rain, which got the rest of us wet—and our gear. Then it began to get colder as the day wore on, but not cold enough to snow. It just continued to rain. It amazes me now to think that we pressed on till we reached Endicott. Details of our misery have evaporated with time, but I am sure the point at which we finally gave up and found a pay phone was at or near Union-Endicott High School. He called his house and someone—it may have been his brother—came and picked us up. We were thoroughly chilled and bedraggled. They dropped me off at the Van Horn apartment on their way up Chenango Street to their house. Ma was shocked at my appearance. I must have looked unwell; I definitely felt that way, aching and feverish. I went to bed immediately and slept into late morning the next day.

This incident causes me to think of the arbitrariness and randomness of memory's selectivity. I remember when I last saw this high school friend. Whole swaths of larger events in my life have slipped the moorings of my memory, but this picayune detail of a young man who was not even one of my closest friends remains firmly lodged. It was in 1959 or 1960 when I was working at the bank. Going about my duties as messenger one day, I came upon him sitting in a chair outside one of the offices. I stopped to talk to him. He was there to see about a student loan to attend the State University of New York at Albany. We exchanged a couple more mundane nothings and with that he was out of my life forever.

Roger K. Miller

Why do I retain memories of this and other commonplace, forgettable occurrences, the kind that happen to everybody every day? Was there something in this particular meeting that to me was anything but ordinary and routine? Was it because he was going on to college and I was stuck in a nothing job (which, actually, was a better job than most for someone just out of high school)? Jealousy, in other words? My plan was to go to college, but in my heart of hearts was I fearful that it would never happen? (Just another of my many fears?) I have always been weirdly impatient; I am anxious to have proposed actions happen *now*, a few seconds after they have been proposed. For instance, the moment I decided to write this book, I wanted it to be finished the next moment. This is a totally impossible and crazy way to think and one I have managed to get over—somewhat—in old age. Maybe what's Coming Next—the Big Sleep, the Long Dirt Nap—is something I am not so eager to have happen *now*. Or the next moment.

§

My joined-at-the-hip buddy Bill and I made a trip to Endicott that was less perilous than the river venture but the equal in ordinariness to my last meeting with my canoeing friend, so naturally I remember it.

The trip had to do with our latest interest, shortwave radio and ham radio. Bill and I were what you might characterize as being in the Boy Scouts but not of it, in that we went to meetings and to activities sporadically but made few attempts to advance in its ranks. Well, Bill did more than I. But there may have been a merit badge or two available in our radio enthusiasm, which in my case had been sparked by Ma having bought me a Silvertone shortwave radio for my birthday—after much nagging by me.

In any case, Bill learned that elements of ham radio were being taught in a night course at IBM in Endicott, where his father worked. We went and about all that I remember of it is that it was taught by a black guy. What, IBM employed black guys? Apparently, as long as they wore white shirts. Bill I think was as surprised as I. I am sure we both tried to act as if it was the most normal thing in the world of 1956 or 1957, and I am equally sure we were not successful. That is the only session we went to, not because of the black guy but because the requirements of ham radio, such as learning Morse code, were too irksome. I have forgotten how we

The Chenango Kid

got to the class, but not how we got home: We walked—probably along Main Street through Endicott, somehow along the Route 17 highway, through Johnson City, into Binghamton, crossing Court Street bridge, through Binghamton, and north on Chenango. I estimate about eight miles to my house, and then Bill had about another mile to his. Not the equivalent of crossing the Sahara without water or head coverings, but it does demonstrate what fifteen- or sixteen-year-old boys were safe in doing on their own at night in the misnamed Boring Decade.

What else did we do, I and my little band of step-brothers—Bill, Tom, Paul, Bob, Jerry, and Don—as we went through our schooldays and weekends? Occasionally movies were shown in the auditorium during the lunch hour, each movie shown in segments over several days. That is where I first saw Lucille Ball and Desi Arnaz in *The Long, Long Trailer*. Adapted (very loosely) from a book, it was made to cash in on Lucy and Desi's television popularity and has long been one of my favorite movies.

We laughed at every new instance of comically intense policing by Officer Moss, known to students everywhere as "Mossy," a Binghamton policeman who seemed to suspect crime going on everywhere at all times, particularly around schools. Perhaps he was right. Deputy Barney Fife of *The Andy Griffith Show* had not yet been created, but if he had and he and Mossy had met, they would have recognized each other as soul mates. A friend tells me about an incident one morning when her father and mother drove her to school. Stopped at the red light at Chenango and Robinson, they were startled when from out of nowhere Mossy jumped on the running board of their car and ordered them to run the red light and chase another car up Robinson Street. She doesn't remember if they caught the miscreant, or what his crime was, but it made her late for school.

We tried to be cool in our dress according to the day's fashion. White bucks or penny loafers or "desert boots" on our feet, khaki pants with a useless little cloth belt just above the butt, which it was *de rigueur* to leave unbuckled and dangling. Sometimes pants pegged at the cuffs, but they were favored more by guys with D.A. ("duck's ass") haircuts, which were kind of hoody. Our hair styles ran more to brush or crew cuts or, more often, the "Princeton," a neat, preppie look. The ensemble could be topped off with an open-collar, button-up shirt underneath a cloth, button-up sweater vest that was left unbuttoned. I had a black one with red trim. We didn't walk with girls, but if we did they most likely would be wearing saddle shoes or penny loafers and a dress that flared slightly or a skirt neither too tight nor too short. Poodle skirts were nowhere near as common as contemporary evocations of the Fifties would have you believe. I confess that, while I defend young persons' right to wear whatever they want or their parents will allow, I prefer the more restrained look of my generation.

Tom and I went to home football games on Saturdays. On Friday before the game the halls were clamorous with excited students scurrying along, ostentatiously dangling from purse or belt or shirt button their tickets for the next day's game. I knew nothing and cared less about football. In fact, I would like to see high school football outlawed for the deleterious effects it has on not-fully-developed young male bodies and for the fraud it perpetuates about team spirit. But it was exciting going to the games amid cheerful crowds in the field behind North with the sky a dazzling bright blue and the air crisp and cold and the cheerleaders cute in their little red-and-blue uniforms, urging us to fight fight fight for dear old North High:

> *You take a leg from some old Indian,*
> *You take an arm from some old squaw,*
> *You take a head from some old totem pole,*
> *And from a tepee take some straw*
> *You take some straw.*
> *And then you put them all to-ge-eh-ther*
> *And with the aid of the Red and Blue-oo-oo*
> *You'll get more fight from the North High boys*
> *Than we'll ever get from you!*

Or something like that, though I assume that particular cheer was for the edification of the Other Side. How very un-PC of us—Indians, squaws. Basketball games were less of a rush, but I went to them with Tom nonetheless.

I did drawings and cartoons for the school newspaper, the *North Star*. I was not *part* of the *North Star*, not part of the staff in that I never got together with others to work on it. I simply submitted the drawings and many of them were published. I also drew covers for the football-game programs. Once I asked Mr. Brennan, the boys' counselor, who had commented favorably on one of my covers, if for an upcoming game it would be all right to do a cover with caricatures of the North coach, Mr. Reutlinger, and the opposing coach. "Caricatures?" he queried. After some verbal stumbling by the two of us I realized he did not know what "caricature" meant. I did not push it further. I wish I had one of those covers now. I liked doing them. I do have several copies of the *North Star*.

In tenth grade I joined with other kids, including Jeff, in painting ghosts and goblins and pumpkins on the Fair Store windows facing Wall Street for Halloween. It was fun, and cold and refreshing, but, as so often, I felt a fraud, an outsider who did not belong with this group.

Almost every marking period I took home a short note from Mr. Brennan congratulating my mother on having a boy who had maintained a "B" average or better for the marking period. It amazes me now that they were individually typed, meaning that his poor secretary had to type dozens of them—sixty-six, it said, in one note that Ma preserved—and their envelopes to the parents. This was long before computers or even programmable typewriters. One of sixty-six out of several hundred boys. Compare that with today, when school administrators, being absurdly inclusive in an attempt not to offend, publicize honor rolls so large that it would make more sense to list those few who did *not* make the roll.

On November 10, 1958, I received a note inviting me to become a member of Ihikona Chapter of the National Honor Society, signed by Alice Fasold, secretary. Subsequently I was given a membership card from the National Honor Society of Secondary Schools, signed by George S. Tate, principal, and Paul E. Elicker, society secretary. I did become a member at a solemn ceremony attended by my mother.

In twelfth grade a kid sitting in the next aisle across from me in one of my classes wanted to go fight for Fidel Castro. He asked me to draw a picture of a Castro camp (from my imagination), which I did and he was pleased. He was a big burly guy and not one of the school's leading scholars, though he liked Kenneth Roberts' *Northwest Passage* because that's what a wanted to be like, one of Robert Rogers' Rangers. I believe he went on to join the U.S. Marines.

That was when Castro was considered a freedom fighter. His revolution to oust the U.S.-aligned dictator Fulgencio Batista from power in Cuba penetrated even teenage brains, but it was not an event that invoked actual discussions, in classrooms and sometimes outside, the way three others did.

Roger K. Miller

The biggest event overall can be stated in one word: Sputnik. When the Soviets launched their 183-pound, basketball-sized aluminum satellite—the first artificial satellite to be sent into Earth orbit—on October 4, 1957, it rocked the country and the world all out of proportion to its modest size. Immediately we heard and debated questions about "how had America fallen behind" and "what is wrong with American education?" Changes in education and federal spending came thick and fast. The most immediate reaction came less than four months later, on January 31, 1958, with the launching of Explorer 1, our first satellite, and two months later, on March 17, the second, Vanguard 1.

Sputnik and its successors altered the course of American history, but probably no more than another event or rather series of events that had the capacity to make even teenagers sit up and take notice: the civil rights movement. It would be foolish to suggest that we high schoolers—and we were more than 95 percent white—were all bleeding-heart civil rights activists, but almost everyone was shocked by incidents such as the 1955-56 bus boycott in Montgomery, Alabama, sparked by Rosa Parks; and the 1957 attempt to integrate Central High School in Little Rock, Arkansas; and the black girl who nearly died in Little Rock because state law prohibited the transfusion of "white blood" into blacks.

However, what really caused us to gawp and grin and gossip was something closer to home: the Big Barbecue, the Gangster Summit, the Mob Meeting—it has been garlanded with many names—just down the road in the small town of Apalachin, New York, on November 14, 1957. About a hundred members of La Cosa Nostra, the American Mafia, met at the home of mobster Joseph Barbara to discuss the narcotics trade and the murder the previous month of mob chieftain Albert Anastasia. State police, made curious by the presence of so many expensive cars with license plates from all over the United States and Canada, raided the meeting. Mafiosi fled in panic into the surrounding woods, chased by police, who rounded up more than sixty. The most lasting effect for the country of the raided meeting was that it confirmed the existence of an American Mafia, which J. Edgar Hoover, apparently not chastened by similar revelations by the Kefauver Committee earlier in the decade, had claimed was a myth. For us the effect was simply the thrill of thinking that all those bad guys had been so close to us.

§

The Chenango Kid

I retain more recollections of national and world happenings from my years in junior and senior high school than I do of any other period. But my brain is like a Jell-O mold, a glop of shimmering, jiggling environment in which bits of colorful events are randomly trapped, revealing nothing about themselves except that they are there. Taken together they must have informed my adolescent view of the world, else they would not have made a lasting, albeit indefinite, impression on me. When I pluck one or the other out of that gelatinous brain to tell about it, it does not come trailing details of why and when, most of which I had to look up.

I was not and never have been a fan of Elvis Presley, but in that I am and ever have been in a distinct minority. Everything he did, every shake of his hips, every thrust of his pelvis, every curl of his lip, from the time of his first appearance on television (January 28, 1956, on Tommy and Jimmy Dorsey's *Stage Show*) made news. And nothing made bigger news than when, two years later (March 24, 1958), he was drafted into the Army. If no girls cried at North, they certainly did elsewhere. Some time after I went to work at *The Milwaukee Journal* I learned that a colleague had served at Fort Chaffee, Arkansas, when Elvis was inducted and witnessed the media frenzy that developed. (My own musical preferences at that point tended more to the likes of the Kingston Trio; "Hang down your head, Tom Dooley," I sang it all the time.)

The day (April 4, 1958), or rather news reports of the day, that fourteen-year-old Cheryl Crane stabbed Johnny Stompanato to death startled us in the way that the Starkweather rampage did. Imagine, a kid committing murder! Crane's act, unlike Starkweather's, was understandable, and eventually ruled justifiable homicide. She was the only child of actress Lana Turner and had defended herself and her mother, she said, from Stompanato, Turner's violent and abusive mob-connected boyfriend.

A disturbing new term entered our lexicon, "The Ugly American," from the 1958 novel of that title by journalists William J. Lederer and Eugene Burdick. Ugly? How could Americans be ugly? We were the good guys. We won World War II for the world, after all. The book (and later movie) had to do with American activities, whether open and putatively benign or clandestine and suspicious, in a fictional Southeast Asian country (read: Vietnam), but the term came to refer to loud and boisterous American tourists in foreign countries.

So that's what they thought of us? Apparently. In May 1958 Vice President Richard Nixon was booed and heckled wherever he went on what was meant as a goodwill tour of South America. In Southeast Asia they were suspicious as to what we were getting up to with all our "advisers" and South Americans didn't like our support of unpopular dictators. And after all we did for them!

Our eighth-grade fears about communists creeping in from the territories were all for naught, because on July 7, 1958, Eisenhower signed legislation allowing Alaska to become the forty-ninth state in the next year. Legislation allowing Hawaiian statehood followed soon thereafter. Some of us got new toys to play with—transistor radios and hula hoops were big. Alvin and his two brother Chipmunks recorded "The Chipmunk Song," thus beginning their fifty-plus-year reign of annoying idiocy.

These recollections can trigger an entire historical tableau in my head. It cannot be explained, for it is like trying to capture in words a smell and a place and an emotion all at once. Happenings and experiences such as these are my "Rosebuds."

§

On the other hand, what an ocean of darkness, what a tall blank wall of silence, the past is! What I have recounted is but the tiniest fraction of the past, and that, I am sure, represents only the dimmest shades of what actually happened. Not to mention what I have not told. Mark Twain had it right, as he usually did: You can't write an honest account of your life until you are dead.

But it nags that I cannot see past those shades. Would it have helped if I had kept a diary, a journal, of those days? Sometimes I envy those few persons—the actress Marilu Henner is one—whose memories are so prodigious that they can summon up exactly what happened and what they were doing on any given day. On the other hand, I have read that total recall, the ability to remember every word that one reads or hears, can cause difficulty in making decisions and in understanding the overall point of a book or lecture due to getting bogged down in a mire of indistinguishable details. Forgetting, according to this research, is good for emotional health and for enabling us to make sense of the world by letting us retain the thoughts that are truly valuable. So, I gather, what I have set down here is what I was *supposed* to set down—according to the dictates of my sieveish memory.

The Chenango Kid

Still, there is one matter about which it would be nice to have a few more details. It is one that I hesitate to go into because more than fifty years later it still seems to irk Nancy. This involves a girl I went with in high school, the *only* girl I went with in high school, and that for just the last couple of months of twelfth grade. It happened years before I ever met Nancy, but she does not like me to bring it up. I suppose she thinks I still carry a torch. Far from it, as I hope this will show her.

I will call the girl Sally, with apologies to anyone named Sally. Apparently Sally, a year behind me, had been admiring me from afar. That in itself surprised me. I think that she got one of her sorority sisters to ask me if I would go with her to her junior prom. Or was it a sorority dance? (It still astounds me that some high schools had sororities and fraternities, junior versions of the college societies.) That inquiry sent me into a panic. A pleasurable one, because it indicated that someone—that is to say, a *girl*—actually liked me, but now I would have to do something about it. *What?* Take a girl to a dance? Me, who almost never talks to girls, much less asks them out? Me, who does not know how to dance? Who thinks he somehow is not good enough to go to formal dances with the sort of high school elite who go to such events? Who lives in a small, shabby apartment that he would be ashamed to have any of the high school elite know he lives in?

Wonder of wonders, I said yes! It could be that the idea that I had been chosen by someone, someone in a social station above me (there weren't many stations below me, in my estimation), overcame the powerful voice in my head and anxiety in my breast impelling me to say no.

But dance? I did not realize that few guys could dance well, but made do with shuffling around the floor. So I thought I had to learn. I turned first to the source I usually do: the library. But pacing out on the kitchen floor the foxtrot and other ancient dances that Modern Teens rarely did anymore while clutching a broom handle and trying to follow the steps diagrammed in the book lying on the table proved less than adequate. Russell's wife Rose (the second of that name), learning of my troubles, sent me to her daughter, a waitress at the restaurant at the Greyhound station (and therefore of my social station, easing any anxiety on that score). She didn't really teach me to dance, but she did impart the valuable information that fancy footwork is fine, but if you can't manage that, girls are just glad if you get up from the table and push them around on the dance floor.

Armed with that assurance and a corsage, and dressed in a the new gray wool graduation suit Ma bought me at Men's Quality Shop in Johnson City, I escorted Sally to her dance in a car driven by a classmate old enough to drive at night. This too, I believe, had been arranged by her and her sorority comrades to allay any objections I might have had about lack of transportation. The female sex is so devious.

One of the details that elude me is where the dance was held. I did dance with her, awkwardly and shyly, and we had our photo taken. I found it difficult to converse over Cokes with the others at our table, none of whom were my particular friends in school. I had the feeling they were being careful to be nice to me for Sally's sake.

We must have had a fairly good time, for it did not end there. So taken was I with the experience of being close to a girl that I pursued her. She seemed willing to be pursued—at first, which gets to the nub of why I go into all this.

A couple of months later we went to my senior prom and then I graduated from North. Ma attended the graduation ceremony and so did Louise, coming down from Hastings in one of those periodic efforts she made to keep connected to me. Did Sally attend? Probably; I can't be sure. I got the job at the bank. We continued to go out that summer and in the fall after she entered twelfth grade. Her parents were nice to me when I went to her house on weekends. Weekday nights were *verboten*, on her orders and those of her parents, because she had homework to do. It was a fairly long trek for me, as she lived near East Junior on the North Side. At first I had no car, so I took the city bus when I could and walked when I could not. When I stayed late—never very late, as her parents hovered—I took an Owl Taxi home, charging it to my Uncle Walter if he happened to be driving for Owl, as he did now and then.

We went together steadily and amicably—and chastely, despite my best efforts—through that fall and winter. Then something began to happen, and here is where I drill into the dark sludge of my memory to try to figure out what it was because it gets to the issue of why I was what I was when young and what I have been since. It is for me now a matter not of faded romance but of the consciousness of my youth.

Sally and I were all right when we were together by ourselves or in the company of her family. Once we all went swimming somewhere; I believe at Ansco Lake. But when we went out with others, with her friends, we increasingly were not all right. And it was me that was the problem, as she told me it was and I did not believe her—and as I only now remember as I write this. The sudden self-revelation makes me a little breathless even now. I resented, felt inferior to, her sorority-fraternity friends from both North and Central, living in their comfortable suburban homes in Morningside Heights or Sunrise Terrace or in the nicer sections of the city. I did not play nice with them because I did not know how to. I thought they were condescending to me, knowing my lower-class circumstances, which they probably were not because they did not. It was just something that a young man ashamed of himself would attribute to others. Interesting that Sally did not feel that way though she did not live in a fancy house in a tony section, but in one side of a duplex in a so-so area. We never had such difficulties when we went out with my friends because we never did go out with them. Other than Tom, they had scattered to the four winds after graduation. And so, while I took her to my senior prom in 1959, when hers came around in 1960 she took someone else.

Doth the gentleman protest too much? Or was it just not that complicated? Most likely it was a simple case of puppy love and she got tired of me, period, because I was me and she had different plans that included going off to college in the fall of 1960 to study to become an elementary school teacher. I was in the working world and she was still in high school. But the breakup left me devastated. Hearing the song "I'm Mr. Blue" by the Fleetwoods made me want to burst into tears, and if I was by myself, I did.

I met her only one more time, a year or so later, in a tavern/hangout called AMPS on Clinton Street. I was drinking a beer and so was she, as I saw to my surprise when with some trepidation I went over to her table to say hello. (At that time the legal drinking age in New York state was eighteen.) I told her I was going to Harpur. That information evoked a flash of sullen interest, probably because the last she knew I had hoped to go to art school. But the interest was only momentary; basically she did not seem at all pleased to see me. I turned on my heel and left.

So you see, Nancy, it is hardly Charles M. Schulz/Charlie Brown pining away lifelong for the red-headed little girl. It is as usual Roger, self-absorbed, trying to figure out how he got this way, using a brief if admittedly piercing slice of the past to illustrate the profound difficulty of unearthing and then understanding it.

§

And so we trudged slowly but inexorably, sometimes to the sounds of the new "exotica music" like Martin Denny's "Quiet Village," toward graduation day, mourning the recent deaths of musicians Buddy Holly, Ritchie Valens, and J.P. ("the Big Bopper") Richardson, in a plane crash in faraway Iowa. Eddie was divorcing Debbie and marrying Liz, Fidel Castro was consolidating the grip on power he would hold for the next half-century, and somewhere college students were stuffing themselves into telephone booths in the latest campus craze.

One of the last images I have of twelfth grade is of sitting in the library on a warm, lovely afternoon shortly before the end of term with the windows open and a balmy breeze wafting over a roomful of restless bodies. But wait. Did we have a library? We must have, because we had a librarian, Miss Dyer. Then if so, where was it, and would the windows open? No matter. My image has the windows open and the library on either the second or third floor. I was reading James Thurber's just-released *The Years With Ross* and thinking, "Now, that's the kind of lively life to lead." The next day, my friend Jerry said this girl whom we all regarded as super smart told him she had seen what I was reading and remarked that "Roger Miller is an intellectual." That puffed me up, to have a smart Jewish girl say that. Of course it was not and is not true and if it were it could not have been determined from a liking of Thurber. Life since then has taught me it was not necessarily a compliment, however much it was meant as one.

And with that and other baggage I went out into the wider world.

—30—

PEOPLE AND PLACES APPEARING IN THE BOOK

Keith G. Miller's family
    Parents: James Lawrence and Alice Amelia Miller
    Sister: Mima Harriet; Walter Smith (husband); Kenneth and Ruth (children)
    Other siblings: Aura, James Lawrence Jr., Howard, Gerald, Clark, William, Frances

Mae Elna Miller's family
    Parents: Frank and Jenny Sheridan
    Children: Roger K. Miller, Louise Sheridan Rogers, unnamed daughter
    Brother: Ralph; Audrey (wife); John and Aubrey (children)
    Brother: Russell; Rose I and Rose II (wives); Winnie (girlfriend)
    Brother: Walter; Lena, Margaret (wives)
    Sister: Anna; Charles Noldy (husband); Donald (son)
    Other sibling: Romayne

Public schools in Binghamton
    Christopher Columbus (south side of Hawley Street between Jay and Fayette streets)
    East Junior High (south side of Robinson Street between Ely Street and Broad Avenue)
    North High (East Frederick Street near corner of Moeller Street)
    Thomas Edison (south side of Robinson Street near corner of Chenango)

Roger K. Miller

Residences of Mae and Roger Miller
- 135 Chenango Street, the Moon Block, west side of street, corner of Lewis
- Eldredge Street, number unknown, east of Chenango, north side of street
- 285 & 289 Chenango, west side of street, between Robinson and Doubleday streets
- 250 Chenango, east side of street, between Doubleday and Eldredge Streets
- 82 Walnut Street, east side of street, not far from Main Street

ACKNOWLEDGMENTS

Three special ladies—

Patricia Sbarra, a longtime friend and a nearly lifelong resident of Broome County, New York, for her dogged encouragement and inexplicable admiration of all my writings;

Carole Edwards, a survivor with me of Mrs. Tice's sixth grade at Thomas Edison School whose acquaintance I renewed (after sixty years) as I was writing this book, for sharpening my recollections of people, places, and things on the old North Side and reminding me of many I had forgotten;

Jane Bednarek, a wonderful friend and equally wonderful mystery novelist (writing as Jane Gillette), for telling me more than occasionally that I needed to get out of the dumps and back to work;

And Harrison E. White, fellow historian manqué and friend of fifty years, a lover of literature who nevertheless agreed to read this book in manuscript and made invaluable contributions, as did his lovely wife Maureen, who is hereby awarded an assist;

Last but first, my beloved wife Nancy—with (adapting from Don Marquis) Nan knows what and Nan knows why.

Made in the USA
Lexington, KY
29 May 2012